Praises for *"Fron Millionaire"*

"This book is a breath of fresh air; Carl's no nonsense approach to building real wealth did everything he promised it would."

-Phillip Hodgson, Massachusetts

"After years of wasting more dollars than I would like to remember on books and programs that where big on theory, but always fell well short in practice, I finally found a program that works. The help and assistance I received from Carl and his team was FANTASTIC. This program changed my life for less than it cost to run my cell phone for one month."

-David Sheppard, New York

"In less than six months, I turned around a 429 credit score with debts of over $50,000 into a 678 credit score with all the debts paid off for less than $6,000. I am truly on the Road to Riches."

-Susan Peterson, Pennsylvania

"This book has changed the way I approach Real Estate Investing. Using this program I am now securing annualized returns of more than 18% without all the problems of dealing with the public. THANK YOU!"

-Joseph Simms, Kansas

"As a family, we had been living from paycheck to paycheck since the day we got married. Thanks to Carl and his life changing program, we are now on the road to riches and living the American dream."

-Barbara Chambers, Nevada

"This is not just another book -- this is a life changing program. The help and encouragement we received from Carl and his team was inspirational. They were always there to help us."

-Peter Foster, Texas

From Credit Despair
To Credit Millionaire

The Road to Riches

From Credit Despair To Credit Millionaire

The Road to Riches

Carl Hampton

LANDMARK PUBLISHING

Library of Congress Cataloging-in-Publication Data

Landmark Publishing
PO Box 5730,
Santa Monica, CA 90409

ISBN 1-59872-336-7

This book is dedicated to my father Keith Arthur (1901-1976). His integrity and compassion for other people left an indelible impression on my life. Thank you for being such a wonderful role model.

TABLE OF CONTENTS

APPENDIX

ACKNOWLEDGMENTS

To my wonderful wife, who tolerated the seemingly endless gestation period that it took to complete this book. I could not have asked for a better partner to spend my life with.

Pat Loveless, her official title is COO (Chief Operating Officer) but she is best described as my "Right Hand". A real estate expert in her own right and affectionately known as the "Millionaire Maker" by our clients. I owe her the greatest debt of gratitude. Without her this book would never have made it to reality.

Robert my long-suffering friend, whose support and encouragement has been steadfast through the good times and the bad. Without him our very successful websites and training systems would have been impossible. No amount of thanks to him could ever be adequate.

Mahdi Tehrani a real team player who worked long and hard on transferring our ideas into such wonderful designs. How he ever made sense of what we were telling him we wanted, I will never know.

Emilia Wright whose exhaustive work through her research and probing questions brought this project to life. She somehow managed to take my disorganized scribble and turn it into something understandable on paper.

Foreword

The Future Really is "Yours" for the Taking

Your journey to a brighter more successful future begins with this truly remarkable book. Carl Hampton and his co-workers are affectionately known as the *"Millionaire Makers"* by their clients. They are all Real Estate experts in their own right.

They have been helping clients with credit scores as low as 409 get home loans and begin their road to financial security for more than 20 years. His unique insight will help you overcome every obstacle you may encounter on the road to fully achieving your financial **Dreams**.

If you put the principles found in this book to use, you will start to reach your financial destiny.

This book is very important for you and your family. You should read it carefully and apply its principles. It will help you reach your destiny. It's time to start living your **Dreams.**

Get your friends to read this book. Every time someone complains about their financial situation suggest they read this book. There is *NO* substitute for *Action*! With *Action,* you can and will overcome your fears, hesitations and accomplish everything you set out to do and more.

START LIVING YOUR DREAMS

CARL HAMPTON

Introduction

<u>You owe it to **Yourself** to live your **Best Life Now.**</u>

How often have you daydreamed of living a more financially secure life? Perhaps, like so many of us, you simply want to accomplish more. Maybe it's your dream to leave that lasting financial legacy for future generations of your family. Like so many Americans, have you written down those **"Goals"** in good faith and then put them off until tomorrow? Well, by now I am sure you are well aware that **"Tomorrow Never Comes".**

To use a familiar term, *"Investing for our long term future is a marathon not a sprint".* We all have a responsibility to improve our financial literacy and develop the required skills and practices for effective financial management. There is a real need to get away from the **"Someday things will get better in my life"** or the **"Someday I will be able to earn enough money to stop worrying about the bills.** There is a lot more to life than that, but it has to be said and understood that the only person that can change your life is **YOU**. There is NO substitute for Action! With Action, you will overcome your fears and hesitations and accomplish everything you set out to do and more.

It is never too late to start building real wealth regardless of how hopeless you think your current situation may be. Most people use the excuse that they need to wait until they have a large amount of money to get going. That excuse is so lame it's comical. These people will normally quote something like "It takes money to earn money" and while that may well be true, there are numerous ways to start small and reach the same goals. Remember, there is NO substitute for Action! With Action, you will overcome your fears and hesitations and accomplish everything you set out to do and more.

There really is nothing that prepares us for the "real world." If your parents were like mine, you were told to work hard at school, get good grades, find a great paying job and enjoy all the benefits along the road to retirement. The world has moved on since those days. With many of the major companies "downsizing" or "outsourcing" to cheaper overseas labor markets, many Americans are now finding themselves falling well short of what they needed for their retirement.

America is considered by many other countries in the world as the land of opportunity, new ideas and hope and in most respects that is as true today as it was sixty years ago. Normally, by the time we embrace a new idea, it is usually anything but new.

The idea has usually traveled a very long and bumpy road enduring lots of examination and plenty of rejection before we finally give it acceptance. Using your credit to purchase real estate products and services to build real long term wealth is no different. These ideas have been around for decades. It's the application and knowledge needed to fulfill your dreams that has changed. Our Road to Riches program outlined for you in the following pages of this book will give you all the required strategies needed to reach your goals regardless of your current financial position.

The purpose of this book is to assist you in overcoming any obstacles that may stop you from reaching your financial goals. The main obstacle to people securing their dreams is fear. A high ranking police officer once told me that FEAR is the biggest crime in America today. You should never allow the fear of getting it wrong or making a mistake, stop you from getting where you deserve to be. That is a crime! The only people who never make mistakes are the people who are doing nothing. It's as simple as that!

There are a large number of reasons why the uninformed fail to secure financial independence. The three main reasons are as follows: (1) Fear, (2) Laziness and (3) Arrogance. All of the most successful people in the world use the two most precious gifts given to us, their minds and their time. The difference between success and failure is our state of mind. If you choose to believe that someone else should do everything for us because we deserve it, then you will die poor. If, on the other hand, you really believe you are the master of your own destiny, there is no limit to what you can achieve.

Chapter 1

It's Time to Get Started

The real decision isn't whether or not this program will work for you (because it will), but rather the only question you should be asking yourself is "are you really serious about **CREATING WEALTH**" for you and your family.

We *all* have tremendous potential, and that potential comes from our two greatest assets, our mind and our time. The way we use these assets determines our destiny. The ability to recognize opportunities when they arise and the time management skills to maximize that opportunity is the real secret to success. For most people, wealth generation is nothing more than a distant dream. Maybe they'll win the lotto or some rich relative will die and leave them the money they need to secure the life they want. I learned from my father at a very young age that we and we alone have full control of our own destiny.

How we manage and use each dollar at our disposal will determine what level we reach in life. If we spend foolishly we will remain poor; spend wisely and you will generate wealth and join the ranks of the rich. The creation and management of a successful long term business is exactly the same -- spend wisely.

Too many businesses overspend on expensive oversized offices that they have no real need for, with more staff than they require. The only thing you should care about is PROFIT and that means buying right, keeping cost down and building wealth. If you look at all the most successful people and companies in the world, you will find that they all managed to build wealth and create passive income. It's the money that should be working hard, not us.

Real Estate has long been the safest and best long term route to real wealth. Markets and trends come and go. The fundamentals of creating wealth with real estate have remained the same for the past sixty years or so. For instance, if you purchased an investment property using finance of around 70% and then rent the property out, if you are lucky, then you could make between 7% and 12% on the investment. For this to happen, you will not only require enough money for the deposit (normally 30%), but also the home markets must continue to rise and the tenants must pay their rent on time.

In a perfect world that would be great, but as most of us know the world is not prefect. Even if you can find the right house at the right price there is always that small problem -- finding the right tenant. Those 2:00 am calls about the plumbing can become a real pain.

Outlined in Chapter (3) Strategy & Implementation, you will find the ultimate program for real estate success. This program has been tried, tested and proven. What you will have is a unique opportunity to guarantee yourself potential earnings in real estate that are well above the average income levels of the past.

The creation of wealth and income from our Real Estate program has two main revenue streams: Tax Liens/Deeds and Mortgage Notes.

Unlike most of the other books on the market that promise to make you rich with systems like "No Money Down" or "Properties for Pennies on the Dollar", our program works. It is being used by people just like you and has been for years. Many of our clients started with very little money and by using the strategy listed in this book, they started to turn from Credit Despair to Credit Millionaires.

There really is no need for you to waste thousands of dollars on outdated tapes and CD sets. That money should be spent on making more money.

This book will supply you with all the information required to get started today. All you need to do is supply the desire, time, energy and enthusiasm! Ladies and Gentleman -- Don't Procrastinate any Longer! In a Lifetime of Chance, Don't Miss This Chance of a Lifetime.

Chapter 2

How to Succeed

This is my simple step-by-step guide on how to succeed. Nobody plans to fail when they start a new business, so why do most businesses fail? Simple, they fail to *plan* correctly. All successful people are paying a price for their success and so will you! How large a price is it? That largely depends on how high a goal you have set. There are some constant elements, however, in every success story.

If you read the stories of the most successful business people in the world, you would see a definite pattern. You'd find formulas that every successful person uses in one variation or another:

    (1)   They Set A Goal;

    (2)   They Establish A Game Plan;

    (3)   They Develop The Required Amount Of Motivation And Determination;

    (4)   They Have A Strong Underlying Belief In Themselves; and

(5) **THEY PUT ALL OF THE ABOVE INTO ACTION!**

These five main ingredients are present in almost every successful person I know or have read about. Of course, however, these principles don't *only* apply to your financial success. They will also apply to success in all areas of your life. The person who follows these formulas and strategies will find the road to success and financial freedom!

(A) SETTING GOALS

It's important that you not only set goals, you must <u>WRITE</u> them down and put them somewhere visible. Put a check box next to each goal. This will help you stay motivated. Set daily, weekly, and monthly goals. We all want to be rich and successful tomorrow, but most so-called overnight success stories took years to achieve. Set realistic goals, not too low, yet not too high. That way you are able to enjoy your success on a daily, weekly, and monthly basis. If you start to reach your goals too easily, then upgrade them and continue on this path until you reach that ultimate success.

(B) ESTABLISH A GAME PLAN

Choose the Investments you feel most comfortable working in before you start. Do your research! Make sure these investments cover all of your requirements. Set out your guidelines before you start such as: What financial limits are you setting for each Investment? Will you be looking for monthly returns on your Investment? I would recommend that you use the *FREE* telephone training sessions at www.lienexchange.com. IT IS VERY IMPORTANT that you understand your markets before investing. A little time here will save you a lot of money in the long term.

MOTIVATION AND DETERMINATION

FOCUS, DEDICATION, DESIRE, AND PERSERVERANCE, a.k.a. "FDDP" will overcome almost any obstacle. All you need to do is DEVELOP THESE FOUR CHARACTERISTICS! On those days when nothing seems to be going right – and we all have them – JUST KEEP GOING! Remember, you are only one conversation away from success!

BELIEVE IN YOURSELF

You are the only person who can and will change your life! Make sure you look at your goals everyday and believe you can achieve them! The *Great American Dream* is there for you! *All you need to do is BELIEVE!*

PUT ALL THE ABOVE INTO ACTION

ACT TODAY, NOT TOMORROW! ACTION REAPS REWARDS! *Please Don't* let another day pass. There really is no substitute for Action. If you act now (today), you will overcome all your fears and hesitations. With Action, you can and will accomplish everything you set out to do and more!

Chapter 3

STRATEGY & IMPLEMENTATION

Strategy

Our program offers a unique opportunity with a guaranteed earning potential well above the average income earned from investment properties. This is "NOT" a get rich quick program! It is a tool to generate real wealth and income from a business plan through smart and safe investing. The more funds you have available, the faster your wealth grows. It's as simple as that! See Chapter (4) How to Secure all the Funding You Will Ever Need.

The following strategy has been successfully used to great effect by thousands of clients from all over the country for many years. What we are about to teach you is an amazing alternative to low paying CD's and risky stock market investments.

Tax Liens/Tax Deeds

Investing in Tax Lien/Deed certificates enables you to realize safe, annualized returns all guaranteed by the United States Government. The collection of Real Estate property taxes is a major priority in every taxing district in the USA. If a county were unable to collect those taxes in a timely fashion, it would be unable to provide the public with important public services such as the police and fire departments and schools for our children. To avoid this problem, all counties in 26 states across the US will place a Tax Lien on any property with delinquent property taxes and then sells the delinquent tax debt to investors. The county gets their money, the tax delinquent taxpayer gets more time to pay their already past due property taxes and the investor gets a Real Estate secured high yielding investment. Tax Liens are often called the "Fort Knox" of investments. Government issued Tax Lien certificates are a safe investment for the reasons stated below.

The constant rise and fall of interest rates do not have any affect whatsoever on Tax Lien Certificates because the interest rates of Tax Lien Certificates are mandated by State law. Basically, you are investing in the Government. When they have collected the past due taxes, you will send them the Tax Lien certificate and in return they will send you a check covering the money you paid for the certificate plus any outstanding interest.

The ups and downs of the stock markets will have no affect whatsoever on the rate of return. Each State has a mandated length of time for the delinquent taxes to be paid. If they are not made current during this time period, the property is sold to pay the debt. There are of course pitfalls and mistakes that the amateur investor can make. We are professionals and have over sixty years of experience between us. The following are examples from three states showing the lucrative business of Tax Liens:

> 16% per year in all 15 counties in Arizona;
> 18% per year in all 67 counties in Florida;
> 50% per year in all 254 counties in Texas.

State of Florida (sec. 197.172)

"In the State of Florida, Real Estate property taxes shall bear interest at the rate of 18 percent per annum from the date of delinquency until a Tax Lien Certificate is sold. In addition to law mandated interest rates, Tax Lien Certificates are secured by Real Estate. In the event the delinquent taxpayer fails to pay the delinquent taxes and interest owed, the investor can seek the property as collateral."

Most properties will have an outstanding mortgage. Generally, the lender will pay these delinquent taxes before it gets to the foreclosure stage. The certificates can also be sold or transferred at a discount before the due date allowing the investor to make a smaller profit on the certificate should there be a need for cash for another project.

The main advantage to the new or smaller investor is that there are many thousands of Tax Liens/Deeds for sale at every budget level. In the old days, you would have to travel thousands of miles across the country to auctions if you wanted to buy Tax Liens/Deeds. Now you can do it from the comfort of your own home. We developed our own trading room at *www.lienexchange.com* and everything you need to know is on the website. We hold regular free telephone training programs covering every aspect of buying and selling Tax Liens/Deeds certificates.

Mortgage Notes

There are a lot of companies in the business of selling training programs about Notes for vast sums of money. It is sometimes called a "Cash Flow" business, meaning they promise large earnings from Notes. The problem with this is that by the time you have given them all your hard earned cash for their program, there are no funds available for you to start making money. Most of these systems require you to find people who want to sell their Notes and then you need to find a buyer, and this is not as simple as it sounds.

Having said that, "Notes" are a super way to earn very high interest returns, all you need to do is "Do it right". Why waste all that money, time and effort on a program when you can use that same money, time and effort to buy your own "Notes". Unlike Tax Lien/Deed certificates, you will be required a larger starting pool of funds. See Chapter (4) How to Secure all the Funding You Will Ever Need.

There are a great many advantages to buying "Notes." For a start, the market is almost unlimited. What is a "Note?" For the purpose of this program, a "Note" is a second mortgage secured by real estate. How much is a "Note?" That could be anything from $10,000 to $1 million. What is the advantage of a "Note" over a Tax Lien/Deed certificate? A "Note" will allow you to collect the interest on a monthly basis; this enables you to reuse the incoming funds to make more money, creating real wealth. Tax Lien/Deed certificates are only paid when the Lien/Deed is redeemed.

When buying "Notes," there are a number of things you will need to keep in mind before letting go of your hard earned money. Not all "Notes" are equal. Doing the right research is very important. See Chapter (6) What to Look for in a Mortgage Note.

You will be able to learn everything you need to know at *www.lienexchange.com*. They hold regular free telephone training calls.

Implementation

Millions of Americans are probably wondering where to invest their hard earned money in these low interest times. Most money market funds, banks, and savings and loans are paying considerably less than 5% interest. After paying taxes and allowing for inflation, a 5% return leaves you with little or nothing to cover that ever increasing cost of living.

Issued by more than 2600 local counties in a majority of states, Tax Lien Certificates are not new. So why haven't you heard about them? Banks, savings and loans and fund managers have been investing in them for years and making lots of money. Why would they want to tell you about them when they can take in *your* money at low interest rates and reinvest *your* funds at a much higher rate receiving huge profits for their shareholders or owners. Now it's your turn to find out about them! It's your turn to start enjoying those huge profits from them!

You Really Can Start Small

We've all heard those sayings "the rich get richer" and "it takes money to make money" and they may well be true in most cases. Investing in Tax Lien Certificates allows you to receive the same high interest rates regardless of your investment. You can start for as little as $200. There will be opportunities for any budget regardless of size.

Many people redirect their IRA or 401K to get started in Tax Lien Certificate investing. The opportunity to double, triple or even quadruple your money in 3, 4 or 5 years depending on which States you invest in, makes this a win-win situation for the Tax Lien Certificate investor.

Even the Rich and Famous Forget to Pay Their Property Taxes

The biggest misconception most people have of Tax Liens is that the only reason people don't pay their property taxes is because they have no money or are deep in debt. As the list below shows, even the rich and famous sometimes overlook their property taxes.

TITLE	AMOUNT
Corporations	
McDonald's Corporation	$11,059.82
Walt Disney World Hospitality & Recreation	$88,156.47
Atlantic Gulf Oil Company	$6,615.87
Amoco Oil	$3,360.37
Bellsouth Mobility Inc.	$13,763.63
Amsouth Bank	$24,478.02
Wells Fargo Bank Minnesota	$1,274.43
Government	
United States of America C/O Property Manager	$1,167.76
United States Postal Service	$9,916.04
City of Hollywood	$146,537.64
Celebrities	
Anna Kournikova	$106,178.89
Stefanie Graf	$17,090.63
Wesley Snipes	$4,943.00
Carrot Top Inc.	$4,683.65

Great Reasons to Invest In Tax Lien Certificates

There are many great reasons to purchase Tax Lien Certificates as part of your investment portfolio. While most Tax Lien Investors emphasize the really high interest rates that can be obtained from Tax Lien Certificates, it should also be remembered that it is possible to become the owner of a property at pennies on the dollar. Does this really happen? Of course it does. Does it happen every day? No, but it does happen and when it does, it's an unexpected joy that will give you bragging rights for years. Listed below are some of the main reasons for investing in Tax Lien Certificates:

1. Security
2. High Interest Rate Returns
3. Ability to Start Small
4. Liquidity
5. Massive availability

The Road to Riches

EARN SUPER HIGH INTEREST RATES INVESTING IN TAX LIEN CERTIFICATES! YOU CAN OBTAIN 100% SAFE AND PREDICTABLE ANNUALIZED RETURNS OF 16% TO 24% ALL GUARANTEED BY THE UNITED STATES GOVERNMENT!

If you put $5000 into a CD (cash deposit) with a local bank in 1975 at 6.02% interest and left it there for 30 years, you would collect $29,541.

If you purchased Tax Liens at the following Rates for 30 years, this is what you would have collected:

In AZ $5000 @ 16% for 30 years $429.249

In FL $5000 @ 18% for 30 years $716,853

In IA $5000 @ 24% for 30 years $5,120,000

Example:

Using rule 72, Divide 72 by the % Interest rate to find out how many years it would take to double your money:

72 divided by 24% = 3 years: *$5000*

> *After 03 years = $10,000*
> *After 06 years = $20,000*
> *After 09 years = $40,000*
> *After 12 years = $80,000*
> *After 15 years = $160,000*
> *After 18 years = $320,000*
> *After 21 years = $640,000*
> *After 24 years = $1,280,000*
> *After 27 years = $2,560,000*
> *After 30 years = $5,120,000*

How many banks are still paying 6% on CD's? NONE. The rate today is around 3%. $5,120,000 or $29,541 which one would *you* choose?

How to Choose the Right Tax Lien Certificates

Like all forms of investments, there are risks involved. The great thing about Tax Lien Certificates is that you can cut your risks down to almost zero. Which Tax Lien Certificate you choose to purchase is a matter of personal choice and will depend on a number of factors. If you keep the following in mind you will be able to sleep at night knowing your hard earned money is safe and earning you a great rate of interest.

All Tax Lien Certificates are secured against the Real Estate property. The property would have been appraised by a government agency at somewhere between 10 and 100 times the amount owed on the Tax Lien.

Tax Lien Certificates take priority over all other forms of liens that can be placed against the property, including any mortgages that may be outstanding on the property. Lenders become your "New Best Friend" if they choose to foreclose on the property. They MUST pay off the Tax Lien first. The lender, in most cases, will pay off the Tax Lien before the redemption date. After all, they are not going to lose a valuable asset over a few thousand dollars.

Should the property owner or the Lender fail to pay off the Tax Lien Certificate before the redemption date, you then receive the right to foreclose on the property. The rules vary from State to State and are outlined in our "Tax Lien States" guide on the lienexchange.com website.

One of two things will now happen: (1) the lender will pay you off or (2) you could get a very nice piece of Real

Estate property for pennies on the dollar. This is a win-win situation for the owner of the Tax Lien Certificate.

Foreclosing On Tax Liens/Deeds

We recommend that you seek the advice of a lawyer or use the services of a Foreclosure specialist. The laws can be very precise and strict about procedure. This is not a time to make mistakes.

Redeeming Your Tax Lien Certificates

This is the easy part of investing in Tax Lien Certificates because all of the work is done by the County Treasurer. Once the owner of the property or lender has paid off the delinquent taxes, the Treasurer will write to you and request that you send in the Tax Lien Certificate.

After the County Treasurer receives the Tax Lien Certificate, their office will mail out your check. It really is as simple as that. Some states may require a "quitclaim deed" in which you confirm you have no further interest in the property. This will be sent to you with the request for the Tax Lien/Deed Certificate. Please ensure that you fully comply with any and all request for information or signed documents before returning the Tax Lien/Deed Certificate. Failure to do so will delay your check.

What Happens If the Property Owner Files For Bankruptcy

The short answer is, YOU WILL GET YOUR INVESTMENT BACK WITH THE INTEREST PAID IN FULL.

The holder of the Tax Lien Certificate is a secured creditor as well as a senior creditor. The Tax Lien Certificate normally always represents only a small fraction of the value of the property. Of course, there is a downside to the property owner filing for bankruptcy and that is the delay in you getting your Tax Lien Certificate redeemed. This can take a few months to a few years. It should be deemed as a small bump in the road and not a major disaster; after all, you are still earning those high interest rates. The thing to remember is that you can always sell the Tax Lien Certificate using the Lienexchange.com marketplace. There will always be investors looking for that type of investment.

There are three commonly used forms of bankruptcy:

1. Chapter 7 can be used by either individuals, or businesses. It can be filed voluntarily or be compelled by creditors. In either case, a trustee is appointed. An individual may use it as a "fresh start;" a business would use it to dissolve in an orderly manner.

2. Chapter 11 is normally used as a "reorganization bankruptcy;" the debtor remains in possession of their property. A committee is appointed to investigate the Debtors financial situation. During the first 120 days, the Debtor has the exclusive right to propose a repayment plan.

3. Chapter 13 can only be used by individuals and is sometimes called the "wage earner" bankruptcy. The guideline for this bankruptcy is $100,000 or less in unsecured and $300,000 or less in secured debts.

You will need to remain alert if you should receive a notice of bankruptcy. You may well need to file a claim to secure your Tax Lien Certificate. We recommend that you seek the advice of an Attorney.

Risk Against Reward

In today's uncertain economy, Tax Lien Certificates surely represents one of the most profitable investments. It is not unusual for investors to double, triple, or even quadruple their initial investment in less than 5 years.

Liquidity

Liquidity is a very important part of any investment. Your ability to be able to sell your investment, should the need arise, often makes the difference between a great investment and a good or average investment.

Before the introduction of the Lienexchange.com website, many knowledgeable investors steered away from investing in Tax Lien Certificates. For most, the unpredictability of when the Tax Lien Certificates would be redeemed outweighed the huge returns. At that time, there was no market place in which to buy or sell their Tax Lien Certificates should they require the return of their investment unexpectedly.

The Lienexchange.com marketplace changed all of this and brought the last essential ingredient (liquidity) to what is an outstanding investment opportunity for investors of all sizes.

Are There Enough Tax Lien/Deed Certificates to Cover Demand

The short and very sweet answer to this question is, YES. The fact is there are billions of dollars in available Tax Lien/Deed Certificates issued by at least 26 States across the US. There has never been a time when demand has outstripped supply.

What Is Your Objective: The Property or the Interest?

What makes Tax Lien Certificates such a unique investment is that they provide a secured high interest rate while at the same time offering you the chance to obtain real estate property for pennies on the dollar. Most investors are investing for the income potential of the Tax

Lien Certificate, but you can maximize your chances of obtaining the property by selecting the states in which you purchase your Tax Lien Certificate or Deed.

You will need to consider the different laws in each state to find out if they assist the owner of the Tax Lien Certificate in obtaining the property from the delinquent taxpayer. You will need to consider both sides of the coin. Let's use Florida and Arizona as examples. Florida allows you to earn a very nice 18% per annum on your investment, but gives the buyer of the Tax Lien Certificate no benefits should you need to foreclose on the property. The Deed goes to the investor who is willing to pay the most for the Deed and of course, you receive your investment plus interest and fees as soon as the sale is complete. In Arizona, if the Tax Lien Certificate is not redeemed by the property owner during the three year redemption period, you can go to court and foreclose on the lien. Should you wait five years, you are no longer required to go to court. At that point, you go to the local county treasurer and apply for a deed. It's as simple as that!

Buying Tax Lien/Deed Certificates at Auction

A well-attended auction can create an intensity of competition and a fear of loss that normally leads to the investor taking a smaller return on their investment. At a "Bid Down" auction where the winner is the investor who will take the lowest percentage rate of interest, this can be a real problem. Auctions can last anywhere from two to five days, so be patient. The better deals are normally found in the last two days of the sale.

Most Counties have a registration procedure in which they charge a fee and there is also a fee for the listings in most cases. It is always a good idea to do your research on the Tax Lien/Deed Certificates you wish to bid on before attending the auction: See "How To Choose The Right Tax Lien/Deed Certificates." You will also need to make sure you understand the "Bidding System" used by the county where you attend the auction. There are four main systems used: See "Bid Down", "Premium Bids", Property Interest" and "Straight Bids" all listed under "Glossary". You can alleviate the expense of traveling to tax lien auctions by using the marketplace of the Lienexchange.com website. The website also provides you with the necessary tools and services for your research.

How to Transfer or Assign your Tax Lien Certificate

Every county that sells a Tax Lien Certificate has put in place a system for transferring or assigning your Tax Lien Certificate. You will need to know what that system is and if there are any charges for the service. In most cases, there is a small charge, but the system itself is very simple to understand.

Chapter 4

How to Secure All the Funding you will Ever Need

This is what it is all about – Money! In this Chapter, I will lay out the four strategies that will allow you to reach your goals and set you off on the "Road to Riches". This is NOT a get rich quick program! It is a tool to generate real wealth and income from a business plan through smart and safe investing. The more funds you have available, the faster your wealth grows. It's as simple as that!

The following strategy has been successfully used to great effect by thousands of our clients from all over the country for many years. What we are about to teach you is an amazing alternative to how most people approach wealth building. I have already pointed out that this is NOT a get rich quick program! You will need to start at "A" and finish at "Z" ensuring that you complete every step on the way. How fast you get there is up to you. Every journey starts with a single step, **no matter now long that journey is,** you are much closer than you think to achieve your dreams. All you need to do is "Take Action Now!"

Your success will depend solely on **you**. The real decision isn't whether or not this program will work for you (because it will), but instead the real question you should be asking yourself is "Am I really serious about **CREATING WEALTH** for me and my family?" Four Simple easy to follow Strategies are:

1. Self-Funding

2. Using your Retirement Dollars

3. Starting your Own Investment Club

4. Using OPM (Other Peoples Money)

The *first* thing you need to do is set your goals and establish a game plan that best suits your own personal circumstances   See Chapter (2) How to Succeed. You will need to be very honest with yourself at this point. Setting goals too high at this stage will only lead to disappointment and that will almost certainly lead to you giving up. Remember, even the longest journey starts with a single step. The thing to keep in mind now is that it's very important for you to GET STARTED right now. Once you start to master the skills required, you will generate momentum and everything begins to get a lot easier and much more enjoyable. There is nothing more satisfying and enjoyable than the pride and pleasure you will feel having reached your goals.

Self-Funding

This is by far the most important phase of the program. Trying to start anywhere else will at best limit your success and at worst lead to complete failure. How much money you start with is almost irrelevant, as I will prove later on in this Chapter. What makes self-funding so important? The world is full of people who talk the talk, but don't or can't walk the walk. To become a credit millionaire, you will need to prove to others that you have gone as far as you can, having used your own money. Again, the amount of money is almost irrelevant because if it works with $500, then it works with $5 million. For those of you with IRA's or 401K's, this is easy. See Chapter (5) Using Your Retirement Dollars on the Road to Riches.

Most of you will start without the benefit of an IRA or 401K, so what you need to do is take some time to work out what available funds you have now, no matter how small. If like many Americans you are living from paycheck to paycheck, then we need to approach this from another direction. How much can you save each week? The most common answer to this question when raised at the training sessions is *"Nothing"*. After more than twenty years of asking that question, I can assure you we always find a figure that you can comfortably save. It really is amazing how much money we spend every day of our lives without thinking.

For the sake of this example, we will start with a modest figure of $25 per week -- not too much for the chance to join the Road to Riches, right?. The first thing you need to do is open a bank account for this project. It's very important that you keep good financial records. This account is your proof to the world that you have started on the Road to Riches. This account should not be used for anything else; this is your business account. What you are trying to prove here is that you have made the effort to start changing your life. By depositing the $25 every week into the account, you are starting to build-up the funds needed to get to the next level. The great American way is to get everything we need instantly. That will not work with this program at this level. It is going to take time to build up, but not as long as you may think. Let's say that you deposit the $25 every week for 12 weeks; you now have $300 sitting in the bank, but more importantly you have proven to yourself that you are serious about creating real wealth for you and your family. You have also given yourself a track record that proves you mean business. When trying to raise credit, a track record is very important.

We are using an example of $25 per week, so imagine what $50, $75, or more would look like on your bank statement.

If you are starting from this level, one way to accelerate this process is to consider joining up with a friend or family member who has the same ideas and desires as you. This way you can double the speed at which you make it to the next level. You can always part company at an agreed level that allows you both to continue on your own. Having got the funds into the bank, you now want to start using this money to make money and this is covered in Chapter (3) Strategy and Implementation.

Using your Retirement Dollars

See Chapter (5) Using your Retirement Dollars on the Road to Riches.

Starting your own Investment Club

Regardless of whatever level you started at, an Investment Club is a great way of increasing the amount of deals you can be involved in. Most existing investment clubs will have high entry levels that may be out of reach for newcomers. As I pointed out earlier, it is almost irrelevant how much money you started with. The benefits of starting your own Investment Club is you get to set the rules and this can be very important at this stage. As a new club, you could make the entry level as low as $500 and set the time limits (minimum time before they can call back the funds). Remember, this is "NOT" a get rich quick program! It is a tool to generate real wealth and income from a business plan through smart and safe investing.

The more people you get to join, the faster you all move up to another level. One way is to set a short time period for inviting new club members to join. I would recommend four weeks. Any longer than that and you are wasting time that should be spent making money. Once this time has arrived, you form a club with like-minded people who have agreed to join you, but leave the door open for new members by inviting them to join in individual projects controlled by the club. What happens is you start generating a fear of loss. Once your family and friends start to see you making money, they will all want to join. Remember, every journey starts with a simple step. What's important is that you START! Action reaps its own rewards!

The great thing about Investment Clubs is once you have fulfilled the time commitment you can leave and go on your own or start another club with the people you worked well with. The only limit to what you can achieve with an Investment Club is your *own* imagination.

Using OPM (Other Peoples Money)

Having completed the self-funding and Investment club levels, you are now ready to start reaching out for OPM (Other Peoples Money). This is where you get to be a credit millionaire. Moving to this level without completing the other two levels almost surely leads to failure and disappointment. Those who have money are always looking to make more than they are getting for their money at that time. Most people are happy to take a small cut in the profit if someone else is doing all the work.

The importance of completing the previous two levels is that you get to hold the high ground. Trying to raise money on an idea that you have no experience with is to say the least, difficult. What will make you different and gain you their respect is the fact that you are already doing it and can show them the profit you have made to date. Like I have said before, the amount of money you started with is almost irrelevant. Money minded people will understand that if it works with $500 it will work with $5 million. Using OPM will allow you to start building up larger reserves and open up more deals and give you the chance to pick and choose the deals you want to invest in. Once you build up a good reputation you will have no problem finding angel investors for your deals.

When dealing with potential investors it is very important that you present the project in a professional way. They will expect to see a well written business plan. A business plan should be broken down into three or four sections each section should outline all the main points and advantages. There are numerous business plan software packages in the market place, so there really is no need to waste time trying to write one. They come in set formats that will allow you to choose the style that best suites your plan.

You really should keep each section to less than two pages, do not over state the facts, this will kill the deal. If you outline any possible downsize to the project and your solution to the problems, should they happen, the investor will feel like they are dealing with someone who really knows what they are talking about.

Chapter 5

Using your Retirement Dollars on the Road to Riches

"In America there are two tax systems, one for the informed and one for the uninformed. Both systems are legal."

One of America's most famous jurists, Justice Learned Hand made this statement over forty years ago. When used today, one would certainly have to include the world of Individual Retirement Accounts (IRA). The point I am making here is that we all need to keep ourselves informed about what IRA alternatives are available to us. Being uniformed about these IRA alternatives almost certainly means we are not taking full advantage of the opportunity to get much safer and considerably higher yield returns than you could ever hope to get from investing in stocks, shares or mutual funds.

Your Broker Doesn't Want You to Know This!

There are many incredible wealth-building opportunities offered by your IRA and 401K's which includes their ability to buy real estate Tax Lien Certificates, Tax Deeds and Notes. The vast majority of Americans since 1974 unfortunately have sat back opting instead to take the easy more passive position. They have allowed their IRAs and 401Ks to be directed by someone else, such as the friendly Broker and their Wall Street affiliates. This easygoing very passive approach "let someone else do it for me" attitude may well have continued forever had it not been for the Wall Street crash of 2000. With more than a trillion dollars lost in IRA and 401K equity alone, it challenged the way we viewed Wall Street. Millions of Americans lost even more trillions in non-IRA, 401K accounts.

If you had used your IRA to purchase Real Estate Tax Lien Certificates, Tax Deeds or Notes!

For most Americans, the difference would be truly alarming. The clear fact is if Americans had known or understood back in 1974 that their IRAs could be used to purchase real estate Tax Lien Certificates, Tax Deeds and Notes, millions of American baby boomers would today be retiring with vast sums of cash and assets inside of their IRAs and 401Ks.

Let's do a few very simple comparisons...

NASDAQ reported on March 10, 2005 that it had risen to 59% of what it was five years earlier! This means

$100,000.00 invested in NASDAQ listed companies in 1999 would now be worth something like **$59,000.00**. That's very sad, but it's where most Americans are today.

If you had put $5000 into a CD, (Cash Deposit), with a local bank in 1975 and secured a 6.02% interest rate and left it there for 30 years you would now be collecting $29,541, a little better than NASDAQ but still not great.

If you had purchased Tax Liens Certificates at the following rates for 30 years, this is what you would have collected:

In AZ $5000 @ 16% for 30 years **$429.249**

In FL $5000 @ 18% for 30 years **$716,853**

In IA $5000 @ 24% for 30 years **$5,120,000**

How many banks are still paying 6% on CD's? NONE, the rate today is around 4%. **$5,120,000** from Tax Lien Certificates; or $29,541 from a CD; or a loss of $41,000 on NASDAQ, which one would you choose?

Your Self-Directed IRA Can Set You Free

Magazine, newspaper and television advertising campaigns have created the illusion to millions of Americans that those Wall Street products were the only financial products you could buy. This is not the fact and as outlined above Wall Street has not preformed well over the last 30 years.

Real Estate has always been a safe investment for the "informed" and with Tax Lien Certificates, Tax Deeds and Notes your retirement dollars are secured by Real Estate.   Real Estate has out performed everything over the last 30 years by a very long way.

IRAs in general have over ninety percent of their funds in financial products.   This may well lead you to ask "Why?" Are the Wall Street financial products superior in any way to real estate investments?" No!   Here are some quotes taken from various financial media.

> "... since the major housing organizations began keeping records in the 1960s, there has never been a year in which the average existing U.S. residence lost value. Not a one."
>
> FORTUNE Magazine, August 12, 2002

> "Real Estate prices have soared over the past years. Latest statistics show that housing prices have increased 60 percent since 1997. The average increase up to 2004 was about 13 percent per year."
>
> THE EPOCH Times January 27-Febuary 2, 2006

> "It is striking that after the longest, strongest bull market in history, the average American built more wealth owning a home than investing in the stock market."
>
> DENVER Post, March 14, 2002

After reading these quotes, it really is hard to understand why IRAs are not 90% real estate versus 10%

Wall Street products. Their very effective marketing has really made all the difference. Wall Street and its affiliates have out-marketed and out spent the real estate markets and as such have succeeded in capturing the trillions of IRA and 401K dollars available. It really is as simple as that.

What Is An IRA?

Employee Retirement Income Security Act (ERISA) was enacted by Congress in 1974. President Ford signed it into law later that year.

To keep it simple an IRA is a personal savings plan that allows you to receive individual tax incentives to set aside earnings for your retirement. Your IRA is a trust or custodial account which must be established in the United States for the exclusive benefit of the holder or its beneficiaries.

Here are five of the most common individual retirement plans, plus one additional plan that covers education:

1. Traditional
2. ROTH
3. SEP (Simplified Employee Pension)
4. SIMPLE (Savings Incentive Match Plan for Employees)
5. Spousal

6. ESA (Coverdell Education Savings Accounts)

1. A Traditional IRA

The Traditional IRA is an IRA that is not one of the following: a ROTH IRA, SIMPLE IRA or Coverdell IRA. A tax paying individual who has earned income and then desires to defer or eliminate taxes on income from funds set aside for their forthcoming retirement is allowed to open a Traditional IRA. You cannot make contributions to a Traditional IRA after the age of 70. Distributions may be taken without any penalties from a Traditional IRA beginning at age 59.

2. The Roth IRA

Unlike the Traditional IRA, the Roth IRA is an after-tax retirement plan which means it is not tax-deductible. The earnings accumulate is tax-free, it should also be remembered that all subsequent distributions are tax-free from the age of 59. Qualified withdrawals can be taken from the account tax-free without any annual limits and there are no minimum distributions required when you reach the age 70. Many CPAs will tell you the Traditional IRA may be better for those taxpayers who expect their tax rate to be lower when withdrawals are due to be taken. Spousal IRA may also be opened as a Roth IRA providing you meet all the qualifications for the ROTH IRA.

3. The SEP IRA

The Simplified Employee Pension (SEP) is the plan

that allows your employer to make contributions toward their employees' retirement plans. Their contributions are paid to the Traditional IRA of each participant in the plan. This plan saves the employer from having to set up a profit sharing or money purchase plan with a trust. The participants under a SEP may establish their own IRA at the institutions of their choice. Due to the fact that the underlying account is an IRA account, covered employees may choose to have a Self-Directed IRA as their SEP IRA. This can be in addition to any other IRA plan the employee may already hold.

4. The Simple IRA

Millions of Americans employed by large corporations already benefit from the small business pension plan (SIMPLE). Savings Incentive Match Plan for Employees is the full name of the plan. As an employee, you can make tax-deductible contributions of up to $8,000.00 per tax year. The employers match the contributions and the money is not taxed until it is withdrawn. Under the "SIMPLE" plan the term "employee" also includes a self-employed individual who received earned income. There are two types of SIMPLE plans, the SIMPLE IRA and the SIMPLE 401(k) Plan. You are allowed to have a Traditional IRA in addition to any other qualified plan or SIMPLE IRA in effect. An IRA opened for a non-working spouse (Spousal IRA) may also be opened as a Traditional IRA.

5. The Spousal IRA

Designed for married couples filing a joint tax return, they can contribute $4,000.00 ($4,500.00 if age 50+), to their IRAs (excluding a SIMPLE IRA) on behalf of each spouse even if one spouse has little or no earned income.

6. The Coverdell Educational Savings Account (ESA)

The Coverdell Educational Savings Account also known as "Coverdell ESA"; is a trust or custodial account. The account is created or organized within the United States exclusively for the sole purpose of paying for qualified higher educational expenses of the designated beneficiary of the ESA Account. This account must be designated as a Coverdell (ESA) when it is established to be treated as a Coverdell (ESA) for IRS tax purposes.

Are All IRAs Created Equally?

The answer to that question is "NO". The type of IRA that is right for you is something you should discuss with your CPA or accountant. In the end choosing the right type of IRA for your needs is your responsibility. The main difference between a typical IRA and a Self-Directed IRA can easily be summed up to - CONTROL. What do we mean by "Control"? We mean *you* control. What happens when you put funds in, what you invest in, and when you take it out? Normally only one of two people would have control of your IRA, the IRA custodian/trustee and you. With over 40,000,000 IRAs in America today, the vast majority of control lies with an IRA custodian/trustee.

Ensuring that you choose the right custodian is very important. It can and will make a big difference to how well your IRA performs. While choosing the wrong custodian or trustee can severely limit the products or category of investment products that it offers to the IRA holder.

Call your IRA custodian and ask them if your IRA is a "Self-Directed IRA". When they ask "why" tell them that you wish to purchase real estate Tax Lien Certificates with your IRA funds. If your IRA custodian/trustee is one of the many stock brokerage houses, banks, mutual fund or insurance companies, it is very likely that they will tell you *"You can't do that with your IRA"*. They like to create the illusion that you cannot buy real estate Tax Lien Certificates, Tax Deeds and Notes with your IRA because they are not equipped to facilitate or service such a purchase. The only reason for this answer is they (the broker) don't make any money from non-financial market products. Their only concern is the fees they (the broker) earn from you, not your wealth.

Big Benefits to Setting up a Self-Directed IRA or SEP with Check Book Control

You will need the assistance of an experienced Self-Directed IRA facilitator to help you set up a single-entity LLC. The formation of the LLC is the most important part of this process and it should be done in full compliance with IRS Regulations. If not formed properly, the IRS could well interpret any IRA funds deposited into the newly created LLC as a prohibited transaction. They may impose fines and a hefty penalty.

After the LLC (you) has been formed, you then elect yourself as the manager to run the fund. As the manger of the LLC you now instruct the Self-Directed IRA to place all, or part, of its funds into the new LLC. As the LLC manager, you would have already opened a bank checking account for the LLC. You now have direct and immediate access to the funds that reside in the LLC checking account. You are now ready to start enjoying the benefits of a Self-Directed IRA with check book control.

As the manager of the LLC, you are empowered to make the investment decisions. These decisions can include, but are not limited to:

• Purchase Real Estate Tax Lien Certificates

• Purchase Real Estate Tax Deeds

- Purchase Real Estate Notes

- Act as a partner in real estate

- Lend money on real estate

- Purchase real estate options

- Purchase a real estate lease

- Consummate a short sale

- Purchase a pre-foreclosure

- Purchase a foreclosure (HUD included)

For more information on this subject you should go to www.lienexchange.com. You will be able to learn more by taking part in their *free* telephone training programs. They also list Tax lien Certificates, Tax Deeds and Notes for sale.

Chapter 6

What to Look for in a Mortgage Note

Five Tips to Buying a "Good" Mortgage Note

Not all mortgage notes are equal. People often laugh when Real Estate Professionals use the phrase "Location, Location, Location". This phrase is mostly used when buying a piece of Real Estate. What most people don't understand is that this still holds true when investing in Mortgage Notes.

Tip #1: Location

You need to check out the location of the property. The mortgage note is secured by the Real Property. Knowing this, the location becomes very important. Most people would agree that they would rather not own a Mortgage Note on a piece of property located in the middle of a desert where the closest form of life is 15 miles away.

Tip #2: LTV (Loan-To-Value)

Loan-To-Value (LTV) means the percentage calculated by dividing the amount borrowed (total of all mortgage liens) by the price or appraised value of the Real Property.

Example:	1st Mortgage	$50,000
	2nd Mortgage	$25,000
	Total Liens:	$75,000 **divided by**
Current Market Value:		$150,000
Equals:		50% LTV

Tip # 3: Lien Position

This is very important. The higher your lien position, the more secure you are. The way it works can be understood using one word, "PRIORITY". Let's say something unfortunate goes wrong with the borrower/homeowner who fails to fulfill their commitment on the payments to the 1st mortgage. The borrower/homeowner has also obtained a 3rd mortgage.

The 1st mortgage holder decides to foreclose. This of course threatens your investment. By law, you have the option as the holder of a mortgage note to pay the delinquent amount to the 1st mortgage holder to protect your investment. Let's say you do this, and now decide to foreclose on the borrower/homeowner.

Referring back to the word "Priority", the only mortgage note you need to maintain is the 1st, because this is the lien before you. In order for the 3rd mortgage holder to protect themselves, they would need to pay all back payments to the 1st mortgage holder as well as to you the (2nd mortgage holder).

Tip #4: Note Terms

You need to know the following:

1) Interest Rate of the Note- To determine the yield spread premium (your return).

2) Terms of Repayment of the Loan- The length of time the borrower/homeowner has to pay off the loan.

3) Loan Type- There are two basic types, Principle and Interest and Interest Only.

> a) With an Interest Only loan, all the payments the borrower/homeowner makes are interest. No payments made affect the principle.

> b) Principle and Interest works the opposite. Each monthly payment affects both the principle balance and the interest. A portion of each payment is applied to the principle and interest.

For example: You lend $10,000 (ten thousand dollars) at 10% for a term of 1 year. You will receive 11 monthly payments of $100.00, while the 12th payment will be $10,100.00. Since all payments were interest only, the original balance remains the same.

Tip #5: Amount of Note

Simply invest at a level of conformability. Let's say you have $150,000 (One Hundred and Fifty Thousand) you want to invest. I suggest instead of investing in one mortgage note of $150,000 you choose to invest in 3 at $50,000 each. That way, should one of the notes become a problem, you are still receiving payments on the other two.

Chapter 7

Understanding Your Credit Report

There are 3 main credit reporting agencies: Equifax, Experian and Trans Union. Mistakes can and sometimes will appear on your credit report. It's very important that you check your report regularly. What can you expect to see on your credit report?

Your personal details: such as name, address, SSN (Social Security Number), employment, DOB (Date of Birth). You will need to check these to ensure they are all correct. Should you find any errors, mail copies of your driver's license, a bank account statement, and a utility bill (if you are employed send a copy of your pay statement).

Open accounts will include your mortgage, car loans, credit cards, store cards and any other loan or line of credit you may have. The information here will show how you handle your accounts; do you pay on time, are you a late payer, as well as how much of your credit line you are using.

Closed accounts will list all the accounts that you or your creditors have closed and the reason why the account was closed.

Derogatory accounts are the accounts that your creditors have put into collection. They can go back as far as ten years. Seven is the normal time limit for these items. It will, for the most part, list the outstanding balance, the creditor who put it into collection and the date the account was opened and went into collection. The main problem with these items is that they can be listed numerous times. It is not unusual to see the same account listed under all three credit agencies.

Public records are the most damaging items on your report. They include things like, IRS liens, Property Tax liens, Judgments and Bankruptcies.

Inquiries list all the companies who have requested your report. Too many of these will effect your credit score.

Can I really repair my credit report?

The answer to this question is **YES.** Many of the clients who have come to us over the years after being turned down for a mortgage or home equity loan by other companies, have successfully used our credit repair clinic.

Most now have the mortgage or home equity loan they wanted at better rates and terms than offered by the companies who first turned them down.

Do Credit Checks or Credit Inquiries Hurt You?

The answer to this question is **YES.** At the very end of your credit report will be a list of inquiries. An inquiry notation is made each time someone requests a copy of your credit report from that credit bureau. Companies that receive a copy of your credit report will be listed under this inquiry section of your report.

Lenders normally don't like to see a lot of inquiries on a credit report. Excessive inquiries often result in a credit denial as easily as bad credit. However, not all inquires are viewed negatively. Below are six origins of inquiries:

Your Existing Creditors (No Problem)

Your existing creditors may do a periodic review of your account for many reasons. These inquiries are not viewed negatively.

Yourself (No Problem)

A notation may be made each time you request a copy of your own file. This notation does not appear on the copy that goes to your potential lender and does not count against you.

The Bureau (No Problem)

Bureaus may compile mailing lists for its subscribers based on the criteria that the lender specifies. Your report may be viewed as a candidate for a particular mailing list. Again, these internal inquiries do not appear on the copy that goes to your potential lenders and therefore do not reflect negatively.

Potential Lenders (negative)

Lenders do not have to have your permission to obtain a copy of your credit file. The law only requires that they reasonably expect to use the information in a credit transaction. Any member of the bureau can obtain your file. All they need is a social security number or a name and address. You should be cautious about giving out any such information until you're serious about doing business.

IRS (negative)

Anyone who has a judgment against them (negative)

The most common inquiries are those by lenders with whom you have applied for credit. A banker will look at them in one of two ways: (1) if they are recent, they are looked at as potential debt pending approval. Lenders have no way of knowing the status of these other pending applications and are likely to take the safest action by denying your application; and (2) If they are more than a couple of months old and it looks as if they turned you down and if there are several previous declines, the banker has to wonder why.

Inquiries will remain on your file for up to 2 years. Those in the last 6 months will count most heavily against you. It is a good idea to review the log to make certain that each inquiry was done with "permissible purpose" as explained in Section 604 of the Fair Credit Reporting Act (FCRA). The FCRA defines the "permissible purposes" for which consumer credit profiles can be provided to others. A credit report may be supplied for the following purposes:

Credit granting considerations

Review or collection of an account

Employment considerations

Insurance underwriting

Application for a government license

With your written permission

Or in response to a court order

FBI investigation

So unless someone fits these categories, they should not be viewing your credit file. Anyone who knowingly and willfully obtains a credit report under false pretenses may be fined under title 18, United States Code, and imprisoned up to two years.

What You Need to Know

The credit score system was developed a number of years ago by a company named Fair Isaac. The system is used by the three main credit bureaus for generating your credit scores. They all use different terms for the scores, Equifax call it your FICO score, Experian calls it your BEACON score and TransUnion calls it your EMPIRICA score.

When you apply for credit, the company will request a copy of your credit report from these bureaus. They then disregard the highest and lowest score and take the *middle score* as your credit score. For example, if your scores were to come in as 592, 612 and 684, your mid score would be 612. There are a number of factors that determine how you are scored, beginning with "Derogatory Accounts." These are accounts that have normally been passed to a collection agency. The next question that might be asked is: Do you have open accounts that have a history of late payments? This is usually shown as 30 days, 60 days, 90 days or 120 days. Another common question is: How close are you to your available credit limits? All of these questions plus situations like bankruptcy or filing Chapter 7 or 13 in the last ten years will affect your score.

Getting your Credit Report

You can apply for your credit reports online from the three bureaus; this is the most cost-effective way. There are a number of online companies that will supply your credit report for you. Most of these are difficult to read and will normally cost you somewhere between $24 and $30. The bureaus will charge you around $8.00 each which is a little more work but this way you get to see very clearly what each bureau is reporting and can take the necessary steps to correct any item that may be reported incorrectly.

Getting a Free Credit Report

If you have been denied credit in the last 60 days you can ask for a free credit report, this will not normally come with a credit score but it will let you see what is causing you to be denied. Some states allow you to receive one free report each year (again, these do not normally come with a credit score). You can apply in writing, over the phone or online.

These are the three main reporting bureaus:

Equifax, PO Box 740241, Atlanta, GA 30374-0241

Telephone: (404) 885 8000

Web site: www.equifax.com

Experian, PO Box 2104, Allen TX 75013-2104

Telephone: (800) 583 4080

Web site: www.experian.com

TransUnion, PO Box 390, Springfield, PA 19064-0390

Telephone: (800) 916 8800

Web site: www.transunion.com

Chapter 8

Can I really repair my credit report?

The answer to this question is **YES.** The higher you can get your credit scores the better. Regardless of how many derogatory items you have on your report, you should at least make the effort to begin clearing them. Everything we do is reflected *in* or dependent *on* our credit reports. Failure to keep them in order can result in you not getting credit, a job or insurance.

Repairing your Credit Report

1st Step
Your Credit Report

The first thing you need to do is obtain a copy of your credit report and check all your personal details. If there are any errors, mail copies of your driver's license, a bank statement and a utility bill (if you are employed also send copy of your pay stub). It is very important that you keep this information updated.

2nd Step

Your Open Accounts

Look at your open accounts and check for payment records. If you see late payments that are not correct, then get the statements and bank records that prove these entries are incorrect and send photocopies to the bureaus using one of the "Dispute Letters" from the "Letters" selection (See Chapter 10). Also, check the balances for accuracy. If these are incorrect, then do the same thing. Creditors can take up to 60 days to list new balances. You are also checking to make sure all the accounts listed are yours.

Try to keep your credit balances on credit cards and store cards to *less* than 50% of your available credit limit. It will cost you points on your credit score when you go over 70% of your available balance.

When you apply for major credit items like a car loan or mortgage, the company will be looking at how you manage your accounts. This is as important as your credit score. Inquiries are generally listed on your credit report for up to 2 years. Four to eight inquires within the last few months will begin to penalize your credit score, so if you are planning on applying for credit, spread your applications out over a period of time to minimize the effect.

Remember to keep copies of every letter you send to the bureaus. If you do not get a reply within 30 days, resend the letter.

3rd Step

Closed Accounts

This section will list all the accounts that you or your creditors have closed and the reason why the accounts were closed. You need to check that all the accounts were closed with a zero balance and were kept in "good standing." Make sure all the accounts listed were yours. If any of the information listed is incorrect, photocopy the closing statements and mail to the bureaus using one of the "Dispute Letters" from the "Letters" section (See Chapter 10).

4th Step

Derogatory Accounts

These are the accounts that your creditors have put into collection. They can go back as far as ten years, although seven is the normal time limit for these items. It will, for the most part, list the balance outstanding, the creditor who put it into collection and the dates the account was opened and went into collection.

The main problem with these items is that they can be listed numerous times. It is not unusual to see the same account listed by 3 or more collection agencies. The reason for this is a collection agency will have the file for a period of time and if they are unable to collect on the debt, they will sell the file to another collection agency but fail to inform the bureaus that they no longer hold the account.

The first thing to do is check the reporting date of the file. The collection agency with the last reporting date will be the company holding the account. Use one of the "Dispute Letters" from the "Letters" section (See Chapter 10). Send the letter to all of the bureaus listing the reference number of the account, the name of the company and the amount of the outstanding balance. Use the following term as the reason for the "Dispute": **"This Company no longer holds this account. Please delete this item from my credit report."** Repeat this formula for all the duplicated accounts.

The bureaus will write back to you normally within 30 days listing all the changes and an updated report. **Persistence** is the name of this game! If for some reason one of the agencies does not reply or fails to remove the item, then re-submit, using one of the "Dispute Letters" from the "Letters" section at the rear of this book.

After you have removed all the duplicated entries, start working on the accounts that you feel are (a) not yours, and (b) not correct -- you may have paid or the amount you owe is incorrect. Using one of the "Dispute Letters" from the "Letters" section (See Chapter 10), send the letter to all of the bureaus listing the reference number of the account, the name of the company and the amount of the outstanding balance and always list the reason for the dispute. This is where real **Persistence is needed!** It may take a number of letters to get these reported correctly, but it's important that you do not give up. Just keep going until you get the matter resolved to your satisfaction.

You are now ready to start calling the companies you owe money. Work out what you can afford and start from there. You should always start by offering as little as possible -- whatever you offer they will ask for more. We always start at 25% of the outstanding balance. When they say "No," ask them for a settlement figure. Never agree to anything there and then. They will say things like "if you pay today by credit card or check by post" -- remember they want your money, and you want the best deal. _NEVER PAY THEM UNTIL YOU HAVE RECEIVED A LETTER ON THEIR LETTERHEAD CONFIRMING YOUR AGREEMENT._

You want their letter to say the following: "We accept (Dollar amount) as a full and final settlement of this account and will report the account as settled to the credit bureaus within the next 30 days.

Always get the name of the person you are talking to. Make a note of the date and time and outline what was said. It can sometimes take 3 or even 4 phone calls to get what you want. Agree on a settlement fee of no more than 60% of the outstanding balance. If you have multiple accounts with this company, then ensure they list all the accounts and balances in the letter. PLEASE DO NOT PAY ANY COLLECTION COMPANY UNTIL YOU HAVE THIS LETTER. *Remember*, you are trying to repair your report, not get into a long dispute over what was agreed over the telephone. Once you have settled and the check has cleared or the payment appears on your credit card statement, using one of the "Dispute Letters" from the "Letters" section (See Chapter 10), send the letter to all of the bureaus listing the reference number of the account, the name of the company and the amount of the outstanding balance. Enclose a copy of the settlement letter and confirmation of payment and request for it to show a zero balance. Do not wait for the collection company to do it for you. No matter what they say on the phone, once they have your money they will have little or no interest in helping you.

5th Step
Public records

These are the most damaging items on your credit report. They can include things like IRS liens, Property Tax liens, Judgments and Bankruptcies. The first thing to do is check that they are yours and reported correctly. If you have any public record entries, it is always a good idea to pay them off or come to an arrangement for payment. Property taxes, once filed, cannot be negotiated. They will continuously accrue interest on the judgment amount, so we always advise our clients to settle these first.

6th Step
Inquiries

This is a list of all the companies who have requested your report. Too many of these will effect your credit score. You should check these carefully. If you find companies other than those you owe money or companies to whom you have made an application for credit, then using one of the "Dispute Letters" from the "Letters" section (See Chapter 10), send the letter to all of the bureaus listing the name of the company and date of the inquiry with the following statement: **"Please remove this inquiry. I did not approve or request this inquiry."**

Chapter 9

How to Establish a Good Credit Score

It will take some time to establish a really good credit score. Most lenders will be looking at your credit report to see how many trade lines you have. Trade lines are open credit accounts. They will be looking at a number of different things: how many, how much, how long and your payment record.

If you are looking to purchase a house or a car, then this is very important to you for a number of reasons. The first is that it will help secure the loan for you. The second is what interest rate they will charge you.

Establishing a good credit record cannot be done overnight. It takes time and you need to be patient. Allow at least six months before you start applying for credit and then do it slowly. Too many inquiries on your report at the same time *will reduce your credit score.*

Open a Bank Account

If you do not have a bank account opened already, then open one. Try and use one of the bigger banks like

Bank of America, Citibank, Wells Fargo, or Citibank. National banks like these will get you a higher credit rating on your accounts.

Build up the account balance over the first month by placing at least half of the funds into a linked savings account. The idea at this stage is to get the account to somewhere around $1000 with between $500 and $600 of this in the savings account.

Open a CD (Cash Deposit) account

Ask the bank to open you a CD account. This is an account where you agree to leave a set amount of money for a set amount of time at a set interest rate. Banks really like this type of account because it allows them to use your money for their business. What you are looking to do is put most of the funds held in your savings account into the CD account. Let's say that you had $600 in your savings account. You would be placing $500 of this into the CD account.

Securing Lines of Credit

Let the funds sit in the account for one month, then go back to the bank and ask for a "secured credit card" for $100 less than the funds in the CD account and tell them you want the card secured by the CD account.

The most important thing here is to use the card wisely by paying off the account before the due date, thus building up a good credit record. You now have a trade line. You will need to repeat this two more times. The 2nd time, the trade line should be a small bank loan for let's say $1000. You will need another CD for $1300 to $1500. Again, you will be securing the loan against the CD account. There are a number of credit card companies that supply secured credit cards, but before applying, find out if they report the account to the credit bureaus. If they do not, then don't apply for their card. The whole idea here is to build up a credit history that is reported.

I would recommend that you wait at least six months before applying for store cards and lines of credit. To ensure that you are not denied credit, apply for your credit report and have a look at the scores. You are trying to get your middle score over 620; this should allow you to apply for credit without disappointment. Please remember -- do not apply for too much credit at the same time because this will affect your score and undo all your hard work. Patience is the key to success here!

Chapter 10

Credit Repair Sample Letters

The following pages are Sample letters that you can use to help repair your credit report

Sample 1 (Disputed items: Personal Details)

Sample 2 (Disputed items: Paid)

Sample 3 (Disputed items: Investigate)

Sample 4 (Disputed items: Re-Investigate))

Sample 5 (Disputed items: Unauthorized Credit Inquiry)

Sample 6 (Direct Letter to Creditor)

REMEMBER YOU MAY NEED TO SEND THE SAME LETTERS MORE THAN ONCE TO GET WHAT YOU WANT

PERSERVERANCE AND PATIENCE WILL PAY OFF!!

For those of you who are not comfortable dealing with collection agencies, we recommend the following company: *www.wcmdirect.com*. Their fees are reasonable and they offer first class service.

Sample 1 Disputed Items: Personal Details

(Enter Your Name)
(Enter Your Address)
(Enter Your City and Zip Code)

Date: (enter date)

Equifax
PO Box 740241
Atlanta GA 30374-0241

Experian   Trans Union
PO Box 2104   PO Box 1000
Allen TX 75013   Chester, PA 19022

Reference: Consumer Report – SSN# (enter your SSN)

Dear Sir/Madam

Change of Address

Would you please be kind enough to update your files to my new address as listed above. I am enclosing a copy of my DL and change of address issued by the DMV/Utility bill/Void Check/Bank Statement.

Date of Birth (Incorrect Report)

Please correct my date of birth as listed on my DL.

Employment Details

Please amend your records to show my correct employment details. I have enclosed a pay stub to confirm this employment.

Please amend my credit report to show the above details and send me an updated copy of my report.

Yours sincerely

(enter your name)

Sample 2 Disputed Items: Paid

(Enter Your Name)
(Enter your Address)
(Enter Your City and Zip Code)

Date: (enter the date)

Equifax
PO Box 740241
Atlanta GA 30374-0241

Experian   Trans Union
PO Box 2104   PO Box 1000
Allen TX 75013   Chester, PA 19022

Reference: Consumer Report – SSN# (enter your SSN)

Dear Sir/Madam

Disputed Items (Incorrect Report)

(I would recommend that you limit this to 3 items per letter).

(Enter Company Name and Account number as listed on your report)

I am disputing the validity of this alleged debt. This account has been settled and should read as a zero balance. I am enclosing confirmation of payment.

(Enter Company Name and Account number as listed on your report)

I am disputing the validity of this alleged debt. This account has been settled and should read as a zero balance. I am enclosing confirmation of payment.

(Enter Company Name and Account number as listed on your report)

I am disputing the validity of this alleged debt. This account has been settled and should read as a zero balance. I am enclosing confirmation of payment.

Please amend my credit report to show the settlement and disputes and send me an updated copy of my credit report.

Yours sincerely

(enter your name)

Sample 3 Disputed Items: Investigate

(Enter you Name)
(Enter your Address)
(Enter Your City and Zip Code)

Date: (enter the date)

Equifax
PO Box 740241
Atlanta GA 30374-0241

Experian   Trans Union
PO Box 2104   PO Box 1000
Allen TX 75013   Chester, PA 19022

Reference: Consumer Report – SSN# (enter your SSN)

Dear Sir/Madam

Disputed Items (Incorrect Report - Please Investigate)

(We recommend that you limit the number of items to 3 per letter).

(Enter Company Name and Account Number)

I am disputing the validity of this alleged debt. I have no knowledge of this company or account. PLEASE INVESTIGATE.

(Enter Company Name and Account Number)

I am disputing the validity of this alleged debt. I have no knowledge of this company or account. PLEASE INVESTIGATE

(Enter Company Name and Account Number)

I am disputing the validity of this alleged debt. I have no knowledge of this company or account. PLEASE INVESTIGATE

Would you please amend my credit report to show these items are in Dispute and send me an updated copy of my credit report.

Yours sincerely

(enter your name)

Sample 4 Disputed Items: Re-Investigate

(Enter you Name)
(Enter your Address)
(Enter Your City and Zip Code)

Date: (enter the date)

Equifax
PO Box 740241
Atlanta GA 30374-0241

Experian   Trans Union
PO Box 2104   PO Box 1000
Allen TX 75013   Chester, PA 19022

Reference: Consumer Report – SSN# (enter your SSN)

Dear Sir/Madam

With reference to your letter dated (enter report date), I am still disputing the following items despite your recent investigations. These items are not being reported correctly and they are injurious to my credit score.

Disputed Items (Incorrect Report - Please Reinvestigate)

(We recommend that you limit the number of items to 3 per letter).

(Enter Company Name and Account Number)

I am disputing the validity of this alleged debt.   PLEASE REINVESTIGATE.

(Enter Company Name and Account Number)

I am disputing the validity of this alleged debt.   PLEASE REINVESTIGATE.

(Enter Company Name and Account Number)

I am disputing the validity of this alleged debt.   PLEASE REINVESTIGATE.

In accordance with the Fair Credit Reporting, please forward me the name and addresses of the person or persons with whom you verified the above information. Please amend my credit report to show these items are in Dispute.

Yours sincerely

(Enter your Name)

Sample 5 Disputed Items: Unauthorized Credit Inquiry

(Enter Your Name)
(Enter your Address)
(Enter Your City and Zip Code)

Date: (enter the date)

Equifax
PO Box 740241
Atlanta GA 30374-0241

Experian   Trans Union
PO Box 2104   PO Box 1000
Allen TX 75013   Chester, PA 19022

Reference: Consumer Report – SSN# (enter your SSN)

Dear Sir/Madam

Disputed Items (Unauthorized Credit Inquiry)

(I would recommend that you limit this to 5 items per letter).

(Enter Company Name and Date of Inquiry as listed on your report)

I am disputing the validity of this Unauthorized Credit Inquiry. Please remove this from my credit report.

(Enter Company Name and Date of Inquiry as listed on your report)

I am disputing the validity of this Unauthorized Credit Inquiry. Please remove this from my credit report.

(Enter Company Name and Date of Inquiry as listed on your report)

I am disputing the validity of this Unauthorized Credit Inquiry Please remove this from my credit report.

Please amend my credit report to show these Inquiries have been deleted and send me an updated copy of my credit report.

Yours sincerely

(enter your name)

Sample 6: Letter Directly to Creditor

(Name)
(Address)
(Address 2)

Date: (enter the date)

Company Name
Address
Address

Reference: Consumer Report – SSN#

Partial Account Number: (enter No)
Original Creditor: (enter Creditor)
Balance Reported: (enter balance)

Dear Sir/Madam

This letter is a formal complaint that you are reporting inaccurate credit information.

I am deeply distressed that you have included the information above in my credit profile. You have failed to maintain reasonable procedures in your operations to assure maximum possible accuracy in the credit reports you publish.

Credit reporting laws ensure that the bureaus should report only 100% accurate credit information. It is your responsibility to ensure you take every step possible to assure the information is completely accurate and correct.

The above listed account urgently needs to be re-investigated. I respectfully request to be provided with proof of this alleged debt, specifically the contact, note or other instrument bearing my signature. Failing that, I demand that this item be deleted from my credit report as soon as possible.

The above listed account is entirely inaccurate and incomplete, and as such represents a very serious error in your reporting. Please delete this misleading information.

Under federal law, you have thirty (30) days to complete your re-investigation. Be advised that the description of the procedure used to determine the accuracy and completeness of the information is hereby requested as well, to be provided within fifteen (15) days of the completion of your re-investigation.

Sincerely

(enter name)

Chapter 11

Direct Access Cheat Sheet

COMPANY	PHONE NUMBER	HOW TO CHEAT
US Finance		
Accredited Home Lenders	(877) 683-4466	Press 0
Advanta (business cards)	800-705-7255	1, 0
America First	800-999-3961	0 or say ""member services
American Education Services	800-233-0557	Select language, then press 2, then 00# at each prompt
American Express	800-528-4800	0 repeatedly
American Funds	800-421-0180	Press 0.
Ameritrade	800-669-3900	3, 3, 0. (Former **Datek** Clients: 800-823-2835)
AT&T Universal Card	800-423-4343	Do not say anything or push any buttons! It takes awhile, but eventually a human comes on-line!
Bank of America	800 900 9000	At ANY Bank of America number, press *0 to get human.
Bank One	877-226-5663	00
Bayview Loan Services	800-457-5105	Press 0.
Bloomingdales Credit	800-295-4057	"Say ""agent."""
Capital One	800-903-3637	For all Capital One #s, press 0 at each prompt or just don't do anything until finally offered option of representative
Charles Schwab	800-435-9050	3, 0
Chase	800-242-7324	At most Chase numbers, press 0 at each prompt; eventually get rep.
Chase Auto Loans	800-346-9670	Press 1, 2, *0
Chase Credit Cards	800-625-5161	Direct to human. (This line is for online issues only.)
Chrysler Financial	800-700-0738	Select language, then press 00
Citi Cards	866-696-5673	Press 0 to get a human is offered at many Citibank numbers.
Citibank	800-756-7047	Otherwise, press 0 at each prompt; eventually get rep.
Citizens Bank	800-922-9999	Press 0,0,0
Columbia Mutual Funds	800-345-6611	"Say ""representative."" "

Commerce Bank	800-937-2000	Press 0.
Countrywide Loans	800-669-5864	Press 0 repeatedly
Decision One Mortgage	888-264-3663	Don't press any keys when prompted; they transfer you
Diner's Club	800-729-5309	Press 2.
Direct Merchants Bank	800-379-7999	Press 0 at each prompt; eventually get rep.
Discover	800-347-2683	****
Dodge and Cox	800-621-3979	Press 0.
e*Trade	800-786-2575	#### (4 pound signs)
Edward Jones	314-515-2000	Worldwide corporate HQ in St. Louis, MO still answers 314-515-2000 with switchboard operators, who announce their name as well
Emigrant direct	800-836-1997	Human answers.
Equifax	866-640-2273	Choose option 3, then press 0 and wait patiently for human.
Exxon Mobil Card	800-344-4355	000 ignoring message
Fidelity	800-544-6666	ignore prompt for social security number, just enter ###
Fidelity NetBenefits	800-581-5800	1,################
Fifth Third Bank	800-972-3030	0,0
First National Bank of Omaha	888-530-3626	Press 0 at each prompt.
Ford Interest Advantage	800-462-2614	Choose option 4, then option 0 to speak to rep.
GE Finance CareCredit	866-893-7864	1, 6, 5, 0, 0
GM MasterCard	800-947-1000	"Press ""0"" at each prompt."
Green Dot Online	866-443-6227	Wait through prompts 3 times, then long wait for rep.
Harris Direct	800-825-5723	Press 0.
Honda Financial Services	800-445-1358	Press 0 at each prompt regardless of the message.
Household Bank (Credit card)	800-771-7339	Press 0 at each prompt to get human.
HSBC	800-477-6000	1, 3, 0
ING	800-464-3473	Direct to human.
Key Bank	800-539-2968	Remain on line; press nothing
M&T Bank	800-724-2440	Press 0 at each prompt.
Marshall Fields Credit Card	800-280-4356	After greeting, choose option #9, and then press 0.
MasterCard	800-MC-ASSIST	000 on each menu
MBNA	800-421-2110	00 when menu starts
Mellon Investor	800-649-3593	Wait through initial recording finishes, select nothing--wait--you will be connected to a live customer service rep

MetLife Bank	866-226-5638	Press # after each menu.
Moneygram	800-926-9400	Press 0 when menu starts.
NAVY FCU	800-914-9494	Press 2, then press * 3 times.
NOVA Information Systems	800 377-3962	Press 0
PayPal	402-935-7733	"Say ""agent.""" See also.
Paypal Buyer Credit	866-571-3012	Be silent and at the end of the options press 6.
PNC Bank	888-762-2265	"Press * till it says ""transferring to customer support;"" takes about 3 *s."
Privacy Guard	800-734-0199	"Say ""agent"" or ""no"" or any word at each prompt."
Prudential Annuity Service Center	888-778-2888	Press *, *. At SSN prompt, press *, *. At end of message will reach rep.
RBS Credit Card Services	800-747-8155	Press 0 at each prompt; eventually get rep.
Smith Barney Benefit access	888-822-6067	Press 0.
Sovereign Bank	877-768-2265	Do not say anything or push any buttons. Eventually a human comes on the line.
State Farm Bank	877-734-2265	Press 0
SunTrust	800-786-8787	Press # after each menu.
T. Rowe Price	800-922-9945	Say 'Representative' at every opportunity
T. Rowe Price	800-225-5132	Press 0 at each prompt.
TD Waterhouse	800-934-4448	Press # after opening prompt, then do it again after prompt to be transferred to rep.
The Student Loan Corp. (Citibank)	800-967-2400	Choose option 5.
The Student Loan People	888-250-6401	Press 0 repeatedly.
TIAA-CREF	800-842-2252	Press 00 at each prompt.
Toyota Financial Services	800-874-8822	"Just stay on the line. Do not hit ""1"" for English or ""0"" for Spanish. "
TransUnion	800-916-8800	No cheat necessary; 2nd prompt offers human contact
US Bank	800-872-2657	0000
USAA	800-531-2265	"Say ""representative"" at every opportunity."
Visa	800-847-2911	000 (ignore prompts saying that it's an invalid entry)
Wachovia	800-922-4684	0, 0
Wal Mart Credit Card	866-888-3868	0
Washington Mutual	800-756-8000	At any time after the announcement(s) press 0,0.

Washington Mutual	800-788-7000	Press 0 at each prompt regardless of the message.
Wells Fargo	800-869-3557	"0,0,0 or when asked for account number say ""I don't know"""
Western Union	800-325-6000	* then ##

US Government

Sallie Mae - Student Loans	888-272-5543	Don't speak or enter anything and you will be transferred to an agent.
US Dept. of Education - Loans	800-848-0979	Say and do nothing at the prompt and you will be transferred to someone.
US Dept. of State - Passports	877-487-2778	Choose English, press 1, 3.
US Dept. of Transportation	800-832-5660	Press 000.
US Dept. of Veterans Affairs	800-827-1000	Press 1, 0.
US Federal Trade Commission	877-382-4357	At each prompt, press 4, 5, 0.
US Homeland Security - FEMA	800-621-FEMA	Select language (1 for English), Don't choose any option, just hold for human; or press 00
US Homeland Security - INS	800-375-5283	Select language, then press 2, 6, 2, 4 at the prompts, then press 0.
US Medicare	800-633-4227	"Say ""agent"" or press 0."
US Postal Service	800-275-8777	Press 3 at each prompt. Press 2 at the next recording.
US Social Security Admin	800-772-1213	Press 00.

US Insurance

Aetna	800-537-9384	"2, then say ""operator"" (check this)"
Aetna	800-680-3566	* then 0 anytime
AIG	877-638-4244	Direct to human.
Blue Cross FEP	800-451-7602	Wait for prompt, then press 0, 3 to reach a CS rep.
CIGNA	800-516-2898	REGARDING A BILL
Cigna	800-849-9000	##
Delta Dental	888-335-8227	00000, wait through message, select language, 4, 0.
GEICO	800-841-3000	Wait for prompt then 6, 1, 5; Or dial 800-555-2752
Medco	800-251-7690	"0000, enter member id or say ""I don't have a member id."""
Medicare	800-633-4227	"After the opening prompt say ""agent""."
Principal Life	800-247-4695	1 for English, 2, then 0 several times.

Appendix

Chapter 12

FAIR CREDIT BILLING ACT

THE FAIR CREDIT BILLING ACT

Public Law 93-49593rd Congress - H.R. 11221

Fair Credit Billing Act.15 USC 1601note.

TITLE III - FAIR CREDIT BILLING

§ 301. Short Title

This title may be cited as the .Fair Credit Billing Act.

§ 302. Declaration of purpose

The last sentence of section 102 of the Truth in Lending Act (15 U.S.C. 1601) is amended by striking out the period and inserting in lieu thereof a comma and the following: .and to protect the consumer against inaccurate and unfair credit billing and credit card practices.

§ 303. Definitions of creditor and open end credit plan

The first sentence of section 103(f) of the Truth in Lending Act (15 U.S.C. 1602(f)) is amended to read as follows: .The term .creditor refers only to creditors who regularly extend, or arrange for the extension of, credit which is payable by agreement in more than four installments or for which the payment of a finance charge is or may be required, whether in connection with loans, sales of property or services, or otherwise. For the purposes of the requirements imposed under Chapter 4 and sections 127(a) (6), 127(a) (7), 127(a) (8), 127(b) (1), 127(b) (2), 127(b) (3), 127(b) (9), and 127(b) (11) of Chapter 2 of this Title, the term .creditor. shall also include card issuers whether or not the amount due is payable by agreement in more than four installments or the payment of a finance charge is or may be required, and the Board shall, by regulation, apply these requirements to such card issuers, to the extent appropriate, even though the requirements are by their terms applicable only to creditors offering open end credit plans. 1

Post, p. 1512. Infra, 15 USC 1637.

PUBLIC LAW 93-495 - October 28, 1974

§ 304. Disclosure of fair credit billing rights

(a) Section 127(a) of the Truth in Lending Act (15 U.S.C. 1637(a)) is amended by adding at the end thereof a new paragraph as follows: .(8) A statement, in a form prescribed by regulations of the Board of the protection provided by sections 161 and 170 to an obligor and the creditors responsibilities under sections 162 and 170. With respect to each of two billing cycles per year, at semiannual intervals, the creditor shall transmit such statement to each obligor to whom the creditor is required to transmit a statement pursuant to sections 127(b) for such billing cycle. (b) Section 127(c) of such Act (15 U.S.C. 1637(c)) is amended to read: .(c) In the case of any existing account under an open end consumer credit plan having an outstanding balance of more than $1 at or after the close of the creditors first full billing cycle under the plan after the effective date of subsection

(a) or any amendments thereto, the items described in subsection (a), to the extent applicable and not previously disclosed, shall be disclosed in a notice mailed or delivered to the obligor not later than the time of mailing the next statement required by subsection (b).§ **305. Disclosure of billing contact**

Section 127(b) of the Truth in Lending Act (15 U.S.C. 1637(b)) is amended by adding at the end thereof a new paragraph as follows: (11) the address to be used by the creditor for the purpose of receiving billing inquiries from the obligor. § **306. Billing practices** The Truth in Lending Act (15 U.S.C. 1601-1665) is amended by adding at the end thereof a new chapter as follows:

Post, pp. 1512,

1515.

PUBLIC LAW 93-495 - October 28, 1974

.Chapter 4.CREDIT BILLING

Sec. 161. Correction of billing errors 162. Regulation of credit reports. 163. Length of billing period. 164. Prompt crediting of payments. 165. Crediting excess payments. 166. Prompt notification of returns. 167. Use of cash discounts. 168. Prohibition of tie-in services. 169. Prohibition of offsets. 170. Rights of credit card customers. 171. Relation to State laws.

§ **161. Correction of billing errors.** (a) If a creditor, within sixty days after having transmitted to an obligor a statement of the obligor's account in connection with an extension of consumer credit, receives at the address disclosed under section 127(b) (11) a written notice (other than notice on a payment stub or other payment medium supplied by the creditor if the creditor so stipulates with the disclosure required under section 127(a) (8)) from the obligor in which the obligor. .(1) sets forth or otherwise enables the creditor to identify the name and account number (if any) of the obligor, .(2) indicates the obligor's belief that the statement contains a billing error and the amount of such billing error, and .(3) sets forth the reasons for the obligor's belief (to the extent applicable) that the statement contains a billing error, the creditor shall, unless the obligor has, after giving such written notice and before the expiration of the time limits herein specified, agreed that the statement was correct. .(A) not later than thirty days after the receipt of the notice, send a written acknowledgment thereof to the obligor, unless the action required in subparagraph (B) is taken within such thirty-day period, and .(B) not later than two complete billing cycles of the 3

15 USC 1666.

Ante, p. 1511.

Ante, p. 1511.

PUBLIC LAW 93-495 - October 28, 1974 creditor (in no event later than ninety days) after the receipt of the notice and prior to taking any action to collect the amount, or any part thereof, indicated by the obligor under paragraph (2) either. .(i) make appropriate corrections in the account of the obligor, including the crediting of any finance charges on amounts erroneously billed, and transmit to the obligor a notification of such corrections and the creditors explanation of any cage in the amount indicated by the obligor under paragraph (2) and, if any such change is made and the obligor so requests, copies of documentary evidence of the obligor's indebtedness; or .(ii) send a written explanation or clarification to the obligor, after having conducted an investigation, setting forth to the extent applicable the reasons why the creditor believes the account of the obligor was correctly shown in the statement and, upon request of the obligor, provide copies of documentary evidence of the obligor's indebtedness. In the case of a billing error where the obligor alleges that the creditors billing statement reflects goods not delivered to the obligor or his designee in accordance with the agreement made at the time of the transaction, a creditor may not construe such amount to be correctly shown unless he determines that such goods were actually delivered, mailed, or otherwise sent to the obligor and provides the obligor with a statement of such determination. After complying with the provisions of this subsection with respect to an alleged billing error, a creditor has no further responsibility under this section if the obligor continues to make substantially the same allegation with respect to such error. . (b) For the purpose of this section, a .billing error. Consists of any of the following:

. (1) A reflection on a statement of an extension of credit

4

Definitions.

PUBLIC LAW 93-495 - October 28, 1974

which was not made to the obligor or, if made, was not in the amount reflected on such statement. . (2) A reflection on a statement of an extension of credit for which the obligor requests additional clarification including documentary evidence thereof. . (3) A reflection on a statement of goods or services not accepted by the obligor or his designee or not delivered to the obligor or his designee in accordance with the agreement made at the time of a transaction. . (4) The creditor's failure to reflect properly on a statement a payment made by the obligor or a credit issued to the obligor. . (5) A computation error or similar error of an accounting nature of the creditor on a statement. . (6) Any other error described in regulations of the Board. . (c) For the purposes of this section, .action to collect the amount, or any part thereof, indicated by an obligor under paragraph (2). does not include the sending of statements of account to the obligor following written notice from the obligor as specified under subsection (a) if. . (1) the obligor's account is not restricted or closed because of the failure of the obligor to pay the amount indicated under paragraph (2) of subsection (a) and . (2) the creditor indicates the payment of such amount is not required pending the creditor's compliance with this section. Nothing in this section shall be construed to prohibit any action by a creditor to collect any amount which has not been indicated by the obligor to contain a billing error. . (d) Pursuant to regulations of the Board, a creditor operating an open end consumer credit plan may not, prior to the sending of the written explanation or clarification required under paragraph (B) (ii), restrict or close an account with respect to which the obligor has indicated pursuant to subsection (a) that he believes such account to contain a billing error solely because of the obligor's failure to pay the amount indicated to be in error. Nothing in this subsection shall

5

PUBLIC LAW 93-495 - October 28, 1974

be deemed to prohibit a creditor from applying against the credit limit on the obligor's account the amount indicated to be in error.

.(e) Any creditor who fails to comply with the requirements of this section or section 162 forfeits any right to collect from the obligor the amount indicated by the obligor under paragraph (2) of subsection (a) of this section, and any finance charges thereon, except that the amount required to be forfeited under this subsection may not exceed $50.

§ 162. Regulation of credit reports

.(a) After receiving a notice from an obligor as provided in section 161(a), a creditor or his agent may not directly or indirectly threaten to report to any person adversely on the obligor's credit rating or credit standing because of the obligor's failure to pay the amount indicated by the obligor under section 161(a) (2) and such amount may not be reported as delinquent to any third party until the creditor has met the requirements of section 161 and has allowed the obligor the same number of days (not less than ten) thereafter to make payment as is provided under the credit agreement with the obligor for the payment of undisputed amounts. .(b) If a creditor receives a further written notice from an obligor that an amount is still in dispute within the time allowed for payment under subsection (a) of this section, a creditor may not report to any third party that the amount of the obligor is delinquent because the obligor has failed to pay an amount which he has indicated under section 161(a) (2), unless the creditor also reports that the amount is in dispute and, at the same time, notifies the obligor of the name and address of each party to whom the creditor is reporting information concerning the delinquency. . (c) A creditor shall report any subsequent resolution of any delinquencies reported pursuant to subsection (b) to the parties to whom such delinquencies were initially reported.

6

Noncompliance.

15 USC 1666a.

PUBLIC LAW 93-495 - October 28, 1974

§ 163. Length of billing period

.(a) If an open end consumer credit plan provides a time period within which an obligor may repay any portion of the credit extended without incurring an additional finance charge, such additional finance charge may not be imposed with respect to such portion of the credit extended for the billing cycle of which such period is a part unless a statement which includes the amount upon which the finance charge for that period is based was mailed at least fourteen days prior to the date specified in the statement by which payment must be made in order to avoid imposition of that finance charge. .(b) Subsection (a) does not apply in any case where a creditor has been prevented, delayed, or hindered in making timely mailing or delivery of such periodic statement within the time period specified in such subsection because of an act of God, war, natural disaster, strike, or other excusable or justifiable cause, as determined under regulations of the Board.

§ 164. Prompt crediting of payments

.Payments received from an obligor under an open end consumer credit plan by the creditor shall be posted promptly to the obligor's account as specified in regulations of the Board. Such regulations shall prevent a finance charge from being imposed on any obligor if the creditor has received the obligor's payment in readily identifiable form in the amount, manner, location, and time indicated by the creditor to avoid the imposition thereof.

§ 165. Crediting excess payments

.Whenever an obligor transmits funds to a creditor in excess of the total balance due on an open end consumer credit account, the creditor shall promptly (1) upon request of the obligor refund the amount of the overpayment, or (2) credit such amount to the obligor's account.

7

15 USC 1666b.

15 USC 1666c.

15 USC 1666d.

PUBLIC LAW 93-495 - October 28, 1974

§ 166. Prompt notification of returns

.With respect to any sales transaction where a credit card has been used to obtain credit, where the seller is a person other than the card issuer, and where the seller accepts or allows a return of the goods or forgiveness of a debit for services which were the subject of such sale, the seller shall promptly transmit to the credit card issuer, a credit statement with respect thereto and the credit card issuer shall credit the account of the obligor for the amount of the transaction.

§ 167. Use of cash discounts

(a) With respect to credit card which may be used for extensions of credit in sales transactions in which the seller is a person other than the card issuer, the card issuer may not, by contract or otherwise, prohibit any such seller from offering a discount to a cardholder to induce the cardholder to pay by cash, check, or similar means rather than use a credit card. . (b) With respect to any sales transaction, any discount not in excess of 5 per centum offered by the seller for the purpose of inducing payment by cash, check, or other means not involving the use of a credit card shall not constitute a finance charge as determined under section 106, if such discount is offered to all prospective buyers and its availability is disclosed to all prospective buyers clearly and conspicuously in accordance with regulations of the Board.

§ 168. Prohibition of tie-in services

.Notwithstanding any agreement to the contrary, a card issuer may not require a seller, as a condition to participating in a credit card plan, to open an account with or procure any other service from the card issuer or its subsidiary or agent.

§ 169. Prohibition of offsets

.(a) A card issuer may not take any action to offset a cardholder's indebtedness arising in connection with a consumer credit transaction under the relevant credit card plan against funds of the cardholder held on deposit with the card 8

15 USC 1666e.

15 USC 1666f.

15 USC 1666g.

15 USC 1666h.

PUBLIC LAW 93-495 - October 28, 1974

issuer unless. . (1) such action was previously authorized in writing by the cardholder in accordance with a credit plan whereby the cardholder agrees periodically to pay debts incurred in his open end credit account by permitting the card issuer periodically to deduct all or a portion of such debt from the cardholder's deposit account, and. (2) such action with respect to any outstanding disputed amount not be taken by the card issuer upon request of the cardholder. In the case of any credit card account in existence on the effective date of this section, the previous written authorization referred to in clause (1) shall not be required until the date (after such effective date) when such account is renewed, but in no case later than one year after such effective date. Such written authorization shall be deemed to exist if the card issuer has previously notified the cardholder that the use of his credit card account will subject any funds which the card issuer holds in deposit accounts of such cardholder to offset against any amounts due and payable on his credit card account which have not been paid in accordance with the terms of the agreement between the card issuer and the cardholder. .(b) This section does not alter or affect the right under State law of a card issuer to attach or otherwise levy upon funds of a cardholder held on deposit with the card issuer if that remedy is constitutionally available to creditors generally.

§ 170. Rights of credit card customers

.(a) Subject to the limitation contained in subsection (b), a card issuer who has issued a credit card to a cardholder pursuant to an open end consumer credit plan shall be subject to all claims (other than tort claims) and defenses arising out of any transaction in which the credit card is used as a method of payment or extension of credit if (1) the obligor has made a good faith attempt to obtain satisfactory resolution of a disagreement or problem relative to the transaction from the person honoring the credit card; (2) the amount of the initial 9

15 USC 1666i.

PUBLIC LAW 93-495 - October 28, 1974

transaction exceeds $50; and (3) the place where the initial transaction occurred was in the same State as the mailing address previously provided by the cardholder or was within 100 miles from such address, except that the limitations set forth in clauses (2) and (3) with respect to an obligor's right to assert claims and defenses against a card issuer shall not be applicable to any transaction in which the person honoring the credit card (A) is the same person as the card issuer, (B) is controlled by the card issuer, (C) is under direct or indirect common control with the card issuer, (D) is a franchised dealer in the card issuer's products or services, or (E) has obtained the order for such transaction through a mail solicitation made by or participated in by the card issuer in which the cardholder is solicited to enter into such transaction by using the credit card issued by the card issuer. .(b) The amount of claims or defenses asserted by the cardholder may not exceed the amount of credit outstanding with respect to such transaction at the time the cardholder first notifies the card issuer or the person honoring the credit card of such claim or defense. For the purpose of determining the amount of credit outstanding in the preceding sentence, payments and credits to the cardholder's account are deemed to have been applied, in the order indicated, to the payment of: (1) late charges in the order of their entry to the account; (2) finance charges in order of their entry to the account; and (3) debits to the account other than those set forth above, in the order in which each debit entry to the account was made.

§ 171. Relation to State laws

.(a) This chapter does not annul, alter, or affect, or exempt any person subject to the provisions of this chapter from complying with, the laws of any State with respect to credit billing practices, except to the extent that those laws are inconsistent with any provision of this chapter, and then only to the extent of the inconsistency. The Board is authorized to determine whether such inconsistencies exist. The Board may not determine that any State law is inconsistent with 10

15 USC 1666j.

PUBLIC LAW 93-495 - October 28, 1974

any provision of this chapter if the Board determines that such law gives greater protection to the consumer. . (b) The Board shall by regulation exempt from the requirements of this chapter any class of credit transactions within any State if it determines that under the law of that State that class of transactions is subject to requirements substantially similar to those imposed under this chapter or that such law gives greater protection to the consumer, and that there is adequate provision for enforcement..

§ 307. Conforming amendments

(a) The table of chapter of the Truth in Lending Act is amended by adding immediately under item 3 the following: .4. CREDIT BILLING

161. (b) Section 111(d) of such Act (15 U.S.C. 1610(d)) is amended by striking out .and 130 and inserting in lieu thereof a comma and the following: .130, and 166. (c) Section 121(a) of such Act (15 U.S.C. 1631(a)) is amended. (1) by striking out .and upon whom a finance charge is or may be imposed; and (2) by inserting .or chapter 4 immediately after .this chapter.. (d) Section 121(b) of such Act (15 U.S.C. 1631(b)) is amended by inserting .or chapter 4 immediately after .this chapter.. (e) Section 122(a) of such Act (15 U.S.C. 1632(a)) is amended by inserting .or chapter 4 immediately after .this chapter.. (f) Section 122(b) of such Act (15 U.S.C. 1632(b)) is amended by inserting .or chapter 4 immediately after .this chapter.

§ 308. Effective date

This title takes effect upon the expiration of one year after the date of its enactment. 11

15 USC 1666

Note.

PUBLIC LAW 93-495 - October 28, 1974

Chapter 13

THE FAIR CREDIT REPORTING ACT

As a public service, the staff of the Federal Trade Commission (FTC) has prepared the following complete text of the Fair Credit Reporting Act (FCRA), 15 U.S.C. § 1681 et seq. Although staff generally followed the format of the U.S. Code as published by the Government Printing Office, the format of this text does differ in minor ways from the Code (and from West's U.S. Code Annotated). For example, this version uses FCRA section numbers (§§ 601-625) in the headings. (The relevant U.S. Code citation is included with each section heading and each reference to the FCRA in the text.)

This version of the FCRA is complete as of January 7, 2002. It includes the amendments to the FCRA set forth in the Consumer Credit Reporting Reform Act of 1996 (Public Law 104-208, the Omnibus Consolidated Appropriations Act for Fiscal Year 1997, Title II, Subtitle D, Chapter 1), Section 311 of the Intelligence Authorization for Fiscal Year 1998 (Public Law 105-107), the Consumer Reporting Employment Clarification Act of 1998 (Public Law 105-347), Section 506 of the Gramm-Leach-Bliley Act (Public Law 106-102), and Sections 358(g) and 505(c) of the Uniting and Strengthening America by Providing Appropriate Tools Required to Intercept and Obstruct Terrorism Act of 2001 (USA PATRIOT Act) (Public Law 107-56).

TABLE OF CONTENTS

§ 601. Short title

This title may be cited as the Fair Credit Reporting Act.

§ 602. Congressional findings and statement of purpose [15 U.S.C. § 1681]

(a) Accuracy and fairness of credit reporting. The Congress makes the following findings:

(1) The banking system is dependent upon fair and accurate credit reporting. Inaccurate credit reports directly impair the efficiency of the banking system, and unfair credit reporting methods undermine the public confidence which is essential to the continued functioning of the banking system.

(2) An elaborate mechanism has been developed for investigating and evaluating the credit worthiness, credit standing, credit capacity, character, and general reputation of consumers.

(3) Consumer reporting agencies have assumed a vital role in assembling and evaluating consumer credit and other information on consumers.

(4) There is a need to insure that consumer reporting agencies exercise their grave responsibilities with fairness, impartiality, and a respect for the consumer's right to privacy.

(b) Reasonable procedures. It is the purpose of this title to require that consumer reporting agencies adopt reasonable procedures for meeting the needs of commerce for consumer credit, personnel, insurance, and other information in a manner which is fair and equitable to the consumer, with regard to the confidentiality, accuracy, relevancy, and proper utilization of such information in accordance with the requirements of this title.

§ 603. Definitions; rules of construction [15 U.S.C. § 1681a]

(a) Definitions and rules of construction set forth in this section are applicable for the purposes of this title.

(b) The term "person" means any individual, partnership, corporation, trust, estate, cooperative, association, government or governmental subdivision or agency, or other entity.

(c) The term "consumer" means an individual.

(d) Consumer report.

(1) In general. The term "consumer report" means any written, oral, or other communication of any information by a consumer reporting agency bearing on a consumer's credit worthiness, credit standing, credit capacity, character, general reputation, personal characteristics, or mode of living which is used or expected to be used or collected in whole or in part for the purpose of serving as a factor in establishing the consumer's eligibility for

(A) credit or insurance to be used primarily for personal, family, or household purposes;

(B) employment purposes; or

(C) any other purpose authorized under section 604 [§ 1681b].

(2) Exclusions. The term "consumer report" does not include

(A) any

(i) report containing information solely as to transactions or experiences between the consumer and the person making the report;

(ii) communication of that information among persons related by common ownership or affiliated by corporate control; or

(iii) communication of other information among persons related by common ownership or affiliated by corporate control, if it is clearly and conspicuously disclosed to the consumer that the information may be communicated among such persons and the consumer is given the opportunity, before the time that the information is initially communicated, to direct that such information not be communicated among such persons;

(B) any authorization or approval of a specific extension of credit directly or indirectly by the issuer of a credit card or similar device;

(C) any report in which a person who has been requested by a third party to make a specific extension of credit directly or indirectly to a consumer conveys his or her decision with respect to such request, if the third party advises the consumer of the name and address of the person to whom the request was made, and such person makes the disclosures to the consumer required under section 615 [§ 1681m]; or

(D) a communication described in subsection (o).

(e) The term "investigative consumer report" means a consumer report or portion thereof in which information on a consumer's character, general reputation, personal characteristics, or mode of living is obtained through personal interviews with neighbors, friends, or associates of the consumer reported on or with others with whom he is acquainted or who may have knowledge concerning any such items of information. However, such information shall not include specific factual information on a consumer's credit record obtained directly from a creditor of the consumer or from a consumer reporting agency when such information was obtained directly from a creditor of the consumer or from the consumer.

(f) The term "consumer reporting agency" means any person which, for monetary fees, dues, or on a cooperative nonprofit basis, regularly engages in whole or in part in the practice of assembling or evaluating consumer credit information or other information on consumers for the purpose of furnishing consumer reports to third parties, and which uses any means or facility of interstate commerce for the purpose of preparing or furnishing consumer reports.

(g) The term "file," when used in connection with information on any consumer, means all of the information on that consumer recorded and retained by a consumer reporting agency regardless of how the information is stored.

(h) The term "employment purposes" when used in connection with a consumer report means a report used for the purpose of evaluating a consumer for employment, promotion, reassignment or retention as an employee.

(i) The term "medical information" means information or records obtained, with the consent of the individual to whom it relates, from licensed physicians or medical practitioners, hospitals, clinics, or other medical or medically related facilities.

(j) Definitions relating to child support obligations.

(1) Overdue support. The term "overdue support" has the meaning given to such term in section 666(e) of title 42 [Social Security Act, 42 U.S.C. § 666(e)].

(2) State or local child support enforcement agency. The term "State or local child support enforcement agency" means a State or local agency which administers a State or local program for establishing and enforcing child support obligations.

(k) Adverse action.

(1) Actions included. The term "adverse action"

(A) has the same meaning as in section 701(d)(6) of the Equal Credit Opportunity Act; and

(B) means

(i) a denial or cancellation of, an increase in any charge for, or a reduction or other adverse or unfavorable change in the terms of coverage or amount of, any insurance, existing or applied for, in connection with the underwriting of insurance;

(ii) a denial of employment or any other decision for employment purposes that adversely affects any current or prospective employee;

(iii) a denial or cancellation of, an increase in any charge for, or any other adverse or unfavorable change in the terms of, any license or benefit described in section 604(a)(3)(D) [§ 1681b]; and

(iv) an action taken or determination that is

(I) made in connection with an application that was made by, or a transaction that was initiated by, any consumer, or in connection with a review of an account under section 604(a)(3)(F)(ii)[§ 1681b]; and

(II) adverse to the interests of the consumer.

(2) Applicable findings, decisions, commentary, and orders. For purposes of any determination of whether an action is an adverse action under paragraph (1)(A), all appropriate final findings, decisions, commentary, and orders issued under section 701(d)(6) of the Equal Credit Opportunity Act by the Board of Governors of the Federal Reserve System or any court shall apply.

(l) Firm offer of credit or insurance. The term "firm offer of credit or insurance" means any offer of credit or insurance to a consumer that will be honored if the consumer is determined, based on information in a consumer report on the consumer, to meet the specific criteria used to select the consumer for the offer, except that the offer may be further conditioned on one or more of the following:

(1) The consumer being determined, based on information in the consumer's application for the credit or insurance, to meet specific criteria bearing on credit worthiness or insurability, as applicable, that are established

(A) before selection of the consumer for the offer; and

(B) for the purpose of determining whether to extend credit or insurance pursuant to the offer.

(2) Verification

(A) that the consumer continues to meet the specific criteria used to select the consumer for the offer, by using information in a consumer report on the consumer, information in the consumer's application for the credit or insurance, or other information bearing on the credit worthiness or insurability of the consumer; or

(B) of the information in the consumer's application for the credit or insurance, to determine that the consumer meets the specific criteria bearing on credit worthiness or insurability.

(3) The consumer furnishing any collateral that is a requirement for the extension of the credit or insurance that was

(A) established before selection of the consumer for the offer of credit or insurance; and

(B) disclosed to the consumer in the offer of credit or insurance.

(m) Credit or insurance transaction that is not initiated by the consumer. The term" credit or insurance transaction that is not initiated by the consumer" does not include the use of a consumer report by a person with which the consumer has an account or insurance policy, for purposes of

(1) reviewing the account or insurance policy; or

(2) collecting the account.

(n) State. The term "State" means any State, the Commonwealth of Puerto Rico, the District of Columbia, and any territory or possession of the United States.

(o) Excluded communications. A communication is described in this subsection if it is a communication

(1) that, but for subsection (d) (2) (D), would be an investigative consumer report;

(2) that is made to a prospective employer for the purpose of

(A) procuring an employee for the employer; or

(B) procuring an opportunity for a natural person to work for the employer;

(3) that is made by a person who regularly performs such procurement;

(4) that is not used by any person for any purpose other than a purpose described in subparagraph (A) or (B) of paragraph (2); and

(5) with respect to which

(A) the consumer who is the subject of the communication

(i) consents orally or in writing to the nature and scope of the communication, before the collection of any information for the purpose of making the communication;

(ii) consents orally or in writing to the making of the communication to a prospective employer, before the making of the communication; and

(iii) in the case of consent under clause (i) or (ii) given orally, is provided written confirmation of that consent by the person making the communication, not later than 3 business days after the receipt of the consent by that person;

(B) the person who makes the communication does not, for the purpose of making the communication, make any inquiry that if made by a prospective employer of the consumer who is the subject of the communication would violate any applicable Federal or State equal employment opportunity law or regulation; and

(C) the person who makes the communication

(i) discloses in writing to the consumer who is the subject of the communication, not later than 5 business days after receiving any request from the consumer for such disclosure, the nature and substance of all information in the consumer's file at the time of the request, except that the sources of any information that is acquired solely for use in making the communication and is actually used for no other purpose, need not be disclosed other than under appropriate discovery procedures in any court of competent jurisdiction in which an action is brought; and

(ii) notifies the consumer who is the subject of the communication, in writing, of the consumer's right to request the information described in clause (i).

(p) Consumer reporting agency that compiles and maintains files on consumers on a nationwide basis. The term "consumer reporting agency that compiles and maintains files on consumers on a nationwide basis" means a consumer reporting agency that regularly engages in the practice of assembling or evaluating, and maintaining, for the purpose of furnishing consumer reports to third parties bearing on a consumer's credit worthiness, credit standing, or credit capacity, each of the following regarding consumers residing nationwide:

(1) Public record information.

(2) Credit account information from persons who furnish that information regularly and in the ordinary course of business.

§ 604. Permissible purposes of consumer reports [15 U.S.C. § 1681b]

(a) In general. Subject to subsection (c), any consumer reporting agency may furnish a consumer report under the following circumstances and no other:

(1) In response to the order of a court having jurisdiction to issue such an order, or a subpoena issued in connection with proceedings before a Federal grand jury.

(2) In accordance with the written instructions of the consumer to whom it relates.

(3) To a person which it has reason to believe

(A) intends to use the information in connection with a credit transaction involving the consumer on whom the information is to be furnished and involving the extension of credit to, or review or collection of an account of, the consumer; or

(B) intends to use the information for employment purposes; or

(C) intends to use the information in connection with the underwriting of insurance involving the consumer; or

(D) intends to use the information in connection with a determination of the consumer's eligibility for a license or other benefit granted by a governmental instrumentality required by law to consider an applicant's financial responsibility or status; or

(E) intends to use the information, as a potential investor or servicer, or current insurer, in connection with a valuation of, or an assessment of the credit or prepayment risks associated with, an existing credit obligation; or

(F) otherwise has a legitimate business need for the information

(i) in connection with a business transaction that is initiated by the consumer; or

(ii) to review an account to determine whether the consumer continues to meet the terms of the account.

(4) In response to a request by the head of a State or local child support enforcement agency (or a State or local government official authorized by the head of such an agency), if the person making the request certifies to the consumer reporting agency that

(A) the consumer report is needed for the purpose of establishing an individual's capacity to make child support payments or determining the appropriate level of such payments;

(B) the paternity of the consumer for the child to which the obligation relates has been established or acknowledged by the consumer in accordance with State laws under which the obligation arises (if required by those laws);

(C) the person has provided at least 10 days' prior notice to the consumer whose report is requested, by certified or registered mail to the last known address of the consumer, that the report will be requested; and

(D) the consumer report will be kept confidential, will be used solely for a purpose described in subparagraph (A), and will not be used in connection with any other civil, administrative, or criminal proceeding, or for any other purpose.

(5) To an agency administering a State plan under Section 454 of the Social Security Act (42 U.S.C. § 654) for use to set an initial or modified child support award.

(b) Conditions for furnishing and using consumer reports for employment purposes.

(1) Certification from user. A consumer reporting agency may furnish a consumer report for employment purposes only if

(A) the person who obtains such report from the agency certifies to the agency that

(i) the person has complied with paragraph (2) with respect to the consumer report, and the person will comply with paragraph (3) with respect to the consumer report if paragraph (3) becomes applicable; and

(ii) information from the consumer report will not be used in violation of any applicable Federal or State equal employment opportunity law or regulation; and

(B) the consumer reporting agency provides with the report, or has previously provided, a summary of the consumer's rights under this title, as prescribed by the Federal Trade Commission under section 609(c)(3) [§ 1681g].

(2) Disclosure to consumer.

(A) In general. Except as provided in subparagraph (B), a person may not procure a consumer report, or cause a consumer report to be procured, for employment purposes with respect to any consumer, unless--

(i) a clear and conspicuous disclosure has been made in writing to the consumer at any time before the report is procured or caused to be procured, in a document that consists solely of the disclosure, that a consumer report may be obtained for employment purposes; and

(ii) the consumer has authorized in writing (which authorization may be made on the document referred to in clause (i)) the procurement of the report by that person.

(B) Application by mail, telephone, computer, or other similar means. If a consumer described in subparagraph (C) applies for employment by mail, telephone, computer, or other similar means, at any time before a consumer report is procured or caused to be procured in connection with that application--

(i) the person who procures the consumer report on the consumer for employment purposes shall provide to the consumer, by oral, written, or electronic means, notice that a consumer report may be obtained for employment purposes, and a summary of the consumer's rights under section 615(a)(3); and

(ii) the consumer shall have consented, orally, in writing, or electronically to the procurement of the report by that person.

(C) Scope. Subparagraph (B) shall apply to a person procuring a consumer report on a consumer in connection with the consumer's application for employment only if--

(i) the consumer is applying for a position over which the Secretary of Transportation has the power to establish qualifications and maximum hours of service pursuant to the provisions of section 31502 of title 49, or a position subject to safety regulation by a State transportation agency; and

(ii) as of the time at which the person procures the report or causes the report to be procured the only interaction between the consumer and the person in connection with that employment application has been by mail, telephone, computer, or other similar means.

(3) Conditions on use for adverse actions.

(A) In general. Except as provided in subparagraph (B), in using a consumer report for employment purposes, before taking any adverse action based in whole or in part on the report, the person intending to take such adverse action shall provide to the consumer to whom the report relates--

(i) a copy of the report; and

(ii) a description in writing of the rights of the consumer under this title, as prescribed by the Federal Trade Commission under section 609(c) (3).

(B) Application by mail, telephone, computer, or other similar means.

(i) If a consumer described in subparagraph (C) applies for employment by mail, telephone, computer, or other similar means, and if a person who has procured a consumer report on the consumer for employment purposes takes adverse action on the employment application based in whole or in part on the report, then the person must provide to the consumer to whom the report relates, in lieu of the notices required under subparagraph (A) of this section and under section 615(a), within 3 business days of taking such action, an oral, written or electronic notification--

(I) that adverse action has been taken based in whole or in part on a consumer report received from a consumer reporting agency;

(II) of the name, address and telephone number of the consumer reporting agency that furnished the consumer report (including a toll-free telephone number established by the agency if the agency compiles and maintains files on consumers on a nationwide basis);

(III) that the consumer reporting agency did not make the decision to take the adverse action and is unable to provide to the consumer the specific reasons why the adverse action was taken; and

(IV) that the consumer may, upon providing proper identification, request a free copy of a report and may dispute with the consumer reporting agency the accuracy or completeness of any information in a report.

(ii) If, under clause (B) (i) (IV), the consumer requests a copy of a consumer report from the person who procured the report, then, within 3 business days of receiving the consumer's request, together with proper identification, the person must send or provide to the consumer a copy of a report and a copy of the consumer's rights as prescribed by the Federal Trade Commission under section 609(c) (3).

(C) Scope. Subparagraph (B) shall apply to a person procuring a consumer report on a consumer in connection with the consumer's application for employment only if--

(i) the consumer is applying for a position over which the Secretary of Transportation has the power to establish qualifications and maximum hours of service pursuant to the provisions of section 31502 of title 49, or a position subject to safety regulation by a State transportation agency; and

(ii) as of the time at which the person procures the report or causes the report to be procured the only interaction between the consumer and the person in connection with that employment application has been by mail, telephone, computer, or other similar means.

(4) Exception for national security investigations.

(A) In general. In the case of an agency or department of the United States Government which seeks to obtain and use a consumer report for employment purposes, paragraph (3) shall not apply to any adverse action by such agency or department which is based in part on such consumer report, if the head of such agency or department makes a written finding that--

(i) the consumer report is relevant to a national security investigation of such agency or department;

(ii) the investigation is within the jurisdiction of such agency or department;

(iii) there is reason to believe that compliance with paragraph (3) will--

(I) endanger the life or physical safety of any person;

(II) result in flight from prosecution;

(III) result in the destruction of, or tampering with, evidence relevant to the investigation;

(IV) result in the intimidation of a potential witness relevant to the investigation;

(V) result in the compromise of classified information; or

(VI) otherwise seriously jeopardize or unduly delay the investigation or another official proceeding.

(B) Notification of consumer upon conclusion of investigation. Upon the conclusion of a national security investigation described in subparagraph (A), or upon the determination that the exception under subparagraph (A) is no longer required for the reasons set forth in such subparagraph, the official exercising the authority in such subparagraph shall provide to the consumer who is the subject of the consumer report with regard to which such finding was made--

(i) a copy of such consumer report with any classified information redacted as necessary;

(ii) notice of any adverse action which is based, in part, on the consumer report; and

(iii) the identification with reasonable specificity of the nature of the investigation for which the consumer report was sought.

(C) Delegation by head of agency or department. For purposes of subparagraphs (A) and (B), the head of any agency or department of the United States Government may delegate his or her authorities under this paragraph to an official of such agency or department who has personnel security responsibilities and is a member of the Senior Executive Service or equivalent civilian or military rank.

(D) Report to the congress. Not later than January 31 of each year, the head of each agency and department of the United States Government that exercised authority under this paragraph during the preceding year shall submit a report to the Congress on the number of times the department or agency exercised such authority during the year.

(E) Definitions. For purposes of this paragraph, the following definitions shall apply:

(i) Classified information. The term 'classified information' means information that is protected from unauthorized disclosure under Executive Order No. 12958 or successor orders.

(ii) National security investigation. The term 'national security investigation' means any official inquiry by an agency or department of the United States Government to determine the eligibility of a consumer to receive access or continued access to classified information or to determine whether classified information has been lost or compromised.

(c) Furnishing reports in connection with credit or insurance transactions that are not initiated by the consumer.

(1) In general. A consumer reporting agency may furnish a consumer report relating to any consumer pursuant to subparagraph (A) or (C) of subsection (a) (3) in connection with any credit or insurance transaction that is not initiated by the consumer only if

(A) the consumer authorizes the agency to provide such report to such person; or

(B) (i) the transaction consists of a firm offer of credit or insurance;

(ii) the consumer reporting agency has complied with subsection (e); and

(iii) there is not in effect an election by the consumer, made in accordance with subsection (e), to have the consumer's name and address excluded from lists of names provided by the agency pursuant to this paragraph.

(2) Limits on information received under paragraph (1) (B). A person may receive pursuant to paragraph (1) (B) only

(A) the name and address of a consumer;

(B) an identifier that is not unique to the consumer and that is used by the person solely for the purpose of verifying the identity of the consumer; and

(C) other information pertaining to a consumer that does not identify the relationship or experience of the consumer with respect to a particular creditor or other entity.

(3) Information regarding inquiries. Except as provided in section 609(a)(5) [§ 1681g], a consumer reporting agency shall not furnish to any person a record of inquiries in connection with a credit or insurance transaction that is not initiated by a consumer.

(d) Reserved.

(e) Election of consumer to be excluded from lists.

(1) In general. A consumer may elect to have the consumer's name and address excluded from any list provided by a consumer reporting agency under subsection (c) (1) (B) in connection with a credit or insurance transaction that is not initiated by the consumer, by notifying the agency in accordance with paragraph (2) that the consumer does not consent to any use of a consumer report relating to the consumer in connection with any credit or insurance transaction that is not initiated by the consumer.

(2) Manner of notification. A consumer shall notify a consumer reporting agency under paragraph (1)

(A) through the notification system maintained by the agency under paragraph (5); or

(B) by submitting to the agency a signed notice of election form issued by the agency for purposes of this subparagraph.

(3) Response of agency after notification through system. Upon receipt of notification of the election of a consumer under paragraph (1) through the notification system maintained by the agency under paragraph (5), a consumer reporting agency shall

(A) inform the consumer that the election is effective only for the 2-year period following the election if the consumer does not submit to the agency a signed notice of election form issued by the agency for purposes of paragraph (2)(B); and

(B) provide to the consumer a notice of election form, if requested by the consumer, not later than 5 business days after receipt of the notification of the election through the system established under paragraph (5), in the case of a request made at the time the consumer provides notification through the system.

(4) Effectiveness of election. An election of a consumer under paragraph (1)

(A) shall be effective with respect to a consumer reporting agency beginning 5 business days after the date on which the consumer notifies the agency in accordance with paragraph (2);

(B) shall be effective with respect to a consumer reporting agency

(i) subject to subparagraph (C), during the 2-year period beginning 5 business days after the date on which the consumer notifies the agency of the election, in the case of an election for which a consumer notifies the agency only in accordance with paragraph (2)(A); or

(ii) until the consumer notifies the agency under subparagraph (C), in the case of an election for which a consumer notifies the agency in accordance with paragraph (2) (B);

(C) shall not be effective after the date on which the consumer notifies the agency, through the notification system established by the agency under paragraph (5), that the election is no longer effective; and

(D) shall be effective with respect to each affiliate of the agency.

(5) Notification system.

(A) In general. Each consumer reporting agency that, under subsection (c) (1) (B), furnishes a consumer report in connection with a credit or insurance transaction that is not initiated by a consumer, shall

(i) establish and maintain a notification system, including a toll-free telephone number, which permits any consumer whose consumer report is maintained by the agency to notify the agency, with appropriate identification, of the consumer's election to have the consumer's name and address excluded from any such list of names and addresses provided by the agency for such a transaction; and

(ii) publish by not later than 365 days after the date of enactment of the Consumer Credit Reporting Reform Act of 1996, and not less than annually thereafter, in a publication of general circulation in the area served by the agency

(I) a notification that information in consumer files maintained by the agency may be used in connection with such transactions; and

(II) the address and toll-free telephone number for consumers to use to notify the agency of the consumer's election under clause (I).

(B) Establishment and maintenance as compliance. Establishment and maintenance of a notification system (including a toll-free telephone number) and publication by a consumer reporting agency on the agency's own behalf and on behalf of any of its affiliates in accordance with this paragraph is deemed to be compliance with this paragraph by each of those affiliates.

(6) Notification system by agencies that operate nationwide. Each consumer reporting agency that compiles and maintains files on consumers on a nationwide basis shall establish and maintain a notification system for purposes of paragraph (5) jointly with other such consumer reporting agencies.

(f) Certain use or obtaining of information prohibited. A person shall not use or obtain a consumer report for any purpose unless

(1) the consumer report is obtained for a purpose for which the consumer report is authorized to be furnished under this section; and

(2) the purpose is certified in accordance with section 607 [§ 1681e] by a prospective user of the report through a general or specific certification.

(g) Furnishing reports containing medical information. A consumer reporting agency shall not furnish for employment purposes, or in connection with a credit or insurance transaction, a consumer report that contains medical information about a consumer, unless the consumer consents to the furnishing of the report.

§ 605. Requirements relating to information contained in consumer reports [15 U.S.C. § 1681c]

(a) Information excluded from consumer reports. Except as authorized under subsection (b) of this section, no consumer reporting agency may make any consumer report containing any of the following items of information:

(1) Cases under title 11 [United States Code] or under the Bankruptcy Act that, from the date of entry of the order for relief or the date of adjudication, as the case may be, antedate the report by more than 10 years.

(2) Civil suits, civil judgments, and records of arrest that from date of entry, antedate the report by more than seven years or until the governing statute of limitations has expired, whichever is the longer period.

(3) Paid tax liens which, from date of payment, antedate the report by more than seven years.

(4) Accounts placed for collection or charged to profit and loss which antedate the report by more than seven years.[1]

(5) Any other adverse item of information, other than records of convictions of crimes which antedates the report by more than seven years.[1]

(b) Exempted cases. The provisions of subsection (a) of this section are not applicable in the case of any consumer credit report to be used in connection with

(1) a credit transaction involving, or which may reasonably be expected to involve, a principal amount of $150,000 or more;

(2) the underwriting of life insurance involving, or which may reasonably be expected to involve, a face amount of $150,000 or more; or

(3) the employment of any individual at an annual salary which equals, or which may reasonably be expected to equal $75,000, or more.

(c) Running of reporting period.

(1) In general. The 7-year period referred to in paragraphs (4) and (6)$^{(2)}$ of subsection (a) shall begin, with respect to any delinquent account that is placed for collection (internally or by referral to a third party, whichever is earlier), charged to profit and loss, or subjected to any similar action, upon the expiration of the 180-day period beginning on the date of the commencement of the delinquency which immediately preceded the collection activity, charge to profit and loss, or similar action.

(2) Effective date. Paragraph (1) shall apply only to items of information added to the file of a consumer on or after the date that is 455 days after the date of enactment of the Consumer Credit Reporting Reform Act of 1996.

(d) Information required to be disclosed. Any consumer reporting agency that furnishes a consumer report that contains information regarding any case involving the consumer that arises under title 11, United States Code, shall include in the report an identification of the chapter of such title 11 under which such case arises if provided by the source of the information. If any case arising or filed under title 11, United States Code, is withdrawn by the consumer before a final judgment, the consumer reporting agency shall include in the report that such case or filing was withdrawn upon receipt of documentation certifying such withdrawal.

(e) Indication of closure of account by consumer. If a consumer reporting agency is notified pursuant to section 623(a)(4) [§ 1681s-2] that a credit account of a consumer was voluntarily closed by the consumer, the agency shall indicate that fact in any consumer report that includes information related to the account.

(f) Indication of dispute by consumer. If a consumer reporting agency is notified pursuant to section 623(a) (3) [§ 1681s-2] that information regarding a consumer who was furnished to the agency is disputed by the consumer, the agency shall indicate that fact in each consumer report that includes the disputed information.

§ 606. Disclosure of investigative consumer reports [15 U.S.C. § 1681d]

(a) Disclosure of fact of preparation. A person may not procure or cause to be prepared an investigative consumer report on any consumer unless

(1) it is clearly and accurately disclosed to the consumer that an investigative consumer report including information as to his character, general reputation, personal characteristics and mode of living, whichever are applicable, may be made, and such disclosure

(A) is made in a writing mailed, or otherwise delivered, to the consumer, not later than three days after the date on which the report was first requested, and

(B) includes a statement informing the consumer of his right to request the additional disclosures provided for under subsection (b) of this section and the written summary of the rights of the consumer prepared pursuant to section 609(c) [§ 1681g]; and

(2) the person certifies or has certified to the consumer reporting agency that

(A) the person has made the disclosures to the consumer required by paragraph (1); and

(B) the person will comply with subsection (b).

(b) Disclosure on request of nature and scope of investigation. Any person who procures or causes to be prepared an investigative consumer report on any consumer shall, upon written request made by the consumer within a reasonable period of time after the receipt by him of the disclosure required by subsection (a) (1) of this section, make a complete and accurate disclosure of the nature and scope of the investigation requested. This disclosure shall be made in a writing mailed, or otherwise delivered, to the consumer not later than five days after the date on which the request for such disclosure was received from the consumer or such report was first requested, whichever is the later.

(c) Limitation on liability upon showing of reasonable procedures for compliance with provisions. No person may be held liable for any violation of subsection (a) or (b) of this section if he shows by a preponderance of the evidence that at the time of the violation he maintained reasonable procedures to assure compliance with subsection (a) or (b) of this section.

(d) Prohibitions.

(1) Certification. A consumer reporting agency shall not prepare or furnish investigative consumer report unless the agency has received a certification under subsection (a) (2) from the person who requested the report.

(2) Inquiries. A consumer reporting agency shall not make an inquiry for the purpose of preparing an investigative consumer report on a consumer for employment purposes if the making of the inquiry by an employer or prospective employer of the consumer would violate any applicable Federal or State equal employment opportunity law or regulation.

(3) Certain public record information. Except as otherwise provided in section 613 [§ 1681k], a consumer reporting agency shall not furnish an investigative consumer report that includes information that is a matter of public record and that relates to an arrest, indictment, conviction, civil judicial action, tax lien, or outstanding judgment, unless the agency has verified the accuracy of the information during the 30-day period ending on the date on which the report is furnished.

(4) Certain adverse information. A consumer reporting agency shall not prepare or furnish an investigative consumer report on a consumer that contains information that is adverse to the interest of the consumer and that is obtained through a personal interview with a neighbor, friend, or associate of the consumer or with another person with whom the consumer is acquainted or who has knowledge of such item of information, unless

(A) the agency has followed reasonable procedures to obtain confirmation of the information, from an additional source that has independent and direct knowledge of the information; or

(B) the person interviewed is the best possible source of the information.

§ 607. Compliance procedures [15 U.S.C. § 1681e]

(a) Identity and purposes of credit users. Every consumer reporting agency shall maintain reasonable procedures designed to avoid violations of section 605 [§ 1681c] and to limit the furnishing of consumer reports to the purposes listed under section 604 [§ 1681b] of this title. These procedures shall require that prospective users of the information identify themselves, certify the purposes for which the information is sought, and certify that the information will be used for no other purpose. Every consumer reporting agency shall make a reasonable effort to verify the identity of a new prospective user and the uses certified by such prospective user prior to furnishing such user a consumer report. No consumer reporting agency may furnish a consumer report to any person if it has reasonable grounds for believing that the consumer report will not be used for a purpose listed in section 604 [§ 1681b] of this title.

(b) Accuracy of report. Whenever a consumer reporting agency prepares a consumer report it shall follow reasonable procedures to assure maximum possible accuracy of the information concerning the individual about whom the report relates.

(c) Disclosure of consumer reports by users allowed. A consumer reporting agency may not prohibit a user of a consumer report furnished by the agency on a consumer from disclosing the contents of the report to the consumer, if adverse action against the consumer has been taken by the user based in whole or in part on the report.

(d) Notice to users and furnishers of information.

(1) Notice requirement. A consumer reporting agency shall provide to any person

(A) who regularly and in the ordinary course of business furnishes information to the agency with respect to any consumer; or

(B) to whom a consumer report is provided by the agency; a notice of such person's responsibilities under this title.

(2) Content of notice. The Federal Trade Commission shall prescribe the content of notices under paragraph (1), and a consumer reporting agency shall be in compliance with this subsection if it provides a notice under paragraph (1) that is substantially similar to the Federal Trade Commission prescription under this paragraph.

(e) Procurement of consumer report for resale.

(1) Disclosure. A person may not procure a consumer report for purposes of reselling the report (or any information in the report) unless the person discloses to the consumer reporting agency that originally furnishes the report

(A) the identity of the end-user of the report (or information); and

(B) each permissible purpose under section 604 [§ 1681b] for which the report is furnished to the end-user of the report (or information).

(2) Responsibilities of procurers for resale. A person who procures a consumer report for purposes of reselling the report (or any information in the report) shall

(A) establish and comply with reasonable procedures designed to ensure that the report (or information) is resold by the person only for a purpose for which the report may be furnished under section 604 [§ 1681b], including by requiring that each person to which the report (or information) is resold and that resells or provides the report (or information) to any other person

(i) identifies each end user of the resold report (or information);

(ii) certifies each purpose for which the report (or information) will be used; and

(iii) certifies that the report (or information) will be used for no other purpose; and

(B) before reselling the report, make reasonable efforts to verify the identifications and certifications made under subparagraph (A).

(3) Resale of consumer report to a federal agency or department. Notwithstanding paragraph (1) or (2), a person who procures a consumer report for purposes of reselling the report (or any information in the report) shall not disclose the identity of the end-user of the report under paragraph (1) or (2) if--

(A) the end user is an agency or department of the United States Government which procures the report from the person for purposes of determining the eligibility of the consumer concerned to receive access or continued access to classified information (as defined in section 604(b)(4)(E)(i)); and

(B) the agency or department certifies in writing to the person reselling the report that nondisclosure is necessary to protect classified information or the safety of persons employed by or contracting with, or undergoing investigation for work or contracting with the agency or department.

§ 608. Disclosures to governmental agencies [15 U.S.C. § 1681f]

Notwithstanding the provisions of section 604 [§ 1681b] of this title, a consumer reporting agency may furnish identifying information respecting any consumer, limited to his name, address, former addresses, places of employment, or former places of employment, to a governmental agency.

§ 609. Disclosures to consumers [15 U.S.C. § 1681g]

(a) Information on file; sources; report recipients. Every consumer reporting agency shall, upon request, and subject to 610(a) (1) [§ 1681h], clearly and accurately disclose to the consumer:

(1) All information in the consumer's file at the time of the request, except that nothing in this paragraph shall be construed to require a consumer reporting agency to disclose to a consumer any information concerning credit scores or any other risk scores or predictors relating to the consumer.

(2) The sources of the information; except that the sources of information acquired solely for use in preparing an investigative consumer report and actually used for no other purpose need not be disclosed: Provided, That in the event an action is brought under this title, such sources shall be available to the plaintiff under appropriate discovery procedures in the court in which the action is brought.

(3)(A) Identification of each person (including each end-user identified under section 607(e) (1) [§ 1681e]) that procured a consumer report

(i) for employment purposes, during the 2-year period preceding the date on which the request is made; or

(ii) for any other purpose, during the 1-year period preceding the date on which the request is made.

(B) An identification of a person under subparagraph (A) shall include

(i) the name of the person or, if applicable, the trade name (written in full) under which such person conducts business; and

(ii) upon request of the consumer, the address and telephone number of the person.

(C) Subparagraph (A) does not apply if--

(i) the end user is an agency or department of the United States Government that procures the report from the person for purposes of determining the eligibility of the consumer to whom the report relates to receive access or continued access to classified information (as defined in section 604(b)(4)(E)(i)); and

(ii) the head of the agency or department makes a written finding as prescribed under section 604(b) (4) (A).

(4) The dates, original payees, and amounts of any checks upon which is based any adverse characterization of the consumer, included in the file at the time of the disclosure.

(5) A record of all inquiries received by the agency during the 1-year period preceding the request that identified the consumer in connection with a credit or insurance transaction that was not initiated by the consumer.

(b) Exempt information. The requirements of subsection (a) of this section respecting the disclosure of sources of information and the recipients of consumer reports do not apply to information received or consumer reports furnished prior to the effective date of this title except to the extent that the matter involved is contained in the files of the consumer reporting agency on that date.

(c) Summary of rights required to be included with disclosure.

(1) Summary of rights. A consumer reporting agency shall provide to a consumer, with each written disclosure by the agency to the consumer under this section

(A) a written summary of all of the rights that the consumer has under this title; and

(B) in the case of a consumer reporting agency that compiles and maintains files on consumers on a nationwide basis, a toll-free telephone number established by the agency, at which personnel are accessible to consumers during normal business hours.

(2) Specific items required to be included. The summary of rights required under paragraph (1) shall include

(A) a brief description of this title and all rights of consumers under this title;

(B) an explanation of how the consumer may exercise the rights of the consumer under this title;

(C) a list of all Federal agencies responsible for enforcing any provision of this title and the address and any appropriate phone number of each such agency, in a form that will assist the consumer in selecting the appropriate agency;

(D) a statement that the consumer may have additional rights under State law and that the consumer may wish to contact a State or local consumer protection agency or a State attorney general to learn of those rights; and

(E) a statement that a consumer reporting agency is not required to remove accurate derogatory information from a consumer's file, unless the information is outdated under section 605 [§ 1681c] or cannot be verified.

(3) Form of summary of rights. For purposes of this subsection and any disclosure by a consumer reporting agency required under this title with respect to consumers' rights, the Federal Trade Commission (after consultation with each Federal agency referred to in section 621(b) [§ 1681s]) shall prescribe the form and content of any such disclosure of the rights of consumers required under this title. A consumer reporting agency shall be in compliance with this subsection if it provides disclosures under paragraph (1) that are substantially similar to the Federal Trade Commission prescription under this paragraph.

(4) Effectiveness. No disclosures shall be required under this subsection until the date on which the Federal Trade Commission prescribes the form and content of such disclosures under paragraph (3).

§ 610. Conditions and form of disclosure to consumers [15 U.S.C. § 1681h]

(a) In general.

(1) Proper identification. A consumer reporting agency shall require, as a condition of making the disclosures required under section 609 [§ 1681g], that the consumer furnish proper identification.

(2) Disclosure in writing. Except as provided in subsection (b), the disclosures required to be made under section 609 [§ 1681g] shall be provided under that section in writing.

(b) Other forms of disclosure.

(1) In general. If authorized by a consumer, a consumer reporting agency may make the disclosures required under 609 [§ 1681g]

(A) other than in writing; and

(B) in such form as may be

(i) specified by the consumer in accordance with paragraph (2); and

(ii) available from the agency.

(2) Form. A consumer may specify pursuant to paragraph (1) that disclosures under section 609 [§ 1681g] shall be made

(A) in person, upon the appearance of the consumer at the place of business of the consumer reporting agency where disclosures are regularly provided, during normal business hours, and on reasonable notice;

(B) by telephone, if the consumer has made a written request for disclosure by telephone;

(C) by electronic means, if available from the agency; or

(D) by any other reasonable means that is available from the agency.

(c) Trained personnel. Any consumer reporting agency shall provide trained personnel to explain to the consumer any information furnished to him pursuant to section 609 [§ 1681g] of this title.

(d) Persons accompanying consumer. The consumer shall be permitted to be accompanied by one other person of his choosing, who shall furnish reasonable identification. A consumer reporting agency may require the consumer to furnish a written statement granting permission to the consumer reporting agency to discuss the consumer's file in such person's presence.

(e) Limitation of liability. Except as provided in sections 616 and 617 [§§ 1681n and 1681o] of this title, no consumer may bring any action or proceeding in the nature of defamation, invasion of privacy, or negligence with respect to the reporting of information against any consumer reporting agency, any user of information, or any person who furnishes information to a consumer reporting agency, based on information disclosed pursuant to section 609, 610, or 615 [§§ 1681g, 1681h, or 1681m] of this title or based on information disclosed by a user of a consumer report to or for a consumer against whom the user has taken adverse action, based in whole or in part on the report, except as to false information furnished with malice or willful intent to injure such consumer.

§ 611. Procedure in case of disputed accuracy [15 U.S.C. § 1681i]

(a) Reinvestigations of disputed information.

(1) Reinvestigation required.

(A) In general. If the completeness or accuracy of any item of information contained in a consumer's file at a consumer reporting agency is disputed by the consumer and the consumer notifies the agency directly of such dispute, the agency shall reinvestigate free of charge and record the current status of the disputed information, or delete the item from the file in accordance with paragraph (5), before the end of the 30-day period beginning on the date on which the agency receives the notice of the dispute from the consumer.

(B) Extension of period to reinvestigate. Except as provided in subparagraph (C), the 30-day period described in subparagraph (A) may be extended for not more than 15 additional days if the consumer reporting agency receives information from the consumer during that 30-day period that is relevant to the reinvestigation.

102 | From Credit Despair to Credit Millionaire

(C) Limitations on extension of period to reinvestigate. Subparagraph (B) shall not apply to any reinvestigation in which, during the 30-day period described in subparagraph (A), the information that is the subject of the reinvestigation is found to be inaccurate or incomplete or the consumer reporting agency determines that the information cannot be verified.

(2) Prompt notice of dispute to furnisher of information.

(A) In general. Before the expiration of the 5-business-day period beginning on the date on which a consumer reporting agency receives notice of a dispute from any consumer in accordance with paragraph (1), the agency shall provide notification of the dispute to any person who provided any item of information in dispute, at the address and in the manner established with the person. The notice shall include all relevant information regarding the dispute that the agency has received from the consumer.

(B) Provision of other information from consumer. The consumer reporting agency shall promptly provide to the person who provided the information in dispute all relevant information regarding the dispute that is received by the agency from the consumer after the period referred to in subparagraph (A) and before the end of the period referred to in paragraph (1)(A).

(3) Determination that dispute is frivolous or irrelevant.

(A) In general. Notwithstanding paragraph (1), a consumer reporting agency may terminate a reinvestigation of information disputed by a consumer under that paragraph if the agency reasonably determines that the dispute by the consumer is frivolous or irrelevant, including by reason of a failure by a consumer to provide sufficient information to investigate the disputed information.

(B) Notice of determination. Upon making any determination in accordance with subparagraph (A) that a dispute is frivolous or irrelevant, a consumer reporting agency shall notify the consumer of such determination not later than 5 business days after making such determination, by mail or, if authorized by the consumer for that purpose, by any other means available to the agency.

(C) Contents of notice. A notice under subparagraph (B) shall include

(i) the reasons for the determination under subparagraph (A); and

(ii) identification of any information required to investigate the disputed information, which may consist of a standardized form describing the general nature of such information.

(4) Consideration of consumer information. In conducting any reinvestigation under paragraph (1) with respect to disputed information in the file of any consumer, the consumer reporting agency shall review and consider all relevant information submitted by the consumer in the period described in paragraph (1)(A) with respect to such disputed information.

(5) Treatment of inaccurate or unverifiable information.

(A) In general. If, after any reinvestigation under paragraph (1) of any information disputed by a consumer, an item of the information is found to be inaccurate or incomplete or cannot be verified, the consumer reporting agency shall promptly delete that item of information from the consumer's file or modify that item of information, as appropriate, based on the results of the reinvestigation.

(B) Requirements relating to reinsertion of previously deleted material.

(i) Certification of accuracy of information. If any information is deleted from a consumer's file pursuant to subparagraph (A), the information may not be reinserted in the file by the consumer reporting agency unless the person who furnishes the information certifies that the information is complete and accurate.

(ii) Notice to consumer. If any information that has been deleted from a consumer's file pursuant to subparagraph (A) is reinserted in the file, the consumer reporting agency shall notify the consumer of the reinsertion in writing not later than 5 business days after the reinsertion or, if authorized by the consumer for that purpose, by any other means available to the agency.

(iii) Additional information. As part of, or in addition to, the notice under clause (ii), a consumer reporting agency shall provide to a consumer in writing not later than 5 business days after the date of the reinsertion

(I) a statement that the disputed information has been reinserted;

(II) the business name and address of any furnisher of information contacted and the telephone number of such furnisher, if reasonably available, or of any furnisher of information that contacted the consumer reporting agency, in connection with the reinsertion of such information; and

(III) a notice that the consumer has the right to add a statement to the consumer's file disputing the accuracy or completeness of the disputed information.

C) Procedures to prevent reappearance. A consumer reporting agency shall maintain reasonable procedures designed to prevent the reappearance in a consumer's file, and in consumer reports on the consumer, of information that is deleted pursuant to this paragraph (other than information that is reinserted in accordance with subparagraph (B)(i)).

D) Automated reinvestigation system. Any consumer reporting agency that compiles and maintains files on consumers on a nationwide basis shall implement an automated system through which furnishers of information to that consumer reporting agency may report the results of a reinvestigation that finds incomplete or inaccurate information in a consumer's file to other such consumer reporting agencies.

(6) Notice of results of reinvestigation.

(A) In general. A consumer reporting agency shall provide written notice to a consumer of the results of a reinvestigation under this subsection not later than 5 business days after the completion of the reinvestigation, by mail or, if authorized by the consumer for that purpose, by other means available to the agency.

(B) Contents. As part of, or in addition to, the notice under subparagraph (A), a consumer reporting agency shall provide to a consumer in writing before the expiration of the 5-day period referred to in subparagraph (A)

(i) a statement that the reinvestigation is completed;

(ii) a consumer report that is based upon the consumer's file as that file is revised as a result of the reinvestigation;

(iii) a notice that, if requested by the consumer, a description of the procedure used to determine the accuracy and completeness of the information shall be provided to the consumer by the agency, including the business name and address of any furnisher of information contacted in connection with such information and the telephone number of such furnisher, if reasonably available;

(iv) a notice that the consumer has the right to add a statement to the consumer's file disputing the accuracy or completeness of the information; and

(v) a notice that the consumer has the right to request under subsection (d) that the consumer reporting agency furnish notifications under that subsection.

(7) Description of reinvestigation procedure. A consumer reporting agency shall provide to a consumer a description referred to in paragraph (6) (B) (iii) by not later than 15 days after receiving a request from the consumer for that description.

(8) Expedited dispute resolution. If a dispute regarding an item of information in a consumer's file at a consumer reporting agency is resolved in accordance with paragraph (5)(A) by the deletion of the disputed information by not later than 3 business days after the date on which the agency receives notice of the dispute from the consumer in accordance with paragraph (1)(A), then the agency shall not be required to comply with paragraphs (2), (6), and (7) with respect to that dispute if the agency

(A) provides prompt notice of the deletion to the consumer by telephone;

(B) includes in that notice, or in a written notice that accompanies a confirmation and consumer report provided in accordance with subparagraph (C), a statement of the consumer's right to request under subsection (d) that the agency furnish notifications under that subsection; and

(C) provides written confirmation of the deletion and a copy of a consumer report on the consumer that is based on the consumer's file after the deletion, not later than 5 business days after making the deletion.

(b) Statement of dispute. If the reinvestigation does not resolve the dispute, the consumer may file a brief statement setting forth the nature of the dispute. The consumer reporting agency may limit such statements to not more than one hundred words if it provides the consumer with assistance in writing a clear summary of the dispute.

(c) Notification of consumer dispute in subsequent consumer reports. Whenever a statement of a dispute is filed, unless there is reasonable grounds to believe that it is frivolous or irrelevant, the consumer reporting agency shall, in any subsequent consumer report containing the information in question, clearly note that it is disputed by the consumer and provide either the consumer's statement or a clear and accurate codification or summary thereof.

(d) Notification of deletion of disputed information. Following any deletion of information which is found to be inaccurate or whose accuracy can no longer be verified or any notation as to disputed information, the consumer reporting agency shall, at the request of the consumer, furnish notification that the item has been deleted or the statement, codification or summary pursuant to subsection (b) or (c) of this section to any person specifically designated by the consumer who has within two years prior thereto received a consumer report for employment purposes, or within six months prior thereto received a consumer report for any other purpose, which contained the deleted or disputed information.

§ 612. Charges for certain disclosures [15 U.S.C. § 1681j]

(a) Reasonable charges allowed for certain disclosures.

(1) In general. Except as provided in subsections (b), (c), and (d), a consumer reporting agency may impose a reasonable charge on a consumer

(A) for making a disclosure to the consumer pursuant to section 609 [§ 1681g], which charge

(i) shall not exceed $8;[1] and

(ii) shall be indicated to the consumer before making the disclosure; and

(B) for furnishing, pursuant to 611(d) [§ 1681i], following a reinvestigation under section 611(a) [§ 1681i], a statement, codification, or summary to a person designated by the consumer under that section after the 30-day period beginning on the date of notification of the consumer under paragraph (6) or (8) of section 611(a) [§ 1681i] with respect to the reinvestigation, which charge

(i) shall not exceed the charge that the agency would impose on each designated recipient for a consumer report; and

(ii) shall be indicated to the consumer before furnishing such information.

(2) Modification of amount. The Federal Trade Commission shall increase the amount referred to in paragraph (1)(A)(I) on January 1 of each year, based proportionally on changes in the Consumer Price Index, with fractional changes rounded to the nearest fifty cents.

(b) Free disclosure after adverse notice to consumer. Each consumer reporting agency that maintains a file on a consumer shall make all disclosures pursuant to section 609 [§ 1681g] without charge to the consumer if, not later than 60 days after receipt by such consumer of a notification pursuant to section 615 [§ 1681m], or of a notification from a debt collection agency affiliated with that consumer reporting agency stating that the consumer's credit rating may be or has been adversely affected, the consumer makes a request under section 609 [§ 1681g].

(c) Free disclosure under certain other circumstances. Upon the request of the consumer, a consumer reporting agency shall make all disclosures pursuant to section 609 [§ 1681g] once during any 12-month period without charge to that consumer if the consumer certifies in writing that the consumer

(1) is unemployed and intends to apply for employment in the 60-day period beginning on the date on which the certification is made;

(2) is a recipient of public welfare assistance; or

(3) has reason to believe that the file on the consumer at the agency contains inaccurate information due to fraud.

(d) Other charges prohibited. A consumer reporting agency shall not impose any charge on a consumer for providing any notification required by this title or making any disclosure required by this title, except as authorized by subsection (a).

§ 613. Public record information for employment purposes [15 U.S.C. § 1681k]

(a) In general. A consumer reporting agency which furnishes a consumer report for employment purposes and which for that purpose compiles and reports items of information on consumers which are matters of public record and are likely to have an adverse effect upon a consumer's ability to obtain employment shall

(1) at the time such public record information is reported to the user of such consumer report, notify the consumer of the fact that public record information is being reported by the consumer reporting agency, together with the name and address of the person to whom such information is being reported; or

(2) maintain strict procedures designed to insure that whenever public record information which is likely to have an adverse effect on a consumer's ability to obtain employment is reported it is complete and up to date. For purposes of this paragraph, items of public record relating to arrests, indictments, convictions, suits, tax liens, and outstanding judgments shall be considered up to date if the current public record status of the item at the time of the report is reported.

(b) Exemption for national security investigations. Subsection (a) does not apply in the case of an agency or department of the United States Government that seeks to obtain and use a consumer report for employment purposes, if the head of the agency or department makes a written finding as prescribed under section 604(b)(4)(A).

§ 614. Restrictions on investigative consumer reports [15 U.S.C. § 1681*l*]

Whenever a consumer reporting agency prepares an investigative consumer report, no adverse information in the consumer report (other than information which is a matter of public record) may be included in a subsequent consumer report unless such adverse information has been verified in the process of making such subsequent consumer report, or the adverse information was received within the three-month period preceding the date the subsequent report is furnished.

§ 615. Requirements on users of consumer reports [15 U.S.C. § 1681m]

(a) Duties of users taking adverse actions on the basis of information contained in consumer reports. If any person takes any adverse action with respect to any consumer that is based in whole or in part on any information contained in a consumer report, the person shall

> (1) provide oral, written, or electronic notice of the adverse action to the consumer;

> (2) provide to the consumer orally, in writing, or electronically

> > (A) the name, address, and telephone number of the consumer reporting agency (including a toll-free telephone number established by the agency if the agency compiles and maintains files on consumers on a nationwide basis) that furnished the report to the person; and

> > (B) a statement that the consumer reporting agency did not make the decision to take the adverse action and is unable to provide the consumer the specific reasons why the adverse action was taken; and

> (3) provide to the consumer an oral, written, or electronic notice of the consumer's right

> > (A) to obtain, under section 612 [§ 1681j], a free copy of a consumer report on the consumer from the consumer reporting agency referred to in paragraph (2), which notice shall include an indication of the 60-day period under that section for obtaining such a copy; and

> > (B) to dispute, under section 611 [§ 1681i], with a consumer reporting agency the accuracy or completeness of any information in a consumer report furnished by the agency.

(b) Adverse action based on information obtained from third parties other than consumer reporting agencies.

> (1) In general. Whenever credit for personal, family, or household purposes involving a consumer is denied or the charge for such credit is increased either wholly or partly because of information obtained from a person other than a consumer reporting agency bearing upon the consumer's credit worthiness, credit standing, credit capacity, character, general reputation, personal characteristics, or mode of living, the user of such information shall, within a reasonable period of time, upon the consumer's written request for the reasons for such adverse action received within sixty days after learning of such adverse action, disclose the nature of the information to the consumer. The user of such information shall clearly and accurately disclose to the consumer his right to make such written request at the time such adverse action is communicated to the consumer.

> (2) Duties of person taking certain actions based on information provided by affiliate.

> > (A) Duties, generally. If a person takes an action described in subparagraph (B) with respect to a consumer, based in whole or in part on information described in subparagraph (C), the person shall

> > > (i) notify the consumer of the action, including a statement that the consumer may obtain the information in accordance with clause (ii); and

(ii) upon a written request from the consumer received within 60 days after transmittal of the notice required by clause (I), disclose to the consumer the nature of the information upon which the action is based by not later than 30 days after receipt of the request.

(B) Action described. An action referred to in subparagraph (A) is an adverse action described in section 603(k)(1)(A) [§ 1681a], taken in connection with a transaction initiated by the consumer, or any adverse action described in clause (i) or (ii) of section 603(k)(1)(B) [§ 1681a].

(C) Information described. Information referred to in subparagraph (A)

(i) except as provided in clause (ii), is information that

(I) is furnished to the person taking the action by a person related by common ownership or affiliated by common corporate control to the person taking the action; and

(II) bears on the credit worthiness, credit standing, credit capacity, character, general reputation, personal characteristics, or mode of living of the consumer; and

(ii) does not include

(I) information solely as to transactions or experiences between the consumer and the person furnishing the information; or

(II) information in a consumer report.

(c) Reasonable procedures to assure compliance. No person shall be held liable for any violation of this section if he shows by a preponderance of the evidence that at the time of the alleged violation he maintained reasonable procedures to assure compliance with the provisions of this section.

(d) Duties of users making written credit or insurance solicitations on the basis of information contained in consumer files.

(1) In general. Any person who uses a consumer report on any consumer in connection with any credit or insurance transaction that is not initiated by the consumer, that is provided to that person under section 604(c)(1)(B) [§ 1681b], shall provide with each written solicitation made to the consumer regarding the transaction a clear and conspicuous statement that

(A) information contained in the consumer's consumer report was used in connection with the transaction;

(B) the consumer received the offer of credit or insurance because the consumer satisfied the criteria for credit worthiness or insurability under which the consumer was selected for the offer;

(C) if applicable, the credit or insurance may not be extended if, after the consumer responds to the offer, the consumer does not meet the criteria used to select the consumer for the offer or any applicable criteria bearing on credit worthiness or insurability or does not furnish any required collateral;

(D) the consumer has a right to prohibit information contained in the consumer's file with any consumer reporting agency from being used in connection with any credit or insurance transaction that is not initiated by the consumer; and

(E) the consumer may exercise the right referred to in subparagraph (D) by notifying a notification system established under section 604(e) [§ 1681b].

(2) Disclosure of address and telephone number. A statement under paragraph (1) shall include the address and toll-free telephone number of the appropriate notification system established under section 604(e) [§ 1681b].

(3) Maintaining criteria on file. A person who makes an offer of credit or insurance to a consumer under a credit or insurance transaction described in paragraph (1) shall maintain on file the criteria used to select the consumer to receive the offer, all criteria bearing on credit worthiness or insurability, as applicable, that are the basis for determining whether or not to extend credit or insurance pursuant to the offer, and any requirement for the furnishing of collateral as a condition of the extension of credit or insurance, until the expiration of the 3-year period beginning on the date on which the offer is made to the consumer.

(4) Authority of federal agencies regarding unfair or deceptive acts or practices not affected. This section is not intended to affect the authority of any Federal or State agency to enforce a prohibition against unfair or deceptive acts or practices, including the making of false or misleading statements in connection with a credit or insurance transaction that is not initiated by the consumer.

§ 616. Civil liability for willful noncompliance [15 U.S.C. § 1681n]

(a) In general. Any person who willfully fails to comply with any requirement imposed under this title with respect to any consumer is liable to that consumer in an amount equal to the sum of

(1)(A) any actual damages sustained by the consumer as a result of the failure or damages of not less than $100 and not more than $1,000; or

(B) in the case of liability of a natural person for obtaining a consumer report under false pretenses or knowingly without a permissible purpose, actual damages sustained by the consumer as a result of the failure or $1,000, whichever is greater;

(2) such amount of punitive damages as the court may allow; and

(3) in the case of any successful action to enforce any liability under this section, the costs of the action together with reasonable attorney's fees as determined by the court.

(b) Civil liability for knowing noncompliance. Any person who obtains a consumer report from a consumer reporting agency under false pretenses or knowingly without a permissible purpose shall be liable to the consumer reporting agency for actual damages sustained by the consumer reporting agency or $1,000, whichever is greater.

(c) Attorney's fees. Upon a finding by the court that an unsuccessful pleading, motion, or other paper filed in connection with an action under this section was filed in bad faith or for purposes of harassment, the court shall award to the prevailing party attorney's fees reasonable in relation to the work expended in responding to the pleading, motion, or other paper.

§ 617. Civil liability for negligent noncompliance [15 U.S.C. § 1681o]

(a) In general. Any person who is negligent in failing to comply with any requirement imposed under this title with respect to any consumer is liable to that consumer in an amount equal to the sum of

(1) any actual damages sustained by the consumer as a result of the failure;

(2) in the case of any successful action to enforce any liability under this section, the costs of the action together with reasonable attorney's fees as determined by the court.

(b) Attorney's fees. On a finding by the court that an unsuccessful pleading, motion, or other paper filed in connection with an action under this section was filed in bad faith or for purposes of harassment, the court shall award to the prevailing party attorney's fees reasonable in relation to the work expended in responding to the pleading, motion, or other paper.

§ 618. Jurisdiction of courts; limitation of actions [15 U.S.C. § 1681p]

An action to enforce any liability created under this title may be brought in any appropriate United States district court without regard to the amount in controversy, or in any other court of competent jurisdiction, within two years from the date on which the liability arises, except that where a defendant has materially and willfully misrepresented any information required under this title to be disclosed to an individual and the information so misrepresented is material to the establishment of the defendant's liability to that individual under this title, the action may be brought at any time within two years after discovery by the individual of the misrepresentation.

§ 619. Obtaining information under false pretenses [15 U.S.C. § 1681q]

Any person who knowingly and willfully obtains information on a consumer from a consumer reporting agency under false pretenses shall be fined under title 18, United States Code, imprisoned for not more than 2 years, or both.

§ 620. Unauthorized disclosures by officers or employees [15 U.S.C. § 1681r]

Any officer or employee of a consumer reporting agency who knowingly and willfully provides information concerning an individual from the agency's files to a person not authorized to receive that information shall be fined under title 18, United States Code, imprisoned for not more than 2 years, or both.

§ 621. Administrative enforcement [15 U.S.C. § 1681s]

(a) (1) Enforcement by Federal Trade Commission. Compliance with the requirements imposed under this title shall be enforced under the Federal Trade Commission Act [15 U.S.C. §§ 41 et seq.] by the Federal Trade Commission with respect to consumer reporting agencies and all other persons subject thereto, except to the extent that enforcement of the requirements imposed under this title is specifically committed to some other government agency under subsection (b) hereof. For the purpose of the exercise by the Federal Trade Commission of its functions and powers under the Federal Trade Commission Act, a violation of any requirement or prohibition imposed under this title shall constitute an unfair or deceptive act or practice in commerce in violation of section 5(a) of the Federal Trade Commission Act [15 U.S.C. § 45(a)] and shall be subject to enforcement by the Federal Trade Commission under section 5(b) thereof [15 U.S.C. § 45(b)] with respect to any consumer reporting agency or person subject to enforcement by the Federal Trade Commission pursuant to this subsection, irrespective of whether that person is engaged in commerce or meets any other jurisdictional tests in the Federal Trade Commission Act. The Federal Trade Commission shall have such procedural, investigative, and enforcement powers, including the power to issue procedural rules in enforcing compliance with the requirements imposed under this title and to require the filing of reports, the production of documents, and the appearance of witnesses as though the applicable terms and conditions of the Federal Trade Commission Act were part of this title. Any person violating any of the provisions of this title shall be subject to the penalties and entitled to the privileges and immunities provided in the Federal Trade Commission Act as though the applicable terms and provisions thereof were part of this title.

(2)(A) In the event of a knowing violation, which constitutes a pattern or practice of violations of this title, the Commission may commence a civil action to recover a civil penalty in a district court of the United States against any person that violates this title. In such action, such person shall be liable for a civil penalty of not more than $2,500 per violation.

(B) In determining the amount of a civil penalty under subparagraph (A), the court shall take into account the degree of culpability, any history of prior such conduct, ability to pay, effect on ability to continue to do business, and such other matters as justice may require.

(3) Notwithstanding paragraph (2), a court may not impose any civil penalty on a person for a violation of section 623(a)(1) [§ 1681s-2] unless the person has been enjoined from committing the violation, or ordered not to commit the violation, in an action or proceeding brought by or on behalf of the Federal Trade Commission, and has violated the injunction or order, and the court may not impose any civil penalty for any violation occurring before the date of the violation of the injunction or order.

(b) Enforcement by other agencies. Compliance with the requirements imposed under this title with respect to consumer reporting agencies, persons who use consumer reports from such agencies, persons who furnish information to such agencies, and users of information that are subject to subsection (d) of section 615 [§ 1681m] shall be enforced under

(1) section 8 of the Federal Deposit Insurance Act [12 U.S.C. § 1818], in the case of

(A) national banks, and Federal branches and Federal agencies of foreign banks, by the Office of the Comptroller of the Currency;

(B) member banks of the Federal Reserve System (other than national banks), branches and agencies of foreign banks (other than Federal branches, Federal agencies, and insured State branches of foreign banks), commercial lending companies owned or controlled by foreign banks, and organizations operating under section 25 or 25(a) [25A] of the Federal Reserve Act [12 U.S.C. §§ 601 et seq., §§ 611 et seq], by the Board of Governors of the Federal Reserve System; and

(C) banks insured by the Federal Deposit Insurance Corporation (other than members of the Federal Reserve System) and insured State branches of foreign banks, by the Board of Directors of the Federal Deposit Insurance Corporation;

(2) section 8 of the Federal Deposit Insurance Act [12 U.S.C. § 1818], by the Director of the Office of Thrift Supervision, in the case of a savings association the deposits of which are insured by the Federal Deposit Insurance Corporation;

(3) the Federal Credit Union Act [12 U.S.C. §§ 1751 et seq.], by the Administrator of the National Credit Union Administration [National Credit Union Administration Board] with respect to any Federal credit union;

(4) subtitle IV of title 49 [49 U.S.C. §§ 10101 et seq.], by the Secretary of Transportation, with respect to all carriers subject to the jurisdiction of the Surface Transportation Board;

(5) the Federal Aviation Act of 1958 [49 U.S.C. Appx §§ 1301 et seq.], by the Secretary of Transportation with respect to any air carrier or foreign air carrier subject to that Act [49 U.S.C. Appx §§ 1301 et seq.]; and

(6) the Packers and Stockyards Act, 1921 [7 U.S.C. §§ 181 et seq.] (except as provided in section 406 of that Act [7 U.S.C. §§ 226 and 227]), by the Secretary of Agriculture with respect to any activities subject to that Act.

The terms used in paragraph (1) that are not defined in this title or otherwise defined in section 3(s) of the Federal Deposit Insurance Act (12 U.S.C. §1813(s)) shall have the meaning given to them in section 1(b) of the International Banking Act of 1978 (12 U.S.C. § 3101).

(c) State action for violations.

(1) Authority of states. In addition to such other remedies as are provided under State law, if the chief law enforcement officer of a State, or an official or agency designated by a State, has reason to believe that any person has violated or is violating this title, the State

(A) may bring an action to enjoin such violation in any appropriate United States district court or in any other court of competent jurisdiction;

(B) subject to paragraph (5), may bring an action on behalf of the residents of the State to recover

(i) damages for which the person is liable to such residents under sections 616 and 617 [§§ 1681n and 1681o] as a result of the violation;

(ii) in the case of a violation of section 623(a) [§ 1681s-2], damages for which the person would, but for section 623(c) [§ 1681s-2], be liable to such residents as a result of the violation; or

(iii) damages of not more than $1,000 for each willful or negligent violation; and

(C) in the case of any successful action under subparagraph (A) or (B), shall be awarded the costs of the action and reasonable attorney fees as determined by the court.

(2) Rights of federal regulators. The State shall serve prior written notice of any action under paragraph (1) upon the Federal Trade Commission or the appropriate Federal regulator determined under subsection (b) and provide the Commission or appropriate Federal regulator with a copy of its complaint, except in any case in which such prior notice is not feasible, in which case the State shall serve such notice immediately upon instituting such action. The Federal Trade Commission or appropriate Federal regulator shall have the right

(A) to intervene in the action;

(B) upon so intervening, to be heard on all matters arising therein;

(C) to remove the action to the appropriate United States district court; and

(D) to file petitions for appeal.

(3) Investigatory powers. For purposes of bringing any action under this subsection, nothing in this subsection shall prevent the chief law enforcement officer, or an official or agency designated by a State, from exercising the powers conferred on the chief law enforcement officer or such official by the laws of such State to conduct investigations or to administer oaths or affirmations or to compel the attendance of witnesses or the production of documentary and other evidence.

(4) Limitation on state action while federal action pending. If the Federal Trade Commission or the appropriate Federal regulator has instituted a civil action or an administrative action under section 8 of the Federal Deposit Insurance Act for a violation of this title, no State may, during the dependency of such action, bring an action under this section against any defendant named in the complaint of the Commission or the appropriate Federal regulator for any violation of this title that is alleged in that complaint.

(5) Limitations on state actions for violation of section 623(a) (1) [§ 1681s-2].

(A) Violation of injunction required. A State may not bring an action against a person under paragraph (1) (B) for a violation of section 623(a) (1) [§ 1681s-2], unless

(i) the person has been enjoined from committing the violation, in an action brought by the State under paragraph (1) (A); and

(ii) the person has violated the injunction.

(B) Limitation on damages recoverable. In an action against a person under paragraph (1) (B) for a violation of section 623(a) (1) [§ 1681s-2], a State may not recover any damages incurred before the date of the violation of an injunction on which the action is based.

(d) Enforcement under other authority. For the purpose of the exercise by any agency referred to in subsection (b) of this section of its powers under any Act referred to in that subsection, a violation of any requirement imposed under this title shall be deemed to be a violation of a requirement imposed under that Act. In addition to its powers under any provision of law specifically referred to in subsection (b) of this section, each of the agencies referred to in that subsection may exercise, for the purpose of enforcing compliance with any requirement imposed under this title any other authority conferred on it by law.

(e) Regulatory authority

(1) The Federal banking agencies referred to in paragraphs (1) and (2) of subsection (b) shall jointly prescribe such regulations as necessary to carry out the purposes of this Act with respect to any persons identified under paragraphs (1) and (2) of subsection (b), and the Board of Governors of the Federal Reserve System shall have authority to prescribe regulations consistent with such joint regulations with respect to bank holding companies and affiliates (other than depository institutions and consumer reporting agencies) of such holding companies.

(2) The Board of the National Credit Union Administration shall prescribe such regulations as necessary to carry out the purposes of this Act with respect to any persons identified under paragraph (3) of subsection (b).

§ 622. Information on overdue child support obligations [15 U.S.C. § 1681s-1]

Notwithstanding any other provision of this title, a consumer reporting agency shall include in any consumer report furnished by the agency in accordance with section 604 [§ 1681b] of this title, any information on the failure of the consumer to pay overdue support which

(1) is provided

(A) to the consumer reporting agency by a State or local child support enforcement agency; or

(B) to the consumer reporting agency and verified by any local, State, or Federal government agency; and

(2) antedates the report by 7 years or less.

§ 623. Responsibilities of furnishers of information to consumer reporting agencies [15 U.S.C. § 1681s-2]

(a) Duty of furnishers of information to provide accurate information.

(1) Prohibition.

(A) Reporting information with actual knowledge of errors. A person shall not furnish any information relating to a consumer to any consumer reporting agency if the person knows or consciously avoids knowing that the information is inaccurate.

(B) Reporting information after notice and confirmation of errors. A person shall not furnish information relating to a consumer to any consumer reporting agency if

(i) the person has been notified by the consumer, at the address specified by the person for such notices, that specific information is inaccurate; and

(ii) the information is, in fact, inaccurate.

(C) No address requirement. A person who clearly and conspicuously specifies to the consumer an address for notices referred to in subparagraph (B) shall not be subject to subparagraph (A); however, nothing in subparagraph (B) shall require a person to specify such an address.

(2) Duty to correct and update information. A person who

(A) regularly and in the ordinary course of business furnishes information to one or more consumer reporting agencies about the person's transactions or experiences with any consumer; and

(B) has furnished to a consumer reporting agency information that the person determines is not complete or accurate, shall promptly notify the consumer reporting agency of that determination and provide to the agency any corrections to that information, or any additional information, that is necessary to make the information provided by the person to the agency complete and accurate, and shall not thereafter furnish to the agency any of the information that remains not complete or accurate.

(3) Duty to provide notice of dispute. If the completeness or accuracy of any information furnished by any person to any consumer reporting agency is disputed to such person by a consumer, the person may not furnish the information to any consumer reporting agency without notice that such information is disputed by the consumer.

(4) Duty to provide notice of closed accounts. A person who regularly and in the ordinary course of business furnishes information to a consumer reporting agency regarding a consumer who has a credit account with that person shall notify the agency of the voluntary closure of the account by the consumer, in information regularly furnished for the period in which the account is closed.

(5) Duty to provide notice of delinquency of accounts. A person who furnishes information to a consumer reporting agency regarding a delinquent account being placed for collection, charged to profit or loss, or subjected to any similar action shall, not later than 90 days after furnishing the information, notify the agency of the month and year of the commencement of the delinquency that immediately preceded the action.

(b) Duties of furnishers of information upon notice of dispute.

(1) In general. After receiving notice pursuant to section 611(a) (2) [§ 1681i] of a dispute with regard to the completeness or accuracy of any information provided by a person to a consumer reporting agency, the person shall

(A) conduct an investigation with respect to the disputed information;

(B) review all relevant information provided by the consumer reporting agency pursuant to section 611(a) (2) [§ 1681i];

(C) report the results of the investigation to the consumer reporting agency; and

(D) if the investigation finds that the information is incomplete or inaccurate, report those results to all other consumer reporting agencies to which the person furnished the information and that compile and maintain files on consumers on a nationwide basis.

(2) Deadline. A person shall complete all investigations, reviews, and reports required under paragraph (1) regarding information provided by the person to a consumer reporting agency, before the expiration of the period under section 611(a)(1) [§ 1681i] within which the consumer reporting agency is required to complete actions required by that section regarding that information.

(c) Limitation on liability. Sections 616 and 617 [§§ 1681n and 1681o] do not apply to any failure to comply with subsection (a), except as provided in section 621(c) (1) (B) [§ 1681s].

(d) Limitation on enforcement. Subsection (a) shall be enforced exclusively under section 621 [§ 1681s] by the Federal agencies and officials and the State officials identified in that section.

§ 624. Relation to State laws [15 U.S.C. § 1681t]

(a) In general. Except as provided in subsections (b) and (c), this title does not annul, alter, affect, or exempt any person subject to the provisions of this title from complying with the laws of any State with respect to the collection, distribution, or use of any information on consumers, except to the extent that those laws are inconsistent with any provision of this title, and then only to the extent of the inconsistency.

(b) General exceptions. No requirement or prohibition may be imposed under the laws of any State

(1) with respect to any subject matter regulated under

(A) subsection (c) or (e) of section 604 [§ 1681b], relating to the prescreening of consumer reports;

(B) section 611 [§ 1681i], relating to the time by which a consumer reporting agency must take any action, including the provision of notification to a consumer or other person, in any procedure related to the disputed accuracy of information in a consumer's file, except that this subparagraph shall not apply to any State law in effect on the date of enactment of the Consumer Credit Reporting Reform Act of 1996;

(C) subsections (a) and (b) of section 615 [§ 1681m], relating to the duties of a person who takes any adverse action with respect to a consumer;

(D) section 615(d) [§ 1681m], relating to the duties of persons who use a consumer report of a consumer in connection with any credit or insurance transaction that is not initiated by the consumer and that consists of a firm offer of credit or insurance;

(E) section 605 [§ 1681c], relating to information contained in consumer reports, except that this subparagraph shall not apply to any State law in effect on the date of enactment of the Consumer Credit Reporting Reform Act of 1996; or

(F) section 623 [§ 1681s-2], relating to the responsibilities of persons who furnish information to consumer reporting agencies, except that this paragraph shall not apply

(i) with respect to section 54A (a) of chapter 93 of the Massachusetts Annotated Laws (as in effect on the date of enactment of the Consumer Credit Reporting Reform Act of 1996); or

(ii) with respect to section 1785.25(a) of the California Civil Code (as in effect on the date of enactment of the Consumer Credit Reporting Reform Act of 1996);

(2) with respect to the exchange of information among persons affiliated by common ownership or common corporate control, except that this paragraph shall not apply with respect to subsection (a) or (c)(1) of section 2480e of title 9, Vermont Statutes Annotated (as in effect on the date of enactment of the Consumer Credit Reporting Reform Act of 1996); or

(3) with respect to the form and content of any disclosure required to be made under section 609(c) [§ 1681g].

(c) Definition of firm offer of credit or insurance. Notwithstanding any definition of the term "firm offer of credit or insurance" (or any equivalent term) under the laws of any State, the definition of that term contained in section 603(l) [§ 1681a] shall be construed to apply in the enforcement and interpretation of the laws of any State governing consumer reports.

(d) Limitations. Subsections (b) and (c)

(1) do not affect any settlement, agreement, or consent judgment between any State Attorney General and any consumer reporting agency in effect on the date of enactment of the Consumer Credit Reporting Reform Act of 1996; and

(2) do not apply to any provision of State law (including any provision of a State constitution) that

(A) is enacted after January 1, 2004;

(B) states explicitly that the provision is intended to supplement this title; and

(C) gives greater protection to consumers than is provided under this title.

§ 625. Disclosures to FBI for counterintelligence purposes [15 U.S.C. § 1681u]

(a) Identity of financial institutions. Notwithstanding section 604 [§ 1681b] or any other provision of this title, a consumer reporting agency shall furnish to the Federal Bureau of Investigation the names and addresses of all financial institutions (as that term is defined in section 1101 of the Right to Financial Privacy Act of 1978 [12 U.S.C. § 3401]) at which a consumer maintains or has maintained an account, to the extent that information is in the files of the agency, when presented with a written request for that information, signed by the Director of the Federal Bureau of Investigation, or the Director's designee in a position not lower than Deputy Assistant Director at Bureau headquarters or a Special Agent in Charge of a Bureau field office designated by the Director, which certifies compliance with this section. The Director or the Director's designee may make such a certification only if the Director or the Director's designee has determined in writing, that such information is sought for the conduct of an authorized investigation to protect against international terrorism or clandestine intelligence activities, provided that such an investigation of a United States person is not conducted solely upon the basis of activities protected by the first amendment to the Constitution of the United States.

(b) Identifying information. Notwithstanding the provisions of section 604 [§ 1681b] or any other provision of this title, a consumer reporting agency shall furnish identifying information respecting a consumer, limited to name, address, former addresses, places of employment, or former places of employment, to the Federal Bureau of Investigation when presented with a written request, signed by the Director or the Director's designee, which certifies compliance with this subsection. The Director or the Director's designee in a position not lower than Deputy Assistant Director at Bureau headquarters or a Special Agent in Charge of a Bureau field office designated by the Director may make such a certification only if the Director or the Director's designee has determined in writing that such information is sought for the conduct of an authorized investigation to protect against international terrorism or clandestine intelligence activities, provided that such an investigation of a United States person is not conducted solely upon the basis of activities protected by the first amendment to the Constitution of the United States.

(c) Court order for disclosure of consumer reports. Notwithstanding section 604 [§ 1681b] or any other provision of this title, if requested in writing by the Director of the Federal Bureau of Investigation, or a designee of the Director in a position not lower than Deputy Assistant Director at Bureau headquarters or a Special Agent in Charge of a Bureau field office designated by the Director, a court may issue an order ex parte directing a consumer reporting agency to furnish a consumer report to the Federal Bureau of Investigation, upon a showing in camera that the consumer report is sought for the conduct of an authorized investigation to protect against international terrorism or clandestine intelligence activities, provided that such an investigation of a United States person is not conducted solely upon the basis of activities protected by the first amendment to the Constitution of the United States.

The terms of an order issued under this subsection shall not disclose that the order is issued for purposes of a counterintelligence investigation.

(d) Confidentiality. No consumer reporting agency or officer, employee, or agent of a consumer reporting agency shall disclose to any person, other than those officers, employees, or agents of a consumer reporting agency necessary to fulfill the requirement to disclose information to the Federal Bureau of Investigation under this section, that the Federal Bureau of Investigation has sought or obtained the identity of financial institutions or a consumer report respecting any consumer under subsection (a), (b), or (c), and no consumer reporting agency or officer, employee, or agent of a consumer reporting agency shall include in any consumer report any information that would indicate that the Federal Bureau of Investigation has sought or obtained such information or a consumer report.

(e) Payment of fees. The Federal Bureau of Investigation shall, subject to the availability of appropriations, pay to the consumer reporting agency assembling or providing report or information in accordance with procedures established under this section a fee for reimbursement for such costs as are reasonably necessary and which have been directly incurred in searching, reproducing, or transporting books, papers, records, or other data required or requested to be produced under this section.

(f) Limit on dissemination. The Federal Bureau of Investigation may not disseminate information obtained pursuant to this section outside of the Federal Bureau of Investigation, except to other Federal agencies as may be necessary for the approval or conduct of a foreign counterintelligence investigation, or, where the information concerns a person subject to the Uniform Code of Military Justice, to appropriate investigative authorities within the military department concerned as may be necessary for the conduct of a joint foreign counterintelligence investigation.

(g) Rules of construction. Nothing in this section shall be construed to prohibit information from being furnished by the Federal Bureau of Investigation pursuant to a subpoena or court order, in connection with a judicial or administrative proceeding to enforce the provisions of this Act. Nothing in this section shall be construed to authorize or permit the withholding of information from the Congress.

(h) Reports to Congress. On a semiannual basis, the Attorney General shall fully inform the Permanent Select Committee on Intelligence and the Committee on Banking, Finance and Urban Affairs of the House of Representatives, and the Select Committee on Intelligence and the Committee on Banking, Housing, and Urban Affairs of the Senate concerning all requests made pursuant to subsections (a), (b), and (c).

(i) Damages. Any agency or department of the United States obtaining or disclosing any consumer reports, records, or information contained therein in violation of this section is liable to the consumer to whom such consumer reports, records, or information relate in an amount equal to the sum of

   (1) $100, without regard to the volume of consumer reports, records, or information involved;

   (2) any actual damages sustained by the consumer as a result of the disclosure;

   (3) if the violation is found to have been willful or intentional, such punitive damages as a court may allow; and

   (4) in the case of any successful action to enforce liability under this subsection, the costs of the action, together with reasonable attorney fees, as determined by the court.

(j) Disciplinary actions for violations. If a court determines that any agency or department of the United States has violated any provision of this section and the court finds that the circumstances surrounding the violation raise questions of whether or not an officer or employee of the agency or department acted willfully or intentionally with respect to the violation, the agency or department shall promptly initiate a proceeding to determine whether or not disciplinary action is warranted against the officer or employee who was responsible for the violation.

(k) Good-faith exception. Notwithstanding any other provision of this title, any consumer reporting agency or agent or employee thereof making disclosure of consumer reports or identifying information pursuant to this subsection in good-faith reliance upon a certification of the Federal Bureau of Investigation pursuant to provisions of this section shall not be liable to any person for such disclosure under this title, the constitution of any State, or any law or regulation of any State or any political subdivision of any State.

(l) Limitation of remedies. Notwithstanding any other provision of this title, the remedies and sanctions set forth in this section shall be the only judicial remedies and sanctions for violation of this section.

(m) Injunctive relief. In addition to any other remedy contained in this section, injunctive relief shall be available to require compliance with the procedures of this section. In the event of any successful action under this subsection, costs together with reasonable attorney fees, as determined by the court, may be recovered.

§ 626. Disclosures to governmental agencies for counterterrorism purposes [15 U.S.C. §1681v]

(a) Disclosure. Notwithstanding section 604 or any other provision of this title, a consumer reporting agency shall furnish a consumer report of a consumer and all other information in a consumer's file to a government agency authorized to conduct investigations of, or intelligence or counterintelligence activities or analysis related to, international terrorism when presented with a written certification by such government agency that such information is necessary for the agency's conduct or such investigation, activity or analysis.

(b) Form of certification. The certification described in subsection (a) shall be signed by a supervisory official designated by the head of a Federal agency or an officer of a Federal agency whose appointment to office is required to be made by the President, by and with the advice and consent of the Senate.

(c) Confidentiality. No consumer reporting agency, or officer, employee, or agent of such consumer reporting agency, shall disclose to any person, or specify in any consumer report, that a government agency has sought or obtained access to information under subsection (a).

(d) Rule of construction. Nothing in section 625 shall be construed to limit the authority of the Director of the Federal Bureau of Investigation under this section.

(e) Safe harbor. Notwithstanding any other provision of this title, any consumer reporting agency or agent or employee thereof making disclosure of consumer reports or other information pursuant to this section in good-faith reliance upon a certification of a governmental agency pursuant to the provisions of this section shall not be liable to any person for such disclosure under this subchapter, the constitution of any State, or any law or regulation of any State or any political subdivision of any State.

Legislative History

House Reports:

>No. 91-975 (Comm. on Banking and Currency) and

>No. 91-1587 (Comm. of Conference)

Senate Reports:

>No. 91-1139 accompanying S. 3678 (Comm. on Banking and Currency)

Congressional Record, Vol. 116 (1970)

>May 25, considered and passed House.

>Sept. 18, considered and passed Senate, amended.

>Oct. 9, Senate agreed to conference report.

>Oct. 13, House agreed to conference report.

Enactment:

>Public Law No. 91-508 (October 26, 1970):

Amendments: Public Law Nos.

>95-473 (October 17, 1978)

>95-598 (November 6, 1978)

>98-443 (October 4, 1984)

>101-73 (August 9, 1989)

>102-242 (December 19, 1991)

>102-537 (October 27, 1992)

>102-550 (October 28, 1992)

>103-325 (September 23, 1994)

>104-88 (December 29, 1995)

104-93 (January 6, 1996)

104-193 (August 22, 1996)

104-208 (September 30, 1996)

105-107 (November 20, 1997)

105-347 (November 2, 1998)

106-102 (November 12, 1999)

107-56 (October 26, 2001)

Endnotes:

1. The reporting periods have been lengthened for certain adverse information pertaining to U.S. Government insured or guaranteed student loans, or pertaining to national direct student loans. See sections 430A (f) and 463(c) (3) of the Higher Education Act of 1965, 20 U.S.C. 1080a (f) and 20 U.S.C. 1087cc(c) (3), respectively.

2. Should read "paragraphs (4) and (5)...." Prior Section 605(a) (6) was amended and re-designated as Section 605(a) (5) in November 1998.

3. The Federal Trade Commission increased the maximum allowable charge to $9.00, effective January 1, 2002. 66 Fed. Reg. 63545 (Dec. 7, 2001).

Chapter 14

FAIR AND ACCURATE CREDIT TRANSACTION ACT

FAIR AND ACCURATE CREDIT TRANSACTIONS ACT OF 2003 Public Law 108-159 108th Congress

An Act To amend the Fair Credit Reporting Act, to prevent identity theft, improve resolution of consumer disputes, improve the accuracy of consumer records, make improvements in the use of, and consumer access to, credit information, and for other purposes. <<NOTE: Dec. 4, 2003 - [H.R. 2622]>>

Be it enacted by the Senate and House of Representatives of the United States of America in Congress <<NOTE: Fair and Accurate Credit Transactions Act of 2003.>> assembled,

SECTION 1. SHORT TITLE; TABLE OF CONTENTS.

(a) Short Title.--This <<NOTE: 15 USC 1601 note.>> Act may be cited as the "Fair and Accurate Credit Transactions Act of 2003".

(b) Table of Contents.--The table of contents for this Act is as follows:

TITLE III--ENHANCING THE ACCURACY OF CONSUMER REPORT INFORMATION

TITLE IV--LIMITING THE USE AND SHARING OF MEDICAL INFORMATION IN THE FINANCIAL SYSTEM

TITLE V--FINANCIAL LITERACY AND EDUCATION IMPROVEMENT

TITLE VI--PROTECTING EMPLOYEE MISCONDUCT INVESTIGATIONS

TITLE VII--RELATION TO STATE LAWS

TITLE VIII--MISCELLANEOUS

SEC. 2. <<NOTE: 15 USC 1681 note.>> DEFINITIONS.

As used in this Act--
(1) the term ``Board'' means the Board of Governors of the Federal Reserve System;
(2) the term ``Commission'', other than as used in title V, means the Federal Trade Commission;
(3) the terms ``consumer'', ``consumer report'', ``consumer reporting agency'', ``creditor'', ``Federal banking agencies'', and ``financial institution'' have the same meanings as in section 603 of the Fair Credit Reporting Act, as amended by this Act; and
(4) the term ``affiliates'' means persons that are related by common ownership or affiliated by corporate control.

SEC. 3. <<NOTE: 15 USC 1681 note.>> EFFECTIVE DATES.

Except as otherwise specifically provided in this Act and the amendments made by this Act--
(1) <<NOTE: Regulations.>> before the end of the 2-month period beginning on the date of enactment of this Act, the Board and the Commission shall jointly prescribe regulations in final form establishing effective dates for each provision of this Act; and

(2) the regulations prescribed under paragraph (1) shall establish effective dates that are as early as possible, while allowing a reasonable time for the implementation of the provisions of this Act, but in no case shall any such effective date be later than 10 months after the date of issuance of such regulations in final form.

TITLE I--IDENTITY THEFT PREVENTION AND CREDIT HISTORY RESTORATION

Subtitle A--Identity Theft Prevention

SEC. 111. AMENDMENT TO DEFINITIONS.

Section 603 of the Fair Credit Reporting Act (15 U.S.C. 1681a) is amended by adding at the end the following:

``(q) Definitions Relating to Fraud Alerts.--

``(1) Active duty military consumer.--The term `active duty military consumer' means a consumer in military service who--``(A) is on active duty (as defined in section 101(d)(1) of title 10, United States Code) or is a reservist performing duty under a call or order to active duty under a provision of law referred to in section 101(a)(13) of title 10, United States Code; and ``(B) is assigned to service away from the usual duty station of the consumer.

``(2) Fraud alert; active duty alert.--The terms `fraud alert' and `active duty alert' mean a statement in the file of a consumer that-- ``(A) notifies all prospective users of a consumer report relating to the consumer that the consumer may be a victim of fraud, including identity theft, or is an active duty military consumer, as applicable; and``(B) is presented in a manner that facilitates a clear and conspicuous view of the statement described in subparagraph (A) by any person requesting such consumer report.

``(3) Identity theft.--The term `identity theft' means a fraud committed using the identifying information of another person, subject to such further definition as the Commission may prescribe, by regulation.

``(4) Identity theft report.--The term `identity theft report' has the meaning given that term by rule of the Commission, and means, at a minimum, a report--``(A) that alleges an identity theft; `(B) that is a copy of an official, valid report filed by a consumer with an appropriate Federal, State, or local law enforcement agency, including the United States Postal Inspection Service, or such other government agency deemed appropriate by the Commission; and ``(C) the filing of which subjects the person filing the report to criminal penalties relating to the filing of false information if, in fact, the information in the report is false.

``(5) New credit plan.--The term `new credit plan' means a new account under an open end credit plan (as defined in section 103(i) of the Truth in Lending Act) or a new credit transaction not under an open end credit plan.

``(r) Credit and Debit Related Terms-- ``(1) Card issuer.--The term `card issuer' means--``(A) a credit card issuer, in the case of a credit card; and`(B) a debit card issuer, in the case of a debit card. ``(2) Credit card.-- The term `credit card' has the same meaning as in section 103 of the Truth in Lending Act. ``(3) Debit card.-- The term `debit card' means any card issued by a financial institution to a consumer for use in initiating an electronic fund transfer from the account of the consumer at such financial institution, for the purpose of transferring money between accounts or obtaining money, Property, labor, or services.

``(4) Account and electronic fund transfer.--The terms`account' and `electronic fund transfer' have the same meanings as in section 903 of the Electronic Fund Transfer Act.

``(5) Credit and creditor.--The terms `credit' and `creditor' have the same meanings as in section 702 of the Equal Credit Opportunity Act.

``(s) Federal Banking Agency.--The term `Federal banking agency' has the same meaning as in section 3 of the Federal Deposit Insurance Act.``(t) Financial Institution.--The term `financial institution' means A State or National bank, a State or Federal savings and loan association, a mutual savings bank, a State or Federal credit union, or any other person that, directly or indirectly, holds a transaction account (as defined in section 19(b) of the Federal Reserve Act) belonging to a consumer.``(u) Reseller.--The term `reseller' means a consumer reporting agency that--

``(1) assembles and merges information contained in the database of another consumer reporting agency or multiple consumer reporting agencies concerning any consumer for purposes of furnishing such information to any third party, to the extent of such activities; and ``(2) does not maintain a database of the assembled or merged information from which new consumer reports are produced.

``(v) Commission.--The term `Commission' means the Federal Trade Commission.

``(w) Nationwide Specialty Consumer Reporting Agency.--The term `nationwide specialty consumer reporting agency' means a consumer reporting agency that compiles and maintains files on consumers on a nationwide basis relating to--

``(1) medical records or payments;

"(2) residential or tenant history;

"(3) check writing history;

"(4) employment history; or

"(5) insurance claims.".

SEC. 112. FRAUD ALERTS AND ACTIVE DUTY ALERTS.

(a) Fraud Alerts.--The Fair Credit Reporting Act (15 U.S.C. 1681 et seq.) is amended by inserting after section 605 the following:

"Sec. 605A. <<NOTE: 15 USC 1681c-1.>> Identity theft prevention; fraud alerts and active duty alerts

"(a) One-Call Fraud Alerts.--

"(1) Initial alerts.--Upon the direct request of a consumer, or an individual acting on behalf of or as a personal representative of a consumer, who asserts in good faith a suspicion that the consumer has been or is about to become a victim of fraud or related crime, including identity theft, a consumer reporting agency described in section 603(p) that maintains a file on the consumer and has received appropriate proof of the identity of the requester shall—(A) include a fraud alert in the file of that consumer, and also provide that alert along with any credit score generated in using that file, for a period of not less than 90 days, beginning on the date of such request, unless the consumer or such representative requests that such fraud alert be removed before the end of such period, and the agency has received appropriate proof of the identity of the requester for such purpose; and(B) refer the information regarding the fraud alert under this paragraph to each of the other consumer reporting agencies described in section 603(p), in accordance with procedures developed under section 621(f)."(2) Access to free reports.--In any case in which a consumer reporting agency includes a fraud alert in the file of a consumer pursuant to this subsection, the consumer reporting agency shall--

"(A) disclose to the consumer that the consumer may request a free copy of the file of the consumer pursuant to section 612(d); and "(B) <<NOTE: Deadline.>> provide to the consumer all disclosures required to be made under section 609, without charge to the consumer, not later than 3 business days after any request described in subparagraph (A).

"(b) Extended Alerts.--

"(1) In general.--Upon the direct request of a consumer, or an individual acting on behalf of or as a personal representative of a consumer, who submits an identity theft report to a consumer reporting agency described in section 603(p) that maintains a file on the consumer, if the agency has received appropriate proof of the identity of the requester, the agency shall--"(A) include a fraud alert in the file of that consumer, and also provide that alert along with any credit score generated in using that file, during the 7-year period beginning on the date of such request, unless the consumer or such representative requests that such fraud alert be removed before the end of such period and the agency has received appropriate proof of the identity of the requester for such purpose; "(B) during the 5-year period beginning on the date of such request, exclude the consumer from any list of consumers prepared by the consumer reporting agency and provided to any third party to offer credit or insurance to the consumer as part of a transaction that was not initiated by the consumer, unless the consumer or such representative requests that such exclusion be rescinded before the end of such period; and"(C) refer the information regarding the extended fraud alert under this paragraph to each of the other consumer reporting agencies described in section 603(p), in accordance with procedures developed under section 621(f)."(2) Access to free reports.--In any case in which a consumer reporting agency includes a fraud alert in the file of a consumer pursuant to this subsection, the consumer reporting agency shall--"(A) disclose to the consumer that the consumer may request 2 free copies of the file of the consumer pursuant to section 612(d) during the 12-month period beginning on the date on which the fraud alert was included in the file; and "(B) <<NOTE: Deadline.>> provide to the consumer all disclosures required to be made under section 609, without charge to the consumer, not later than 3 business days after any request described in subparagraph (A).

"(c) Active Duty Alerts.--Upon the direct request of an active duty military consumer, or an individual acting on behalf of or as a personal representative of an active duty military consumer, a consumer reporting agency described in section 603(p) that maintains a file on the active duty military consumer and has received appropriate proof of the identity of the requester shall--

"(1) include an active duty alert in the file of that active duty military consumer, and also provide that alert along with any credit score generated in using that file, during a period of not less than 12 months, or such longer period as the Commission shall determine, by regulation, beginning on the date of the request, unless the active duty military consumer or such representative requests that such fraud alert be removed before the end of such period, and the agency has received appropriate proof of the identity of the requester for such purpose; "(2) during the 2-year period beginning on the date of such request, exclude the active duty military consumer from any list of consumers prepared by the consumer reporting agency and provided to any third party to offer credit or insurance to the consumer as part of a transaction that was not initiated by the consumer, unless the consumer requests that such exclusion be rescinded before the end of such period; and``(3) refer the information regarding the active duty alert to each of the other consumer reporting agencies described in section 603(p), in accordance with procedures developed under section 621(f). ``(d) Procedures.--Each consumer reporting agency described in section 603(p) shall establish policies and procedures to comply with this section, including procedures that inform consumers of the availability of initial, extended, and active duty alerts and procedures that allow consumers and active duty military consumers to request initial, extended, or active duty alerts (as applicable) in a simple and easy manner, including by telephone. ``(e) Referrals of Alerts.--Each consumer reporting agency described in section 603(p) that receives a referral of a fraud alert or active duty alert from another consumer reporting agency pursuant to this section shall, as though the agency received the request from the consumer directly, follow the procedures required under--

``(1) paragraphs (1)(A) and (2) of subsection (a), in the case of a referral under subsection (a)(1)(B);``(2) paragraphs (1)(A), (1)(B), and (2) of subsection (b), in the case of a referral under subsection (b)(1)(C); and``(3) paragraphs (1) and (2) of subsection (c), in the case of a referral under subsection (c)(3). ``(f) Duty of Reseller To Re-convey Alert.--A reseller shall include in its report any fraud alert or active duty alert placed in the file of a consumer pursuant to this section by another consumer reporting agency. ``(g) Duty of Other Consumer Reporting Agencies To Provide Contact Information.--If a consumer contacts any consumer reporting agency that is not described in section 603(p) to communicate a suspicion that the consumer has been or is about to become a victim of fraud or related crime, including identity theft, the agency shall provide information to the consumer on how to contact the Commission and the consumer reporting agencies described in section 603(p) to obtain more detailed information and request alerts under this section.``(h) Limitations on Use of Information for Credit Extensions.--

``(1) Requirements for initial and active duty alerts.--

``(A) Notification.--Each initial fraud alert and active duty alert under this section shall include information that notifies all prospective users of a consumer report on the consumer to which the alert relates that the consumer does not authorize the establishment of any new credit plan or extension of credit, other than under an open-end credit plan (as defined in section 103(i)), in the name of the consumer, or issuance of an additional card on an existing credit account requested by a consumer, or any increase in credit limit on an existing credit account requested by a consumer, except in accordance with subparagraph (B).``(B) Limitation on users.--

``(i) In general.--No prospective user of a consumer report that includes an initial fraud alert or an active duty alert in accordance with this section may establish a new credit plan or extension of credit, other than under an open-end credit plan (as defined in section 103(i)), in the name of the consumer, or issue an additional card on an existing credit account requested by a consumer, or grant any increase in credit limit on an existing credit account requested by a consumer, unless the user utilizes reasonable policies and procedures to form a reasonable belief that the user knows the identity of the person making the request.

``(ii) Verification.--If a consumer requesting the alert has specified a telephone number to be used for identity verification purposes, before authorizing any new credit plan or extension described in clause (i) in the name of such consumer, a user of such consumer report shall contact the consumer using that telephone number or take reasonable steps to verify the consumer's identity and confirm that the application for a new credit plan is not the result of identity theft.``(2) Requirements for extended alerts.--

``(A) Notification.--Each extended alert under this section shall include information that provides all prospective users of a consumer report relating to a consumer with--``(i) notification that the consumer does not authorize the establishment of any new credit plan or extension of credit described in clause (i), other than under an open-end credit plan (as defined in section 103(i)), in the name of the consumer, or issuance of an additional card on an existing credit account requested by a consumer, or any increase in credit limit on an existing credit account requested by a consumer, except in accordance with subparagraph (B); and``(ii) a telephone number or other reasonable contact method designated by the consumer.``(B) Limitation on users.--No prospective user of a consumer report or of a credit score generated using the information in the file of a consumer that includes an extended fraud alert in accordance with this section may establish a new credit plan or extension of credit, other than under an open-end credit plan (as defined in section 103(i)), in the name of the consumer, or issue an additional card on an existing credit account requested by a consumer, or any increase in credit limit on an existing credit account requested by a consumer, unless the user contacts the consumer in person or using the contact method described in subparagraph (A)(ii) to confirm that the application for a new credit plan or increase in credit limit, or request for an additional card is not the result of identity theft.''.

(b) Rulemaking.--The <<NOTE: 15 USC 1681c-1 note.>> Commission shall prescribe regulations to define what constitutes appropriate proof of identity for purposes of sections 605A, 605B, and 609(a)(1) of the Fair Credit Reporting Act, as amended by this Act.

SEC. 113. TRUNCATION OF CREDIT CARD AND DEBIT CARD ACCOUNT NUMBERS.

Section 605 of the Fair Credit Reporting Act (15 U.S.C. 1681c) is amended by adding at the end the following: ``(g) Truncation of Credit Card and Debit Card Numbers.--

``(1) In general.--Except as otherwise provided in this subsection, no person that accepts credit cards or debit cards for the transaction of business shall print more than the last 5 digits of the card number or the expiration date upon any receipt provided to the cardholder at the point of the sale or transaction.

``(2) Limitation.--This <<NOTE: Applicability.>> subsection shall apply only to receipts that are electronically printed, and shall not apply to transactions in which the sole means of recording a credit card or debit card account number is by handwriting or by an imprint or copy of the card.

``(3) Effective date.--This subsection shall become effective--

``(A) 3 years after the date of enactment of this subsection, with respect to any cash register or other machine or device that electronically prints receipts for credit card or debit card transactions that is in use before January 1, 2005; and ``(B) 1 year after the date of enactment of this subsection, with respect to any cash register or other machine or device that electronically prints receipts for credit card or debit card transactions that is first put into use on or after January 1, 2005.''.

SEC. 114. ESTABLISHMENT OF PROCEDURES FOR THE IDENTIFICATION OF POSSIBLE INSTANCES OF IDENTITY THEFT.

Section 615 of the Fair Credit Reporting Act (15 U.S.C. 1681m) is amended--

(1) by striking ``(e)'' at the end; and

(2) by adding at the end the following:

``(e) Red Flag Guidelines and Regulations Required.--

``(1) Guidelines.--The Federal banking agencies, the National Credit Union Administration, and the Commission shall jointly, with respect to the entities that are subject to their respective enforcement authority under section 621--

``(A) establish and maintain guidelines for use by each financial institution and each creditor regarding identity theft with respect to account holders at, or customers of, such entities, and update such guidelines as often as necessary;

``(B) prescribe regulations requiring each financial institution and each creditor to establish reasonable policies and procedures for implementing the guidelines established pursuant to subparagraph (A), to identify possible risks to account holders or customers or to the safety and soundness of the institution or customers; and ``(C) prescribe regulations applicable to card issuers to ensure that, if a card issuer receives notification of a change of address for an existing account, and within a short period of time (during at least the first 30 days after such notification is) receives a request for an additional or replacement card for the same account, the card issuer may not issue the additional or replacement card, unless the card issuer, in accordance with reasonable policies and procedures-- ``(i) notifies the cardholder of the request at the former address of the cardholder and provides to the cardholder a means of promptly reporting incorrect address changes;

``(ii) notifies the cardholder of the request by such other means of communication as the cardholder and the card issuer previously agreed to; or ``(iii) uses other means of assessing the validity of the change of address, in accordance with reasonable policies and procedures established by the card issuer in accordance with the regulations prescribed under subparagraph (B).

``(2) Criteria.--

``(A) In general.--In developing the guidelines required by paragraph (1)(A), the agencies described in paragraph (1) shall identify patterns, practices, and specific forms of activity that indicate the possible existence of identity theft. ``(B) Inactive accounts.--In developing the guidelines required by paragraph (1)(A), the agencies described in paragraph (1) shall consider including reasonable guidelines providing that when a transaction occurs with respect to a credit or deposit account that has been inactive for more than 2 years, the creditor or financial institution shall follow reasonable policies and procedures that provide for notice to be given to a consumer in a manner reasonably designed to reduce the likelihood of identity theft with respect to such account. ``(3) Consistency with verification requirements.--Guidelines established pursuant to paragraph (1) shall not be inconsistent with the policies and procedures required under section 5318(l) of title 31, United States Code.''.

SEC. 115. AUTHORITY TO TRUNCATE SOCIAL SECURITY NUMBERS.

Section 609(a)(1) of the Fair Credit Reporting Act (15 U.S.C. 1681g(a)(1)) is amended by striking ``except that nothing'' and inserting the following: ``except that-- ``(A) if the consumer to whom the file relates requests that the first 5 digits of the social security number (or similar identification number) of the consumer not be included in the disclosure and the consumer reporting agency has received appropriate proof of the identity of the requester, the consumer reporting agency shall so truncate such number in such disclosure; and ``(B) nothing''.

Subtitle B--Protection and Restoration of Identity Theft Victim Credit History

SEC. 151. SUMMARY OF RIGHTS OF IDENTITY THEFT VICTIMS.

(a) In General.--

(1) Summary.--Section 609 of the Fair Credit Reporting Act (15 U.S.C. 1681g) is amended by adding at the end the following:''(d) Summary of Rights of Identity Theft Victims.--''(1) In general.--The Commission, in consultation with the Federal banking agencies and the National Credit Union Administration, shall prepare a model summary of the rights of consumers under this title with respect to the procedures for remedying the effects of fraud or identity theft involving credit, an electronic fund transfer, or an account or transaction at or with a financial institution or other creditor.

''(2) Summary <<NOTE: Effective date.>> of rights and contact information.--Beginning 60 days after the date on which the model summary of rights is prescribed in final form by the Commission pursuant to paragraph (1), if any consumer contacts a consumer reporting agency and expresses a belief that the consumer is a victim of fraud or identity theft involving credit, an electronic fund transfer, or an account or transaction at or with a financial institution or other creditor, the consumer reporting agency shall, in addition to any other action that the agency may take, provide the consumer with a summary of rights that contains all of the information required by the Commission under paragraph (1), and information on how to contact the Commission to obtain more detailed information.

''(e) Information Available to Victims.--''(1) In general.--For <<NOTE: Deadline.>> the purpose of documenting fraudulent transactions resulting from identity theft, not later than30 days after the date of receipt of a request from a victim in accordance with paragraph (3), and subject to verification of the identity of the victim and the claim of identity theft in accordance with paragraph (2), a business entity that has provided credit to, provided for consideration products, goods, or services to, accepted payment from, or otherwise entered into a commercial transaction for consideration with, a person who has allegedly made unauthorized use of the means of identification of the victim, shall provide a copy of application and business transaction records in the control of the business entity, whether maintained by the business entity or by another person on behalf of the business entity, evidencing any transaction alleged to be a result of identity theft to--''(A) the victim;''(B) any Federal, State, or local government law enforcement agency or officer specified by the victim in such a request; or''(C) any law enforcement agency investigating the identity theft and authorized by the victim to take receipt of records provided under this subsection.

''(2) Verification of identity and claim.--Before a business entity provides any information under paragraph (1), unless the business entity, at its discretion, otherwise has a high degree of confidence that it knows the identity of the victim making a request under paragraph (1), the victim shall provide to the business entity--
''(A) as proof of positive identification of the victim, at the election of the business entity--''(i) the presentation of a government-issued identification card;''(ii) personally identifying information of the same type as was provided to the business entity by the unauthorized person; or''(iii) personally identifying information that the business entity typically requests from new applicants or for new transactions, at the time of the victim's request for information, including any documentation described in clauses (i) and (ii); and''(B) as proof of a claim of identity theft, at the election of the business entity--''(i) a copy of a police report evidencing the claim of the victim of identity theft; and ''(ii) a properly completed—
''(I) copy of a standardized affidavit of identity theft developed   and made available by the Commission; or''(II) an affidavit of fact that is acceptable to the business entity for that purpose.

''(3) Procedures.--The request of a victim under paragraph (1) shall--''(A) be in writing;''(B) be mailed to an address specified by the business entity, if any; and''(C) if asked by the business entity, include relevant information about any transaction alleged to be a result of identity theft to facilitate compliance with this section including--i) if known by the victim (or if readily obtainable by the victim), the date of the application or transaction; and''(ii) if known by the victim (or if readily obtainable by the victim), any other identifying information such as an account or transaction number.

''(4) No charge to victim.--Information required to be provided under paragraph (1) shall be so provided without charge.''(5) Authority to decline to provide information.--A business entity may decline to provide information under paragraph (1) if, in the exercise of good faith, the business entity determines that--''(A) this subsection does not require disclosure of the information; B) after reviewing the information provided pursuant to paragraph (2), the business entity does not have a high degree of confidence in knowing the true identity of the individual requesting the information;

``(C) the request for the information is based on a misrepresentation of fact by the individual requesting the information relevant to the request for information; or``(D) the information requested is Internet navigational data or similar information about a person's visit to a website or online service.

``(6) Limitation on liability.--Except as provided in section 621, sections 616 and 617 do not apply to any violation of this subsection.

``(7) Limitation on civil liability.--No business entity may be held civilly liable under any provision of Federal, State, or other law for disclosure, made in good faith pursuant to this subsection.

``(8) No new recordkeeping obligation.--Nothing in this subsection creates an obligation on the part of a business entity to obtain, retain, or maintain information or records that are not otherwise required to be obtained, retained, or maintained in the ordinary course of its business or under other applicable law.

``(9) Rule of construction.--

``(A) In general.--No provision of subtitle A of title V of Public Law 106-102, prohibiting the disclosure of financial information by a business entity to third parties shall be used to deny disclosure of information to the victim under this subsection.``(B) Limitation.--Except as provided in subparagraph (A), nothing in this subsection permits a business entity to disclose information, including information to law enforcement under subparagraphs (B) and (C) of paragraph (1), that the business entity is otherwise prohibited from disclosing under any other applicable provision of Federal or State law.

``(10) Affirmative defense.--In any civil action brought to enforce this subsection, it is an affirmative defense (which the defendant must establish by a preponderance of the evidence) for a business entity to file an affidavit or answer stating that--``(A) the business entity has made a reasonably diligent search of its available business records; and``(B) the records requested under this subsection do not exist or are not reasonably available.

``(11) Definition of victim.--For purposes of this subsection, the term `victim' means a consumer whose means of identification or financial information has been used or transferred (or has been alleged to have been used or transferred) without the authority of that consumer, with the intent to commit, or to aid or abet, an identity theft or a similar crime.

``(12) Effective date.--This subsection shall become effective 180 days after the date of enactment of this subsection.

``(13) Effectiveness study.--

Not <<NOTE: Deadline. Reports.>> later than 18 months after the date of enactment of this subsection, the Comptroller General of the United States shall submit a report to Congress assessing the effectiveness of this provision.".

(2) Relation to state laws.--Section 625(b)(1) of the Fair Credit Reporting Act (15 U.S.C. 1681t(b)(1), as so re-designated) is amended by adding at the end the following new subparagraph:``(G) section 609(e), relating to information available to victims under section 609(e);".

(b) Public <<NOTE: Deadline. 15 USC 1681c-1 note.>> Campaign To Prevent Identity Theft.--Not later than 2 years after the date of enactment of this Act, the Commission shall establish and implement a media and distribution campaign to teach the public how to prevent identity theft. Such campaign shall include existing Commission education materials, as well as radio, television, and print public service announcements, video cassettes, interactive digital video discs (DVD's) or compact audio discs (CD's), and Internet resources.

SEC. 152. BLOCKING OF INFORMATION RESULTING FROM IDENTITY THEFT.

(a) In General.--The Fair Credit Reporting Act (15 U.S.C. 1681 et seq.) is amended by inserting after section 605A, as added by this Act, the following:

``Sec. 605B. <<NOTE: 15 USC 1681c-2.>> Block of information resulting from identity theft

a) Block.--Except <<NOTE: Deadline.>> as otherwise provided in this section, a consumer reporting agency shall block the reporting of any information in the file of a consumer that the consumer identifies as information that resulted from an alleged identity theft, not later than 4 business days after the date of receipt by such agency of--

``(1) appropriate proof of the identity of the consumer;

``(2) a copy of an identity theft report;

``(3) the identification of such information by the consumer; and

``(4) a statement by the consumer that the information is not information relating to any transaction by the consumer.

``(b) Notification.--A consumer reporting agency shall promptly notify the furnisher of information identified by the consumer under subsection (a)--``(1) that the information may be a result of identity theft;``(2) that an

identity theft report has been filed;``(3) that a block has been requested under this section; and 4) of the effective dates of the block.
``(c) Authority To Decline or Rescind.—

``(1) In general.--A consumer reporting agency may decline to block, or may rescind any block, of information relating to a consumer under this section, if the consumer reporting agency reasonably determines that—``(A) the information was blocked in error or a block was requested by the consumer in error;``(B) the information was blocked, or a block was requested by the consumer, on the basis of a material misrepresentation of fact by the consumer relevant to the request to block; or``(C) the consumer obtained possession of goods, services, or money as a result of the blocked transaction or transactions. ``

(2) Notification to consumer.--If a block of information is declined or rescinded under this subsection, the affected consumer shall be notified promptly, in the same manner as consumers are notified of the reinsertion of information under section 611(a)(5)(B). ``

(3) Significance of block.--For purposes of this subsection, if a consumer reporting agency rescinds a block, the presence of information in the file of a consumer prior to the blocking of such information is not evidence of whether the consumer knew or should have known that the consumer obtained possession of any goods, services, or money as a result of the block.

``(d) Exception for Resellers.--
``(1) No reseller file.--This section shall not apply to a consumer reporting agency, if the consumer reporting agency--``(A) is a reseller;``(B) is not, at the time of the request of the consumer under subsection (a), otherwise furnishing or reselling a consumer report concerning the information identified by the consumer; and``(C) informs the consumer, by any means, that the consumer may report the identity theft to the Commission to obtain consumer information regarding identity theft.

``(2) Reseller with file.--The sole obligation of the consumer reporting agency under this section, with regard to any request of a consumer under this section, shall be to block the consumer report maintained by the consumer reporting agency from any subsequent use, if--``(A) the consumer, in accordance with the provisions of subsection (a), identifies, to a consumer reporting agency, information in the file of the consumer that resulted from identity theft; and``(B) the consumer reporting agency is a reseller of the identified information.

``(3) Notice.--In carrying out its obligation under paragraph (2), the reseller shall promptly provide a notice to the consumer of the decision to block the file. Such notice shall contain the name, address, and telephone number of each consumer reporting agency from which the consumer information was obtained for resale.

``(e) Exception for Verification Companies.--The provisions of this section do not apply to a check services company, acting as such, which issues authorizations for the purpose of approving or processing negotiable instruments, electronic fund transfers, or similar methods of payments, except that, beginning 4 business days after receipt of information described in paragraphs (1) through (3) of subsection (a), a check services company shall not report to a national consumer reporting agency described in section 603(p), any information identified in the subject identity theft report as resulting from identity theft.

``(f) Access to Blocked Information by Law Enforcement Agencies.--No provision of this section shall be construed as requiring a consumer reporting agency to prevent a Federal, State, or local law enforcement agency from accessing blocked information in a consumer file to which the agency could otherwise obtain access under this title.".
(b) Clerical Amendment.--The table of sections for the Fair Credit
Reporting Act (15 U.S.C. 1681 et seq.) is amended by inserting after the item relating to section 605 the following new items:

``605A. Identity theft prevention; fraud alerts and active duty alerts.
``605B. Block of information resulting from identity theft.".

SEC. 153. <<NOTE: Procedures.>> COORDINATION OF IDENTITY THEFT COMPLAINT INVESTIGATIONS.

Section 621 of the Fair Credit Reporting Act (15 U.S.C. 1681s) is amended by adding at the end the following:
``(f) Coordination of Consumer Complaint Investigations.--

``(1) In general.--Each consumer reporting agency described in section 603(p) shall develop and maintain procedures for the referral to each other such agency of any consumer complaint received by the agency alleging identity theft, or requesting a fraud alert under section 605A or a block under section 605B.

``(2) Model form and procedure for reporting identity theft.--The Commission, in consultation with the Federal banking agencies and the National Credit Union Administration, shall develop a model form and model procedures to be used by consumers who are victims of identity theft for contacting and informing creditors and consumer reporting agencies of the fraud.

``(3) Annual summary reports.--Each consumer reporting agency described in section 603(p) shall submit an annual summary report to the Commission on consumer complaints received by the agency on identity theft or fraud alerts.''.

SEC. 154. PREVENTION OF REPOLLUTION OF CONSUMER REPORTS.

(a) Prevention of Reinsertion of Erroneous Information.--Section 623(a) of the Fair Credit Reporting Act (15 U.S.C. 1681s-2(a)) is amended by adding at the end the following:

``(6) Duties of furnishers upon notice of identity theft-related information.--

``(A) Reasonable procedures.--A person that furnishes information to any consumer reporting agency shall have in place reasonable procedures to respond to any notification that it receives from a consumer reporting agency under section 605B relating to information resulting from identity theft, to prevent that person from refurnishing such blocked information.

``(B) Information alleged to result from identity theft.--If a consumer submits an identity theft report to a person who furnishes information to a consumer reporting agency at the address specified by that person for receiving such reports stating that information maintained by such person that purports to relate to the consumer resulted from identity theft, the person may not furnish such information that purports to relate to the consumer to any consumer reporting agency, unless the person subsequently knows or is informed by the consumer that the information is correct.''.

(b) Prohibition on Sale or Transfer of Debt Caused by Identity Theft.--Section 615 of the Fair Credit Reporting Act (15 U.S.C. 1681m), as amended by this Act, is amended by adding at the end the following:

``(f) Prohibition on Sale or Transfer of Debt Caused by Identity Theft.--

``(1) In general.--No person shall sell, transfer for consideration, or place for collection a debt that such person has been notified under section 605B has resulted from identity theft.

``(2) Applicability.--The prohibitions of this subsection shall apply to all persons collecting a debt described in paragraph (1) after the date of a notification under paragraph (1).

``(3) Rule of construction.--Nothing in this subsection shall be construed to prohibit--

``(A) the repurchase of a debt in any case in which the assignee of the debt requires such repurchase because the debt has resulted from identity theft;

``(B) the securitization of a debt or the pledging of a portfolio of debt as collateral in connection with a borrowing; or

``(C) the transfer of debt as a result of a merger, acquisition, purchase and assumption transaction, or transfer of substantially all of the assets of an entity.''.

SEC. 155. NOTICE BY DEBT COLLECTORS WITH RESPECT TO FRAUDULENT INFORMATION.

Section 615 of the Fair Credit Reporting Act (15 U.S.C. 1681m), as amended by this Act, is amended by adding at the end the following:

``(g) Debt Collector Communications Concerning Identity Theft.--If a person acting as a debt collector (as that term is defined in title VIII) on behalf of a third party that is a creditor or other user of a consumer report is notified that any information relating to a debt that the person is attempting to collect may be fraudulent or may be the result of identity theft, that person shall--

``(1) notify the third party that the information may be fraudulent or may be the result of identity theft; and

``(2) upon request of the consumer to whom the debt purportedly relates, provide to the consumer all information to which the consumer would otherwise be entitled if the consumer were not a victim of identity theft, but wished to dispute the debt under provisions of law applicable to that person.''.

SEC. 156. STATUTE OF LIMITATIONS.

Section 618 of the Fair Credit Reporting Act (15 U.S.C. 1681p) is amended to read as follows:

``Sec. 618. Jurisdiction of courts; limitation of actions

``An action to enforce any liability created under this title may be brought in any appropriate United States district court, without regard to the amount in controversy, or in any other court of competent jurisdiction, not later than the earlier of--

``(1) 2 years after the date of discovery by the plaintiff of the violation that is the basis for such liability; or

``(2) 5 years after the date on which the violation that is the basis for such liability occurs.''.

SEC. 157. STUDY ON THE USE OF TECHNOLOGY TO COMBAT IDENTITY THEFT.

(a) Study Required.--The Secretary of the Treasury shall conduct a study of the use of biometrics and other similar technologies to reduce the incidence and costs to society of identity theft by providing convincing evidence of who actually performed a given financial transaction.

(b) Consultation.--The Secretary of the Treasury shall consult with Federal banking agencies, the Commission, and representatives of financial institutions, consumer reporting agencies, Federal, State, and local government agencies that issue official forms or means of identification, State prosecutors, law enforcement agencies, the biometric industry, and the general public in formulating and conducting the study required by subsection (a).

(c) Authorization of Appropriations.--There are authorized to be appropriated to the Secretary of the Treasury for fiscal year 2004, such sums as may be necessary to carry out the provisions of this section.

(d) Report Required.--Before <<NOTE: Deadline.>> the end of the 180-day period beginning on the date of enactment of this Act, the Secretary shall submit a report to Congress containing the findings and conclusions of the study required under subsection (a), together with such recommendations for legislative or administrative actions as may be appropriate.

TITLE II--IMPROVEMENTS IN USE OF AND CONSUMER ACCESS TO CREDIT INFORMATION

SEC. 211. FREE CONSUMER REPORTS.

(a) In General.--Section 612 of the Fair Credit Reporting Act (15 U.S.C. 1681j) is amended--

(1) by re-designating subsection (a) as subsection (f), and transferring it to the end of the section;

(2) by inserting before subsection (b) the following:

``(a) Free Annual Disclosure.--

``(1) Nationwide consumer reporting agencies.--

``(A) In general.--All consumer reporting agencies described in subsections (p) and (w) of section 603 shall make all disclosures pursuant to section 609 once during any 12-month period upon request of the consumer and without charge to the consumer.

``(B) Centralized <<NOTE: Applicability.>> source.--Subparagraph (A) shall apply with respect to a consumer reporting agency described in section 603(p) only if the request from the consumer is made using the centralized source established for such purpose in accordance with section 211(c) of the Fair and Accurate Credit Transactions Act of 2003.

``(C) Nationwide specialty consumer reporting agency.--``(i) In general.--The <<NOTE: Regulations.>> Commission shall prescribe regulations applicable to each consumer reporting agency described in section 603(w) to require the establishment of a streamlined process for consumers to request consumer reports under subparagraph (A), which shall include, at a minimum, the establishment by each such agency of a toll-free telephone number for such requests. ``(ii) Considerations.--In prescribing regulations under clause (i), the Commission shall consider--``(I) the significant demands that may be placed on consumer reporting agencies in providing such consumer reports;``(II) appropriate means to ensure that consumer reporting agencies can satisfactorily meet those demands, including the efficacy of a system of staggering the availability to consumers of such consumer reports; and``(III) the ease by which consumers should be able to contact consumer reporting agencies with respect to access to such consumer reports.``(iii) Date of issuance.--The <<NOTE: Deadline.>> Commission shall issue the regulations required by this subparagraph in final form not later than 6 months after the date of enactment of the Fair and Accurate Credit Transactions Act of 2003. ``(iv) Consideration <<NOTE: Effective date.>> of ability to comply.--The regulations of the Commission under this subparagraph shall establish an effective date by which each nationwide specialty consumer reporting agency (as defined in section 603(w)) shall be required to comply with subsection (a), which effective date--

``(I) shall be established after consideration of the ability of each nationwide specialty consumer reporting agency to comply with subsection (a); and``(II) <<NOTE: Deadline.>> shall be not later than 6 months after the date on which such regulations are issued in final form (or such additional period not to exceed 3 months, as the Commission determines appropriate).

``(2) Timing.--A <<NOTE: Deadline.>> consumer reporting agency shall provide a consumer report under paragraph (1) not later than 15 days after the date on which the request is received under paragraph (1).

``(3) Reinvestigations.--Notwithstanding <<NOTE: Deadline.>> the time periods specified in section 611(a)(1), a reinvestigation under that section by a consumer reporting agency upon a request of a consumer that is made after receiving a consumer report under this subsection shall be completed not later than 45 days after the date on which the request is received.

``(4) Exception for first 12 months of operation.--This subsection shall not apply to a consumer reporting agency that has not been furnishing consumer reports to third parties on a continuing basis during the 12-month period preceding a request under paragraph (1), with respect to consumers residing nationwide.''; (3) by re-designating subsection (d) as subsection (e); (4) by inserting before subsection (e), as re-designated, the following:

``(d) Free Disclosures in Connection With Fraud Alerts.--Upon the request of a consumer, a consumer reporting agency described in section 603(p) shall make all disclosures pursuant to section 609 without charge to the consumer, as provided in subsections (a)(2) and (b)(2) of section 605A, as applicable.'';

(5) in subsection (e), as re-designated, by striking ``subsection (a)'' and inserting ``subsection (f)''; and (6) in subsection (f), as re-designated, by striking ``Except as provided in subsections (b), (c), and (d), a'' and inserting ``In the case of a request from a consumer other than a request that is covered by any of subsections (a) through (d), a''. (b) Circumvention Prohibited.--The Fair Credit Reporting Act (15 U.S.C. 1681 et seq.) is amended by adding after section 628, as added by section 216 of this Act, the following new section:

``Sec. 629. <<NOTE: 15 USC 1681x.>> Corporate and technological circumvention prohibited

``The <<NOTE: Regulations. Effective date.>> Commission shall prescribe regulations, to become effective not later than 90 days after the date of enactment of this section, to prevent a consumer reporting agency from circumventing or evading treatment as a consumer reporting agency described in section 603(p) for purposes of this title, including--

``(1) by means of a corporate reorganization or restructuring, including a merger, acquisition, dissolution, divestiture, or asset sale of a consumer reporting agency; or

``(2) by maintaining or merging public record and credit account information in a manner that is substantially equivalent to that described in paragraphs (1) and (2) of section 603(p), in the manner described in section 603(p).''.

(c) Summary of Rights To Obtain and Dispute Information in Consumer Reports and To Obtain Credit Scores.--Section 609(c) of the Fair Credit Reporting Act (15 U.S.C. 1681g) is amended to read as follows:

``(c) Summary of Rights To Obtain and Dispute Information in Consumer Reports and To Obtain Credit Scores.--

``(1) Commission summary of rights required.--

``(A) In general.--The Commission shall prepare a model summary of the rights of consumers under this title.``(B) Content of summary.--The summary of rights prepared under subparagraph (A) shall include a description of--``(i) the right of a consumer to obtain a copy of a consumer report under subsection (a) from each consumer reporting agency;``(ii) the frequency and circumstances under which a consumer is entitled to receive a consumer report without charge under section 612;``(iii) the right of a consumer to dispute information in the file of the consumer under section 611;``(iv) the right of a consumer to obtain a credit score from a consumer reporting agency, and a description of how to obtain a credit score;``(v) the method by which a consumer can contact, and obtain a consumer report from, a consumer reporting agency without charge, as provided in the regulations of the Commission prescribed under section 211(c) of the Fair and Accurate Credit Transactions Act of 2003; and``(vi) the method by which a consumer can contact, and obtain a consumer report from, a consumer reporting agency described in section 603(w), as provided in the regulations of the Commission prescribed under section 612(a)(1)(C).``(C) Availability <<NOTE: Public information.>> of summary of rights.--The Commission shall--``(i) actively publicize the availability of the summary of rights prepared under this paragraph;``(ii) conspicuously post on its Internet website the availability of such summary of rights; and``(iii) promptly make such summary of rights available to consumers, on request.

``(2) Summary of rights required to be included with agency disclosures.--A consumer reporting agency shall provide to a consumer, with each written disclosure by the agency to the consumer under this section--

``(A) the summary of rights prepared by the Commission under paragraph (1);

``(B) in the case of a consumer reporting agency described in section 603(p), a toll-free telephone number established by the agency, at which personnel are accessible to consumers during normal business hours;

``(C) a list of all Federal agencies responsible for enforcing any provision of this title, and the address and any appropriate phone number of each such agency, in a form that will assist the consumer in selecting the appropriate agency;

``(D) a statement that the consumer may have additional rights under State law, and that the consumer may wish to contact a State or local consumer protection agency or a State attorney general (or the equivalent thereof) to learn of those rights; and

``(E) a statement that a consumer reporting agency is not required to remove accurate derogatory information from the file of a consumer, unless the information is outdated under section 605 or cannot be verified.''.

(d) Rulemaking <<NOTE: 15 USC 1681j note.>> Required.--

(1) In general.--The Commission shall prescribe regulations applicable to consumer reporting agencies described in section 603(p) of the Fair Credit Reporting Act, to require the establishment of-- (A) a centralized source through which consumers may obtain a consumer report from each such consumer reporting agency, using a single request, and without charge to the consumer, as provided in section 612(a) of the Fair Credit Reporting Act (as amended by this section); and(B) a standardized form for a consumer to make such a request for a consumer report by mail or through an internet website.

(2) Considerations.--In prescribing regulations under paragraph (1), the Commission shall consider--(A) the significant demands that may be placed on consumer reporting agencies in providing such consumer reports; (B) appropriate means to ensure that consumer reporting agencies can satisfactorily meet those demands, including the efficacy of a system of staggering the availability to consumers of such consumer reports; and(C) the ease by which consumers should be able to contact consumer reporting agencies with respect to access to such consumer reports.

(3) Centralized source.--The centralized source for a request for a consumer report from a consumer required by this subsection shall provide for--(A) a toll-free telephone number for such purpose;(B) use of an Internet website for such purpose; and(C) a process for requests by mail for such purpose.

(4) Transition.--The regulations of the Commission under paragraph (1) shall provide for an orderly transition by consumer reporting agencies described in section 603(p) of the Fair Credit Reporting Act to the centralized source for consumer report distribution required by section 612(a)(1)(B), as amended by this section, in a manner that-- (A) does not temporarily overwhelm such consumer reporting agencies with requests for disclosures of consumer reports beyond their capacity to deliver; and (B) does not deny creditors, other users, and consumers access to consumer reports on a time-sensitive basis for specific purposes, such as home purchases or suspicions of identity theft, during the transition period.

(5) Timing.--Regulations required by this subsection shall-- (A) <<NOTE: Deadline.>> be issued in final form not later than 6 months after the date of enactment of this Act; and (B) <<NOTE: Effective date.>> become effective not later than 6 months after the date on which they are issued in final form.

(6) Scope of regulations.--(A) In general.--The Commission shall, by rule, determine whether to require a consumer reporting agency that compiles and maintains files on consumers on substantially a nationwide basis, other than one described in section603(p) of the Fair Credit Reporting Act, to make free consumer reports available upon consumer request, and if so, whether such consumer reporting agencies should make such free reports available through the centralized source described in paragraph (1)(A). (B) Considerations.--Before making any determination under subparagraph (A), the Commission shall consider--(i) the number of requests for consumer reports to, and the number of consumer reports generated by, the consumer reporting agency, in comparison with consumer reporting agencies described in subsections (p) and (w) of section 603 of the Fair Credit Reporting Act;(ii) the overall scope of the operations of the consumer reporting agency; (iii) the needs of consumers for access to consumer reports provided by consumer reporting agencies free of charge; (iv) the costs of providing access to consumer reports by consumer reporting agencies free of charge; and(v) the effects on the ongoing competitive viability of such consumer reporting agencies if such free access is required.

SEC. 212. DISCLOSURE OF CREDIT SCORES.

(a) Statement on Availability of Credit Scores.--Section 609(a) of the Fair Credit Reporting Act (15 U.S.C. 1681g a)) is amended by adding at the end the following new paragraph:
``(6) If the consumer requests the credit file and not the credit score, a statement that the consumer may request and obtain a credit score.''.

(b) Disclosure of Credit Scores.--Section 609 of the Fair Credit Reporting Act (15 U.S.C. 1681g), as amended by this Act, is amended by adding at the end the following:
``(f) Disclosure of Credit Scores.--
``

``(1) In general.--Upon the request of a consumer for a credit score, a consumer reporting agency shall supply to the consumer a statement indicating that the information and credit scoring model may be different than the credit score that may be used by the lender, and a notice which shall include--
``(A) the current credit score of the consumer or the most recent credit score of the consumer that was previously calculated by the credit reporting agency for a purpose related to the extension of credit; ``(B) the range of possible credit scores under the model used; ``(C) all of the key factors that adversely affected the credit score of the consumer in the model used, the total number of which shall not exceed 4, subject to paragraph (9); ``(D) the date on which the credit score was created; and ``(E) the name of the person or entity that provided the credit score or credit file upon which the credit score was created.

``(2) Definitions.--For purposes of this subsection, the following definitions shall apply:
``(A) Credit score.--The term `credit score'--
``(i) means a numerical value or a categorization derived from a statistical tool or modeling system used by a person who makes or arranges a loan to predict the likelihood of certain credit behaviors, including default (and the numerical value or the categorization derived from such analysis may also be referred to as a `risk predictor' or `risk score'); and ``(ii) does not include--``(I) any mortgage score or rating of an automated underwriting system that considers one or more factors in addition to credit information, including the loan to value ratio, the amount of down payment, or the financial assets of a consumer; or
``(II) any other elements of the underwriting process or underwriting decision.
``(B) Key factors.--The term `key factors' means all relevant elements or reasons adversely affecting the credit score for the particular individual, listed in the order of their importance based on their effect on credit score.

``(3) Timeframe and manner of disclosure.--The information required by this subsection shall be provided in the same timeframe and manner as the information described in subsection (a).

``(4) Applicability to certain uses.--This subsection shall not be construed so as to compel a consumer reporting agency to develop or disclose a score if the agency does not--
``(A) distribute scores that are used in connection with residential real property loans; or
``(B) develop scores that assist credit providers in understanding the general credit behavior of a consumer and predicting the future credit behavior of the consumer.

``(5) Applicability to credit scores developed by another person.--
``(A) In general.--This subsection shall not be construed to require a consumer reporting agency that distributes credit scores developed by another person or entity to provide a further explanation of them, or to except that the consumer reporting agency shall provide the consumer with the name and address and website for contacting the person or entity who developed the score or developed the methodology of the score.
``(B) Exception.--This paragraph shall not apply to a consumer reporting agency that develops or modifies scores that are developed by another person or entity.

``(6) Maintenance of credit scores not required.--This subsection shall not be construed to require a consumer

``(7) Compliance in certain cases.--In complying with this subsection, a consumer reporting agency shall--
``(A) supply the consumer with a credit score that is derived from a credit scoring model that is widely distributed to users by that consumer reporting agency in connection with residential real property loans or with a credit score that assists the consumer in understanding the credit scoring assessment of the credit behavior of the consumer and predictions about the future credit behavior of the consumer; and
``(B) a statement indicating that the information and credit scoring model may be different than that used by the lender.

``(8) Fair and reasonable fee.--A consumer reporting agency may charge a fair and reasonable fee, as determined by the Commission, for providing the information required under this subsection.

``(9) Use of enquiries as a key factor.--If a key factor that adversely affects the credit score of a consumer consists of the number of enquiries made with respect to a consumer report, that factor shall be included in the disclosure pursuant to paragraph (1)(C) without regard to the numerical limitation in such paragraph.''.

(c) Disclosure of Credit Scores by Certain Mortgage Lenders.--Section 609 of the Fair Credit Reporting Act (15 U.S.C. 1681g), as amended by this Act, is amended by adding at the end the following:``(g) Disclosure of Credit Scores by Certain Mortgage Lenders.--``(1) In general.--Any person who makes or arranges loans and who uses a consumer credit score, as defined in subsection (f), in connection with an application initiated or sought by a consumer for a closed end loan or the establishment of an open end loan for a consumer purpose that is secured by 1 to 4 units of residential real property (hereafter in this subsection referred to as the `lender') shall provide the following to the consumer as soon as reasonably practicable:`

`(A) Information required under subsection (f).--``(i) In general.--A copy of the information identified in subsection (f) that was obtained from a consumer reporting agency or was developed and used by the user of the information.``(ii) Notice under subparagraph (d).--In addition to the information provided to it by a third party that provided the credit score or scores, a lender is only required to provide the notice contained in subparagraph (D).``

(B) Disclosures in case of automated underwriting system.--``(i) In general.--If a person that is subject to this subsection uses an automated underwriting system to underwrite a loan, that person may satisfy the obligation to provide a credit score by disclosing a credit score and associated key factors supplied by a consumer reporting agency.``(ii) Numerical credit score.--However, if a numerical credit score is generated by an automated underwriting system used by an enterprise, and that score is disclosed to the person, the score shall be disclosed to the consumer consistent with subparagraph (C).``(iii) Enterprise defined.--For purposes of this subparagraph, the term `enterprise' has the same meaning as in paragraph (6) of section 1303 of the Federal Housing Enterprises Financial Safety and Soundness Act of 1992.

``(C) Disclosures of credit scores not obtained from a consumer reporting agency.--A person that is subject to the provisions of this subsection and that uses a credit score, other than a credit score provided by a consumer reporting agency, may satisfy the obligation to provide a credit score by disclosing a credit score and associated key factors supplied by a consumer reporting agency.

``(D) Notice to home loan applicants.--A copy of the following notice, which shall include the name, address, and telephone number of each consumer reporting agency providing a credit score that was used `notice to the home loan applicant.` In connection with your application for a home loan, the lender must disclose to you the score that a consumer reporting agency distributed to users and the lender used in connection with your home loan, and the key factors affecting your credit scores.`
The credit score is a computer generated summary calculated at the time of the request and based on information that a consumer reporting agency or lender has on file. The scores are based on data about your credit history and payment patterns. Credit scores are important because they are used to assist the lender in determining whether you will obtain a loan. They may also be used to determine what interest rate you may be offered on the mortgage. Credit scores can change over time, depending on your conduct, how your credit history and payment patterns change, and how credit scoring technologies change.
`Because the score is based on information in your credit history, it is very important that you review the credit-related information that is being furnished to make sure it is accurate. Credit records may vary from one company to another.
`If you have questions about your credit score or the credit information that is furnished to you, contact the consumer reporting agency at the address and telephone number provided with this notice, or contact the lender, if the lender developed or generated the credit score. The consumer reporting agency plays no part in the decision to take any action on the loan application and is unable to provide you with specific reasons for the decision on a loan application.
`If you have questions concerning the terms of the loan, contact the lender.'.

``(E) Actions not required under this subsection.--This subsection shall not require any person to--``(i) explain the information provided pursuant to subsection (f);``(ii) disclose any information other than a credit score or key factors, as defined in subsection (f);``(iii) disclose any credit score or related information obtained by the user after a loan has closed;``(iv) provide more than 1 disclosure per loan transaction; or``(v) provide the disclosure required by this subsection when another person has made the disclosure to the consumer for that loan transaction.

``(F) No obligation for content.--``(i) In general.--The obligation of any person pursuant to this subsection shall be limited solely to providing a copy of the information that was received from the consumer reporting agency.``(ii) Limit on liability.--No person has liability under this subsection for the content of that information or for the omission of any information within the report provided by the consumer reporting agency.

``(G) Person defined as excluding enterprise.--As used in this subsection, the term `person' does not include an enterprise (as defined in paragraph (6) of section 1303 of the Federal Housing Enterprises Financial Safety and Soundness Act of 1992).

``(2) Prohibition on disclosure clauses null and void.--

``(A) In general.--Any provision in a contract that prohibits the disclosure of a credit score by a person who makes or arranges loans or a consumer reporting agency is void.

``(B) No liability for disclosure under this subsection.--A lender shall not have liability under any contractual provision for disclosure of a credit score pursuant to this subsection.''.(d) Inclusion of Key Factor in Credit Score Information in Consumer Report.--Section 605(d) of the Fair Credit Reporting Act (15 U.S.C. 1681c(d)) is amended-- (1) by striking ``Disclosed.--Any consumer reporting agency'' and inserting ``Disclosed.--``(1) Title 11 information.--Any consumer reporting agency''; and (2) by adding at the end the following new paragraph:``(2) Key factor in credit score information.--Any consumer reporting agency that furnishes a consumer report that contains any credit score or any other risk score or predictor on any consumer shall include in the report a clear and conspicuous statement that a key factor (as defined in section 609(f)(2)(B)) that adversely affected such score or predictor was the number of enquiries, if such a predictor was in fact a key factor that adversely affected such score. This paragraph shall not apply to a check services company, acting as such, which issues authorizations for the purpose of approving or processing negotiable instruments, electronic fund transfers, or similar methods of payments, but only to the extent that such company is engaged in such activities.''.(e) Technical and Conforming Amendments.--Section 625(b) of the Fair Credit Reporting Act (15 U.S.C. 1681t(b)), as so designated by section 214 of this Act, is amended--(1) by striking ``or'' at the end of paragraph (2); and (2) by striking paragraph (3) and inserting the following:

``(3) with respect to the disclosures required to be made under subsection (c), (d), (e), or (g) of section 609, or subsection (f) of section 609 relating to the disclosure of credit scores for credit granting purposes, except that this paragraph--

``(A) shall not apply with respect to sections 1785.10, 1785.16, and 1785.20.2 of the California Civil Code (as in effect on the date of enactment of the Fair and Accurate Credit Transactions Act of 2003) and section 1785.15 through section 1785.15.2 of such Code (as in effect on such date);

``(B) shall not apply with respect to sections 5-3-106(2) and 212-14.3-104.3 of the Colorado Revised Statutes (as in effect on the date of enactment of the Fair and Accurate Credit Transactions Act of 2003); and

``(C) shall not be construed as limiting, annulling, affecting, or superseding any provision of the laws of any State regulating the use in an insurance activity, or regulating disclosures concerning such use, of a credit-based insurance score of a consumer by any person engaged in the business of insurance;

``(4) with respect to the frequency of any disclosure under section 612(a), except that this paragraph shall not apply--

``(A) with respect to section 12-14.3-105(1)(d) of the Colorado Revised Statutes (as in effect on the date of enactment of the Fair and Accurate Credit Transactions Act of 2003);

``(B) with respect to section 10-1-393(29)(C) of the Georgia Code (as in effect on the date of enactment of the Fair and Accurate Credit Transactions Act of 2003);

``(C) with respect to section 1316.2 of title 10 of the Maine Revised Statutes (as in effect on the date of enactment of the Fair and Accurate Credit Transactions Act of 2003);

``(D) with respect to sections 14-1209(a)(1) and 14-1209(b)(1)(i) of the Commercial Law Article of the Code of Maryland (as in effect on the date of enactment of the Fair and Accurate Credit Transactions Act of 2003);

``(E) with respect to section 59(d) and section 59(e) of chapter 93 of the General Laws of Massachusetts (as in effect on the date of enactment of the Fair and Accurate Credit Transactions Act of 2003);

``(F) with respect to section 56:11-37.10(a)(1) of the New Jersey Revised Statutes (as in effect on the date of enactment of the Fair and Accurate Credit Transactions Act of 2003); or

``(G) with respect to section 2480c(a)(1) of title 9 of the Vermont Statutes Annotated (as in effect on the date of enactment of the Fair and Accurate Credit Transactions Act of 2003); or''.

SEC. 213. ENHANCED DISCLOSURE OF THE MEANS AVAILABLE TO OPT OUT OF PRESCREENED LISTS.

(a) Notice and Response Format for Users of Reports.--Section 615(d)(2) of the Fair Credit Reporting Act (15 U.S.C. 1681m(d)(2)) is amended to read as follows:

``(2) Disclosure of address and telephone number; format.--A statement under paragraph (1) shall--

``(A) include the address and toll-free telephone number of the appropriate notification system established under section 604(e); and

``(B) be presented in such format and in such type size and manner as to be simple and easy to understand, as established by the Commission, by rule, in consultation with the Federal banking agencies and the National Credit Union Administration.''.

(b) Rulemaking <<NOTE: Deadline. 15 USC 1681m note.>> Schedule.--Regulations required by section 615(d)(2) of the Fair Credit Reporting Act, as amended by this section, shall be issued in final form not later than 1 year after the date of enactment of this Act.

(c) Duration of Elections.--Section 604(e) of the Fair Credit Reporting Act (15 U.S.C. 1681b(e)) is amended in each of paragraphs (3)(A) and (4)(B)(i)), by striking ``2-year period'' each place that term appears and inserting ``5-year period''.

(d) Public <<NOTE: Internet. 15 USC 1681b note.>> Awareness Campaign.--The Commission shall actively publicize and conspicuously post on its website any address and the toll-free telephone number established as part of a notification system for opting out of prescreening under section 604(e) of the Fair Credit Reporting Act (15 U.S.C. 1681b(e)), and otherwise take measures to increase public awareness regarding the availability of the right to opt out of prescreening.

(e) Analysis <<NOTE: 15 USC 1601 note.>> of Further Restrictions on Offers of Credit or Insurance.--

(1) In general.--The Board shall conduct a study of--

(A) the ability of consumers to avoid receiving written offers of credit or insurance in connection with transactions not initiated by the consumer; and

(B) the potential impact that any further restrictions on providing consumers with such written offers of credit or insurance would have on consumers.

(2) Report.--The <<NOTE: Deadline.>> Board shall submit a report summarizing the results of the study required under paragraph (1) to the Congress not later than 12 months after the date of enactment of this Act, together with such recommendations for legislative or administrative action as the Board may determine to be appropriate.

(3) Content of report.--The report described in paragraph

(2) shall address the following issues:

(A) The current statutory or voluntary mechanisms that are available to a consumer to notify lenders and insurance providers that the consumer does not wish to receive written offers of credit or insurance.

(B) The extent to which consumers are currently utilizing existing statutory and voluntary mechanisms to avoid receiving offers of credit or insurance.

(C) The benefits provided to consumers as a result of receiving written offers of credit or insurance.

(D) Whether consumers incur significant costs or are otherwise adversely affected by the receipt of written offers of credit or insurance.

(E) Whether further restricting the ability of lenders and insurers to provide written offers of credit or insurance to consumers would affect--

(i) the cost consumers pay to obtain credit or insurance;

(ii) the availability of credit or insurance;

(iii) consumers' knowledge about new or alternative products and services;

(iv) the ability of lenders or insurers to compete with one another; and

(v) the ability to offer credit or insurance products to consumers who have been traditionally underserved.

SEC. 214. AFFILIATE SHARING.

(a) Limitation.--The Fair Credit Reporting Act (15 U.S.C. 1601 et seq.) is amended--

(1) by re-designating sections 624 (15 U.S.C. 1681t), 625 (15 U.S.C. 1681u), and 626 (15 U.S.C. 6181v) as sections 625, 626, and 627, respectively; and

(2) by inserting after section 623 the following:

``Sec. 624. <<NOTE: 15 USC 1681s-3.>> Affiliate sharing

``(a) Special Rule for Solicitation for Purposes of Marketing.--

``(1) Notice.--Any person that receives from another person related to it by common ownership or affiliated by corporate control a communication of information that would be a consumer report, but for clauses (i), (ii), and (iii) of section 603(d)(2)(A), may not use the information to make a solicitation for marketing purposes to a consumer about its products or services, unless--

''(A) it is clearly and conspicuously disclosed to the consumer that the information may be communicated among such persons for purposes of making such solicitations to the consumer; and

''(B) the consumer is provided an opportunity and a simple method to prohibit the making of such solicitations to the consumer by such person.

''(2) Consumer choice.--

''(A) In general.--The notice required under paragraph (1) shall allow the consumer the opportunity to prohibit all solicitations referred to in such paragraph, and may allow the consumer to choose from different options when electing to prohibit the sending of such solicitations, including options regarding the types of entities and information covered, and which methods of delivering solicitations the consumer elects to prohibit.

''(B) Format.--Notwithstanding subparagraph (A), the notice required under paragraph (1) shall be clear, conspicuous, and concise, and any method provided under paragraph (1)(B) shall be simple. The regulations prescribed to implement this section shall provide specific guidance regarding how to comply with such standards.

''(3) Duration.--

''(A) In general.--The election of a consumer pursuant to paragraph (1)(B) to prohibit the making of solicitations shall be effective for at least 5 years, beginning on the date on which the person receives the election of the consumer, unless the consumer requests that such election be revoked.

''(B) Notice upon expiration of effective period.--At such time as the election of a consumer pursuant to paragraph (1)(B) is no longer effective, a person may not use information that the person receives in the manner described in paragraph (1) to make any solicitation for marketing purposes to the consumer, unless the consumer receives a notice and an opportunity, using a simple method, to extend the opt-out for another period of at least 5 years, pursuant to the procedures described in paragraph (1).

''(4) Scope.--This section shall not apply to a person--

''(A) using information to make a solicitation for marketing purposes to a consumer with whom the person has a pre-existing business relationship;

''(B) using information to facilitate communications to an individual for whose benefit the person provides employee benefit or other services pursuant to a contract with an employer related to and arising out of the current employment relationship or status of the individual as a participant or beneficiary of an employee benefit plan;

''(C) using information to perform services on behalf of another person related by common ownership or affiliated by corporate control, except that this subparagraph shall not be construed as permitting a person to send solicitations on behalf of another person, if such other person would not be permitted to send the solicitation on its own behalf as a result of the election of the consumer to prohibit solicitations under paragraph (1)(B);

''(D) using information in response to a communication initiated by the consumer;

''(E) using information in response to solicitations authorized or requested by the consumer; or

''(F) if compliance with this section by that person would prevent compliance by that person with any provision of State insurance laws pertaining to unfair discrimination in any State in which the person is lawfully doing business.

''(5) No retroactivity.--This subsection shall not prohibit the use of information to send a solicitation to a consumer if such information was received prior to the date on which persons are required to comply with regulations implementing this subsection.

''(b) Notice for Other Purposes Permissible.--A notice or other disclosure under this section may be coordinated and consolidated with any other notice required to be issued under any other provision of law by a person that is subject to this section, and a notice or other disclosure that is equivalent to the notice required by subsection (a), and that is provided by a person described in subsection (a) to a consumer together with disclosures required by any other provision of law, shall satisfy the requirements of subsection (a).

''(c) User Requirements.--Requirements with respect to the use by a person of information received from another person related to it by common ownership or affiliated by corporate control, such as the requirements of this section, constitute requirements with respect to the exchange of information among persons affiliated by common ownership or common corporate control, within the meaning of section 625(b)(2).

''(d) Definitions.--For purposes of this section, the following definitions shall apply:

''(1) Pre-existing business relationship.--The term 'pre-existing business relationship' means a relationship between a person, or a person's licensed agent, and a consumer, based on--

''(A) a financial contract between a person and a consumer which is in force;

''(B) the purchase, rental, or lease by the consumer of that person's goods or services, or a financial transaction (including holding an active account or a policy in force or having another continuing relationship) between the consumer and that person during the 18-month period immediately preceding the date on which the consumer is sent a solicitation covered by this section;

``(C) an inquiry or application by the consumer regarding a product or service offered by that person, during the 3-month period immediately preceding the date on which the consumer is sent a solicitation covered by this section; or

``(D) any other pre-existing customer relationship defined in the regulations implementing this section.

``(2) Solicitation.--The term `solicitation' means the marketing of a product or service initiated by a person to a particular consumer that is based on an exchange of information described in subsection (a), and is intended to encourage the consumer to purchase such product or service, but does not include communications that are directed at the general public or determined not to be a solicitation by the regulations prescribed under this section.".

(b) Rulemaking <<NOTE: 15 USC 1681s-3 note.>> Required.--

(1) In general.--The Federal banking agencies, the National Credit Union Administration, and the Commission, with respect to the entities that are subject to their respective enforcement authority under section 621 of the Fair Credit Reporting Act and the Securities and Exchange Commission, and in coordination as described in paragraph (2), shall prescribe regulations to implement section 624 of the Fair Credit Reporting Act, as added by this section.

(2) Coordination.--Each agency required to prescribe regulations under paragraph (1) shall consult and coordinate with each other such agency so that, to the extent possible, the regulations prescribed by each such entity are consistent and comparable with the regulations prescribed by each other such agency.

(3) Considerations.--In promulgating regulations under this subsection, each agency referred to in paragraph (1) shall--

(A) ensure that affiliate sharing notification methods provide a simple means for consumers to make determinations and choices under section 624 of the Fair Credit Reporting Act, as added by this section;

(B) consider the affiliate sharing notification practices employed on the date of enactment of this Act by persons that will be subject to that section 624; and

(C) ensure that notices and disclosures may be coordinated and consolidated, as provided in subsection

(b) of that section 624.

(4) Timing.--Regulations required by this subsection shall--

(A) <<NOTE: Deadline.>> be issued in final form not later than 9 months after the date of enactment of this Act; and

(B) <<NOTE: Effective date.>> become effective not later than 6 months after the date on which they are issued in final form.

(c) Technical and Conforming Amendments.--

(1) Definitions.--Section 603(d)(2)(A) of the Fair Credit Reporting Act (15 U.S.C. 1681(d)(2)(A))<<NOTE: 15 USC 1681a.>> is amended by inserting ``subject to section 624,'' after ``(A)''.

(2) Relation to state laws.--Section 625(b)(1) of the Fair Credit Reporting Act (15 U.S.C. 1681t(b)(1)), as so designated by subsection (a) of this section, is amended--

(A) by striking ``or'' after the semicolon at the end of subparagraph (E); and

(B) by adding at the end the following new subparagraph:

``(H) section 624, relating to the exchange and use of information to make a solicitation for marketing purposes; or''.

(3) Cross reference correction.--Section 627(d) of the Fair Credit Reporting Act (15 U.S.C. 1681v(d)), as so designated by subsection (a) of this section, is amended by striking ``section 625'' and inserting ``section 626''.

(4) Table of sections.--The table of sections for title VI of the Consumer Credit Protection Act (15 U.S.C. 1601 et seq.) is amended by striking the items relating to sections 624 through 626 and inserting the following:

``624. Affiliate sharing.
``625. Relation to State laws.
``626. Disclosures to FBI for counterintelligence purposes.
``627. Disclosures to governmental agencies for counterintelligence purposes.''.

(e) Studies <<NOTE: 15 USC 1681s-3 note.>> of Information Sharing Practices.--

(1) In general.--The Federal banking agencies, the National Credit Union Administration, and the Commission shall jointly conduct regular studies of the consumer information sharing practices by financial institutions and other persons that are creditors or users of consumer reports with their affiliates.

(2) Matters for study.--In conducting the studies required by paragraph (1), the agencies described in paragraph (1) shall--

(A) identify--

(i) the purposes for which financial institutions and other creditors and users of consumer reports share consumer information;

(ii) the types of information shared by such entities with their affiliates;

(iii) the number of choices provided to consumers with respect to the control of such sharing, and the degree to and manner in which consumers exercise such choices, if at all; and

(iv) whether such entities share or may share personally identifiable transaction or experience information with affiliates for purposes--

(I) that are related to employment or hiring, including whether the person that is the subject of such information is given notice of such sharing, and the specific uses of such shared information; or

(II) of general publication of such information; and

(B) specifically examine the information sharing practices that financial institutions and other creditors and users of consumer reports and their   affiliates employ for the purpose of making underwriting decisions or credit evaluations of consumers.

(3) Reports.--

(A) Initial report.--Not <<NOTE: Deadlines.>> later than 3 years after the date of enactment of this Act, the Federal banking agencies, the National Credit Union Administration, and the Commission shall jointly submit a report to the Congress on the results of the initial study conducted in accordance with this subsection, together with any recommendations for legislative or regulatory action.

(B) Follow-up reports.--The Federal banking agencies, the National Credit Union Administration, and the Commission shall, not less frequently than once every 3 years following the date of submission of the initial report under subparagraph (A), jointly submit a report to the Congress that, together with any recommendations for legislative or regulatory action--

(i) documents any changes in the areas of study referred to in paragraph (2)(A) occurring since the date of submission of the previous report;

(ii) identifies any changes in the practices of financial institutions and other creditors and users of consumer reports in sharing consumer information with their affiliates for the purpose of making underwriting decisions or credit evaluations of consumers occurring since the date of submission of the previous report; and

(iii) examines the effects that changes described in clause (ii) have had, if any, on the degree to which such affiliate sharing practices reduce the need for financial institutions, creditors, and other users of consumer reports to rely on consumer reports for such decisions.

SEC. 215. <<NOTE: 15 USC 1681 note.>> STUDY OF EFFECTS OF CREDIT SCORES AND CREDIT-BASED INSURANCE SCORES ON AVAILABILITY AND AFFORDABILITY OF FINANCIAL PRODUCTS.

(a) Study Required.--The Commission and the Board, in consultation with the Office of Fair Housing and Equal Opportunity of the Department of Housing and Urban Development, shall conduct a study of--

(1) the effects of the use of credit scores and credit-based insurance scores on the availability and affordability of financial products and services, including credit cards, mortgages, auto loans, and property and casualty insurance;

(2) the statistical relationship, utilizing a multivariate analysis that controls for prohibited factors under the Equal Credit Opportunity Act and other known risk factors, between credit scores and credit-based insurance scores and the quantifiable risks and actual losses experienced by businesses;

(3) the extent to which, if any, the use of credit scoring models, credit scores, and credit-based insurance scores impact on the availability and affordability of credit and insurance to the extent information is currently available or is available through proxies, by geography, income, ethnicity, race, color, religion, national origin, age, sex, marital status, and creed, including the extent to which the consideration or lack of consideration of certain factors by credit scoring systems could result in negative or differential treatment of protected classes under the Equal Credit Opportunity Act, and the extent to which, if any, the use of underwriting systems relying on these models could achieve comparable results through the use of factors with less negative impact; and

(4) the extent to which credit scoring systems are used by businesses, the factors considered by such systems, and the effects of variables which are not considered by such systems.

(b) Public Participation.--The Commission shall seek public input about the prescribed methodology and research design of the study described in subsection (a), including from relevant Federal regulators, State insurance regulators, community, civil rights, consumer, and housing groups.

(c) Report Required.--

(1) In general.--Before <<NOTE: Deadline.>> the end of the 24-month period beginning on the date of enactment of this Act, the Commission shall submit a detailed report on the study conducted pursuant to subsection (a) to the Committee on Financial Services of the House of Representatives and the Committee on Banking, Housing, and Urban Affairs of the Senate.

(2) Contents of report.--The report submitted under paragraph (1) shall include the findings and conclusions of the Commission, recommendations to address specific areas of concerns addressed in the study, and recommendations for legislative or administrative action that the Commission may determine to be necessary to ensure that credit and credit-based insurance scores are used appropriately and fairly to avoid negative effects.

SEC. 216. DISPOSAL OF CONSUMER REPORT INFORMATION AND RECORDS.

(a) In General.--The Fair Credit Reporting Act (15 U.S.C. 1681 et seq.), as amended by this Act, is amended by adding at the end the following:

``Sec. 628. <<NOTE: 15 USC 1681w.>> Disposal of records

``(a) Regulations.--

``(1) In general.--Not <<NOTE: Deadline.>> later than 1 year after the date of enactment of this section, the Federal banking agencies, the National Credit Union Administration, and the Commission with respect to the entities that are subject to their respective enforcement authority under section 621, and the Securities and Exchange Commission, and in coordination as described in paragraph (2), shall issue final regulations requiring any person that maintains or otherwise possesses consumer information, or any compilation of consumer information, derived from consumer reports for a business purpose to properly dispose of any such information or compilation.

``(2) Coordination.--Each agency required to prescribe regulations under paragraph (1) shall--

``(A) consult and coordinate with each other such agency so that, to the extent possible, the regulations prescribed by each such agency are consistent and comparable with the regulations by each such other agency; and

``(B) ensure that such regulations are consistent with the requirements and regulations issued pursuant to Public Law 106-102 and other provisions of Federal law.

``(3) Exemption authority.--In issuing regulations under this section, the Federal banking agencies, the National Credit Union Administration, the Commission, and the Securities and Exchange Commission may exempt any person or class of persons from application of those regulations, as such agency deems appropriate to carry out the purpose of this section.

``(b) Rule of Construction.--Nothing in this section shall be construed--

``(1) to require a person to maintain or destroy any record   pertaining to a consumer that is not imposed under other law; or

``(2) to alter or affect any requirement imposed under any other provision of law to maintain or destroy such a record.''.

(b) Clerical Amendment.--The table of sections for title VI of the Consumer Credit Protection Act (15 U.S.C. 1601 et seq.) is amended by inserting after the item relating to section 627, as added by section 14 of this Act, the following:

``628. Disposal of records.
``629. Corporate and technological circumvention prohibited.''.

SEC. 217. REQUIREMENT TO DISCLOSE COMMUNICATIONS TO A CONSUMER REPORTING AGENCY.

(a) In General.--Section 623(a) of the Fair Credit Reporting Act (15 U.S.C. 1681s-2(a)) as amended by this Act, is amended by inserting after paragraph (6), the following new paragraph:

``(7) Negative information.--

``(A) Notice to consumer required.--

``(i) In general.--If any financial institution that extends credit and regularly and in the ordinary course of business furnishes information to a consumer reporting agency described in section 603(p) furnishes negative   information to such an agency regarding credit extended to a customer, the financial institution shall provide a notice of such furnishing of negative information, in writing, to the customer.

``(ii) Notice effective for subsequent submissions.--After providing such notice, the financial institution may submit additional negative information to a consumer reporting agency described in section 603(p) with respect to the same transaction, extension of credit, account, or customer without providing additional notice to the customer.

``(B) Time of notice.--

``(i) In <<NOTE: Deadline.>> general.--The notice required under subparagraph (A) shall be provided to the customer prior to, or no later than 30 days after, furnishing the negative information to a consumer reporting agency described in section 603(p).

``(ii) Coordination with new account disclosures.--If the notice is provided to the customer prior to furnishing the negative information to a consumer reporting agency, the notice may not be included in the initial disclosures provided under section 127(a) of the Truth in Lending Act.

``(C) Coordination with other disclosures.--The notice required under subparagraph (A)--

``(i) may be included on or with any notice of default, any billing statement, or any other materials provided to the customer; and

``(ii) must be clear and conspicuous.

``(D) Model disclosure.--

``(i) Duty of board to prepare.--The Board shall prescribe a brief model disclosure a financial institution may use to comply with subparagraph (A), which shall not exceed 30 words.

``(ii) Use of model not required.--No provision of this paragraph shall be construed as requiring a financial institution to use any such model form prescribed by the Board.

``(iii) Compliance using model.--A financial institution shall be deemed to be in compliance with subparagraph (A) if the financial institution uses any such model form prescribed by the Board, or the financial institution uses any such model form and rearranges its format.

``(E) Use of notice without submitting negative information.--No provision of this paragraph shall be construed as requiring a financial institution that has provided a customer with a notice described in subparagraph (A) to furnish negative information about the customer to a consumer reporting agency.

``(F) Safe harbor.--A financial institution shall not be liable for failure to perform the duties required by this paragraph if, at the time of the failure, the financial institution maintained reasonable policies and procedures to comply with this paragraph or the financial institution reasonably believed that the institution is prohibited, by law, from contacting the consumer.

``(G) Definitions.--For purposes of this paragraph, the following definitions shall apply:

``(i) Negative information.--The term `negative information' means information concerning a customer's delinquencies, late payments, insolvency, or any form of default.

``(ii) Customer; financial institution.--The terms `customer' and `financial institution' have the same meanings as in section 509 Public Law 106-102.''.

(b) Model Disclosure Form.--Before <<NOTE: Deadline. Federal Register, publication. 15 USC 1681s-2 note.>> the end of the 6-month period beginning on the date of enactment of this Act, the Board shall adopt the model disclosure required under the amendment made by subsection (a) after notice duly given in the Federal Register and an opportunity for public comment in accordance with section 553 of title 5, United States Code.

TITLE III--ENHANCING THE ACCURACY OF CONSUMER REPORT INFORMATION

SEC. 311. RISK-BASED PRICING NOTICE.

(a) Duties of Users.--Section 615 of the Fair Credit Reporting Act (15 U.S.C. 1681m), as amended by this Act, is amended by adding at the end the following:

``(h) Duties of Users in Certain Credit Transactions.--

``(1) In general.--Subject to rules prescribed as provided in paragraph (6), if any person uses a consumer report in connection with an application for, or a grant, extension, or other provision of, credit on material terms that are materially less favorable than the most favorable terms available to a substantial proportion of consumers from or through that person, based in whole or in part on a consumer report, the person shall provide an oral, written, or electronic notice to the consumer in the form and manner required by regulations prescribed in accordance with this subsection.

``(2) Timing.--The notice required under paragraph (1) may be provided at the time of an application for, or a grant, extension, or other provision of, credit or the time of communication of an approval of an application for, or grant, extension, or other provision of, credit, except as provided in the regulations prescribed under paragraph (6).

``(3) Exceptions.--No notice shall be required from a person under this subsection if--

``(A) the consumer applied for specific material terms and was granted those terms, unless those terms were initially specified by the person after the transaction was initiated by the consumer and after the person obtained a consumer report; or

``(B) the person has provided or will provide a notice to the consumer under subsection (a) in connection with the transaction.

``(4) Other notice not sufficient.--A person that is required to provide a notice under subsection (a) cannot meet that requirement by providing a notice under this subsection.

``(5) Content and delivery of notice.--A notice under this subsection shall, at a minimum--

``(A) include a statement informing the consumer that the terms offered to the consumer are set based on information from a consumer report;

``(B) identify the consumer reporting agency furnishing the report;

``(C) include a statement informing the consumer that the consumer may obtain a copy of a consumer report from that consumer reporting agency without charge; and

``(D) include the contact information specified by that consumer reporting agency for obtaining such consumer reports (including a toll-free telephone number established by the agency in the case of a consumer reporting agency described in section 603(p)).

``(6) Rulemaking.--

``(A) Rules required.--The Commission and the Board shall jointly prescribe rules.

``(B) Content.--Rules required by subparagraph (A) shall address, but are not limited to--

``(i) the form, content, time, and manner of delivery of any notice under this subsection;

``(ii) clarification of the meaning of terms used in this subsection, including what credit terms are material, and when credit terms are materially less favorable;

``(iii) exceptions to the notice requirement under this subsection for classes of persons or transactions regarding which the agencies determine that notice would not significantly benefit consumers;

``(iv) a model notice that may be used to comply with this subsection; and

``(v) the timing of the notice required under paragraph (1), including the circumstances under which the notice must be provided after the terms offered to the consumer were set based on information from a consumer report.

``(7) Compliance.--A person shall not be liable for failure to perform the duties required by this section if, at the time of the failure, the person maintained reasonable policies and procedures to comply with this section.

``(8) Enforcement.--

``(A) No civil actions.--Sections 616 and 617 shall not apply to any failure by any person to comply with this section.

``(B) Administrative enforcement.--This section shall be enforced exclusively under section 621 by the Federal agencies and officials identified in that section.''.

(b) Relation to State Laws.--Section 625(b)(1) of the Fair Credit Reporting Act (15 U.S.C. 1681t(b)(1)), as so designated by section 214 of this Act, is amended by adding at the end the following:

``(I) section 615(h), relating to the duties of users of consumer reports to provide notice with respect to terms in certain credit transactions;''.

SEC. 312. PROCEDURES TO ENHANCE THE ACCURACY AND INTEGRITY OF INFORMATION FURNISHED TO CONSUMER REPORTING AGENCIES.

(a) Accuracy Guidelines and Regulations.--Section 623 of the Fair Credit Reporting Act (15 U.S.C. 1681s-2) is amended by adding at the end the following:

``(e) Accuracy Guidelines and Regulations Required.--

``(1) Guidelines.--The Federal banking agencies, the National Credit Union Administration, and the Commission shall, with respect to the entities that are subject to their respective enforcement authority under section 621, and in coordination as described in paragraph (2)--

``(A) establish and maintain guidelines for use by each person that furnishes information to a consumer reporting agency regarding the accuracy and integrity of the information relating to consumers that such entities furnish to consumer reporting agencies, and update such guidelines as often as necessary; and

``(B) prescribe regulations requiring each person that furnishes information to a consumer reporting agency to establish reasonable policies and procedures for implementing the guidelines established pursuant to subparagraph (A).

``(2) Coordination.--Each agency required to prescribe regulations under paragraph (1) shall consult and coordinate with each other such agency so that, to the extent possible, the regulations prescribed by each such entity are consistent and comparable with the regulations prescribed by each other such agency.

``(3) Criteria.--In developing the guidelines required by paragraph (1)(A), the agencies described in paragraph (1) shall--

``(A) identify patterns, practices, and specific forms of activity that can compromise the accuracy and integrity of information furnished to consumer reporting agencies;

``(B) review the methods (including technological means) used to furnish information relating to consumers to consumer reporting agencies;

``(C) determine whether persons that furnish information to consumer reporting agencies maintain and enforce policies to assure the accuracy and integrity of information furnished to consumer reporting agencies; and

``(D) examine the policies and processes that persons that furnish information to consumer reporting agencies employ to conduct reinvestigations and correct inaccurate information relating to consumers that has been furnished to consumer reporting agencies.''.

(b) Duty of Furnishers To Provide Accurate Information.--Section 623(a)(1) of the Fair Credit Reporting Act (15 U.S.C. 1681s-2(a)(1)) is amended--

(1) in subparagraph (A), by striking ``knows or consciously avoids knowing that the information is inaccurate'' and inserting ``knows or has reasonable cause to believe that the information is inaccurate''; and

(2) by adding at the end the following:

``(D) Definition.--For purposes of subparagraph (A), the term `reasonable cause to believe that the information is inaccurate' means having specific knowledge, other than solely allegations by the consumer, that would cause a reasonable person to have substantial doubts about the accuracy of the information.''.

(c) Ability of Consumer To Dispute Information Directly With Furnisher.--Section 623(a) of the Fair Credit Reporting Act (15 U.S.C. 1681s-2(a)), as amended by this Act, is amended by adding at the end the following:

``(8) Ability of consumer to dispute information directly with furnisher.--

``(A) In general.--The <<NOTE: Regulations.>> Federal banking agencies, the National Credit Union Administration, and the Commission shall jointly prescribe regulations that shall identify the circumstances under which a furnisher shall be required to reinvestigate a dispute concerning the accuracy of information contained in a consumer report on the consumer, based on a direct request of a consumer.

``(B) Considerations.--In prescribing regulations under subparagraph (A), the agencies shall weigh--

``(i) the benefits to consumers with the costs on furnishers and the credit reporting system;

``(ii) the impact on the overall accuracy and integrity of consumer reports of any such requirements;

``(iii) whether direct contact by the consumer with the furnisher would likely result in the most expeditious resolution of any such dispute; and

``(iv) the potential impact on the credit reporting process if credit repair organizations, as defined in section 403(3), including entities that would be a credit repair organization, but for section 403(3)(B)(i), are able to circumvent the prohibition in subparagraph (G).

``(C) Applicability.--Subparagraphs (D) through (G) shall apply in any circumstance identified under the regulations promulgated under subparagraph (A).

``(D) Submitting a notice of dispute.--A consumer who seeks to dispute the accuracy of information shall provide a dispute notice directly to such person at the address specified by the person for such notices that--

``(i) identifies the specific information that is being disputed;

``(ii) explains the basis for the dispute; and

``(iii) includes all supporting documentation required by the furnisher to substantiate the basis of the dispute.

``(E) Duty of person after receiving notice of dispute.--After receiving a notice of dispute from a consumer pursuant to subparagraph (D), the person that provided the information in dispute to a consumer reporting agency shall--

``(i) conduct an investigation with respect to the disputed information;

``(ii) review all relevant information provided by the consumer with the notice;

``(iii) complete such person's investigation of the dispute and report the results of the investigation to the consumer before the expiration of the period under section 611(a)(1) within which a consumer reporting agency would be required to complete its action if the consumer had elected to dispute the information under that section; and ``(iv) if the investigation finds that the information reported was inaccurate, promptly notify each consumer reporting agency to which the person furnished the inaccurate information of that determination and provide to the agency any correction to that information that is necessary to make the information provided by the person accurate.

``(F) Frivolous or irrelevant dispute.--

``(i) In general.--This paragraph shall not apply if the person receiving a notice of a dispute from a consumer reasonably determines that the dispute is frivolous or irrelevant, including--

``(I) by reason of the failure of a consumer to provide sufficient information to investigate the disputed information; or

``(II) the submission by a consumer of a dispute that is substantially the same as a dispute previously submitted by or for the consumer, either directly to the person or through a consumer reporting agency under subsection (b), with respect to which the person has already performed the person's duties under this paragraph or subsection (b), as applicable.

``(ii) Notice <<NOTE: Deadline.>> of determination.--Upon making any determination under clause (i) that a dispute is frivolous or irrelevant, the person shall notify the consumer of such determination not later than 5 business days after making such determination, by mail or, if authorized by the consumer for that purpose, by any other means available to the person.

``(iii) Contents of notice.--A notice under clause (ii) shall include--

``(I) the reasons for the determination under clause (i); and

``(II) identification of any information required to investigate the disputed information, which may consist of a standardized form describing the general nature of such information.

``(G) Exclusion of credit repair organizations.--This paragraph shall not apply if the notice of the dispute is submitted by, is prepared on behalf of the consumer by, or is submitted on a form supplied to the consumer by, a credit repair organization, as defined in section 403(3), or an entity that would be a credit repair organization, but for section 403(3)(B)(i).''.

(d) Furnisher Liability Exception.--Section 623(a)(5) of the Fair Credit Reporting Act (15 U.S.C. 1681s-2(a)(5)) is amended--

(1) by striking ``A person'' and inserting the following:

``(A) In general.--A person'';

(2) by inserting ``date of delinquency on the account, which shall be the'' before ``month'';

(3) by inserting ``on the account'' before ``that immediately preceded''; and

(4) by adding at the end the following:

``(B) Rule of construction.--For purposes of this paragraph only, and provided that the consumer does not dispute the information, a person that furnishes information on a delinquent account that is placed for collection, charged for profit or loss, or subjected to any similar action, complies with this paragraph, if--

``(i) the person reports the same date of delinquency as that provided by the creditor to which the account was owed at the time at which the commencement of the delinquency occurred, if the creditor previously reported that date of delinquency to a consumer reporting agency;

``(ii) the creditor did not previously report the date of delinquency to a consumer reporting agency, and the person establishes and follows reasonable procedures to obtain the date of delinquency from the creditor or another reliable source and reports that date to a consumer reporting agency as the date of delinquency; or

``(iii) the creditor did not previously report the date of delinquency to a consumer reporting agency and the date of delinquency cannot be reasonably obtained as provided in clause (ii), the person establishes and follows reasonable procedures to ensure the date reported as the date of delinquency precedes the date on which the account is placed for collection, charged to profit or loss, or subjected to any similar action, and reports such date to the credit reporting agency.''.

(e) Liability and Enforcement.--

(1) Civil liability.--Section 623 of the Fair Credit Reporting Act (15 U.S.C. 1681s-2) is amended by striking subsections (c) and (d) and inserting the following:

``(c) Limitation on Liability.--Except as provided in section 621(c)(1)(B), sections 616 and 617 do not apply to any violation of--

``(1) subsection (a) of this section, including any regulations issued there under;

``(2) subsection (e) of this section, except that nothing in this paragraph shall limit, expand, or otherwise affect liability under section 616 or 617, as applicable, for violations of subsection (b) of this section; or

``(3) subsection (e) of section 615.

``(d) Limitation on Enforcement.--The provisions of law described in paragraphs (1) through (3) of subsection (c) (other than with respect to the exception described in paragraph (2) of subsection (c)) shall be enforced exclusively as provided under section 621 by the Federal agencies and officials and the State officials identified in section 621.''.

(2) State actions.--Section 621(c) of the Fair Credit Reporting Act (15 U.S.C. 1681s(c)) is amended-- (A) in paragraph (1)(B)(ii), by striking ``of section 623(a)'' and inserting ``described in any of paragraphs (1) through (3) of section 623(c)''; and

(B) in paragraph (5)--

(i) in each of subparagraphs (A) and (B), by striking ``of section 623(a)(1)'' each place that term appears and inserting ``described in any of paragraphs (1) through (3) of section 623(c)''; and

(ii) by amending the paragraph heading to read as follows:

``(5) Limitations on state actions for certain violations.--

(f) Rule of Construction.--Nothing <<NOTE: 15 USC 1681n note.>> in this section, the amendments made by this section, or any other provision of this Act shall be construed to affect any liability under section 616 or 617 of the Fair Credit Reporting Act (15 U.S.C. 1681n, 1681o) that existed on the day before the date of enactment of this Act.

SEC. 313. FTC AND CONSUMER REPORTING AGENCY ACTION CONCERNING COMPLAINTS.

(a) In General.--Section 611 of the Fair Credit Reporting Act (15 U.S.C. 1681i) is amended by adding at the end the following:

``(e) Treatment of Complaints and Report to Congress.--

``(1) In general.--The Commission shall--

``(A) <<NOTE: Records.>> compile all complaints that it receives that a file of a consumer that is maintained by a consumer reporting agency described in section 603(p) contains incomplete or inaccurate information, with respect to which, the consumer appears to have disputed the completeness or accuracy with the consumer reporting agency or otherwise utilized the procedures provided by subsection (a); and

``(B) transmit each such complaint to each consumer reporting agency involved.

``(2) Exclusion.--Complaints received or obtained by the Commission pursuant to its investigative authority under the Federal Trade Commission Act shall not be subject to paragraph (1).

``(3) Agency responsibilities.--Each consumer reporting agency described in section 603(p) that receives a complaint transmitted by the Commission pursuant to paragraph (1) shall--

``(A) review each such complaint to determine whether all legal obligations imposed on the consumer reporting agency under this title (including any obligation imposed by an applicable court or administrative order) have been met with respect to the subject matter of the complaint;

``(B) provide reports on a regular basis to the Commission regarding the determinations of and actions taken by the consumer reporting agency, if any, in connection with its review of such complaints; and

``(C) <<NOTE: Records.>> maintain, for a reasonable time period, records regarding the disposition of each such complaint that is sufficient to demonstrate compliance with this subsection.

``(4) Rulemaking authority.--The Commission may prescribe regulations, as appropriate to implement this subsection.

``(5) Annual report.--The Commission shall submit to the Committee on Banking, Housing, and Urban Affairs of the Senate and the Committee on Financial Services of the House of Representatives an annual report regarding information gathered by the Commission under this subsection.''.

(b) Prompt <<NOTE: 15 USC 1681i note.>> Investigation of Disputed Consumer Information.--

(1) Study required.--The Board and the Commission shall jointly study the extent to which, and the manner in which, consumer reporting agencies and furnishers of consumer information to consumer reporting agencies are complying with the procedures, time lines, and requirements under the Fair Credit Reporting Act for the prompt investigation of the disputed accuracy of any consumer information, the completeness of the information provided to consumer reporting agencies, and the prompt correction or deletion, in accordance with such Act, of any inaccurate or incomplete information or information that cannot be verified.

(2) Report required.--Before <<NOTE: Deadline.>> the end of the 12-month period beginning on the date of enactment of this Act, the Board and the Commission shall jointly submit a progress report to the Congress on the results of the study required under paragraph (1).

(3) Considerations.--In preparing the report required under paragraph (2), the Board and the Commission shall consider information relating to complaints compiled by the Commission under section 611(e) of the Fair Credit Reporting Act, as added by this section.

(4) Recommendations.--The report required under paragraph (2) shall include such recommendations as the Board and the Commission jointly determine to be appropriate for legislative or administrative action, to ensure that--

(A) consumer disputes with consumer reporting agencies over the accuracy or completeness of information in a consumer's file are promptly and fully investigated and any incorrect, incomplete, or unverifiable information is corrected or deleted immediately thereafter;

(B) furnishers of information to consumer reporting agencies maintain full and prompt compliance with the duties and responsibilities established under section 623 of the Fair Credit Reporting Act; and

(C) consumer reporting agencies establish and maintain appropriate internal controls and management review procedures for maintaining full and continuous compliance with the procedures, time lines, and requirements under the Fair Credit Reporting Act for the prompt investigation of the disputed accuracy of any consumer information and the prompt correction or deletion, in accordance with such Act, of any inaccurate or incomplete information or information that cannot be verified.

SEC. 314. IMPROVED DISCLOSURE OF THE RESULTS OF REINVESTIGATION.

(a) In General.--Section 611(a)(5)(A) of the Fair Credit Reporting Act (15 U.S.C. 1681i(a)(5)(A)) is amended by striking ``shall'' and all that follows through the end of the subparagraph, and inserting the following: ``shall-

``(i) promptly delete that item of information from the file of the consumer, or modify that item of information, as appropriate, based on the results of the reinvestigation; and

``(ii) <<NOTE: Notification.>> promptly notify the furnisher of that information that the file of the consumer.''.

(b) Furnisher Requirements Relating to Inaccurate, Incomplete, or Unverifiable Information.--Section 623(b)(1) of the Fair Credit Reporting Act (15 U.S.C. 1681s-2(b)(1)) is amended--

(1) in subparagraph (C), by striking ``and'' at the end; and

(2) in subparagraph (D), by striking the period at the end and inserting the following: ``; and

``(E) if an item of information disputed by a consumer is found to be inaccurate or incomplete or cannot be verified after any reinvestigation under paragraph (1), for purpose of reporting to a consumer reporting agency only, as appropriate, based on the results of the reinvestigation promptly--

``(i) modify that item of information;

``(ii) delete that item of information; or

``(iii) permanently block the reporting of that item of information.''.

SEC. 315. RECONCILING ADDRESSES.

Section 605 of the Fair Credit Reporting Act (15 U.S.C. 1681c), as amended by this Act, is amended by adding at the end the following:

``(h) Notice of Discrepancy in Address.--

``(1) In general.--If a person has requested a consumer report relating to a consumer from a consumer reporting agency described in section 603(p), the request includes an address for the consumer that substantially differs from the addresses in the file of the consumer, and the agency provides a consumer report in response to the request, the consumer reporting agency shall notify the requester of the existence of the discrepancy.

``(2) Regulations.--

``(A) Regulations required.--The Federal banking agencies, the National Credit Union Administration, and the Commission shall jointly, with respect to the entities that are subject to their respective enforcement authority under section 621, prescribe regulations providing guidance regarding reasonable policies and procedures that a user of a consumer report should employ when such user has received a notice of discrepancy under paragraph (1).

``(B) Policies and procedures to be included.--The regulations prescribed under subparagraph (A) shall describe reasonable policies and procedures for use by a user of a consumer report--

``(i) to form a reasonable belief that the user knows the identity of the person to whom the consumer report pertains; and

``(ii) if the user establishes a continuing relationship with the consumer, and the user regularly and in the ordinary course of business furnishes information to the consumer reporting agency from which the notice of discrepancy pertaining to the consumer was obtained, to reconcile the address of the consumer with the consumer reporting agency by furnishing such address to such consumer reporting agency as part of information regularly furnished by the user for the period in which the relationship is established.''.

SEC. 316. NOTICE OF DISPUTE THROUGH RESELLER.

(a) Requirement for Reinvestigation of Disputed Information Upon Notice From a Reseller.--Section 611(a) of the Fair Credit Reporting Act (15 U.S.C. 1681i (a)(1)(A)) is amended--

(1) in paragraph (1)(A)--
(A) by striking ``If the completeness'' and inserting ``Subject to subsection (f), if the completeness'';
(B) by inserting ``, or indirectly through a reseller,'' after ``notifies the agency directly''; and

(C) by inserting ``or reseller'' before the period at the end;
(2) in paragraph (2)(A)--
(A) by inserting ``or a reseller'' after ``dispute from any consumer''; and
(B) by inserting ``or reseller'' before the period at the end; and
(3) in paragraph (2)(B), by inserting ``or the reseller'' after ``from the consumer''.

(b) Reinvestigation Requirement Applicable to Resellers.--Section 611 of the Fair Credit Reporting Act (15 U.S.C. 1681i), as amended by this Act, is amended by adding at the end the following:
``(f) Reinvestigation Requirement Applicable to Resellers.--
``(1) Exemption from general reinvestigation requirement.--Except as provided in paragraph (2), a reseller shall be exempt from the requirements of this section.
``(2) Action <<NOTE: Deadline.>> required upon receiving notice of a dispute.--If a reseller receives a notice from a consumer of a dispute concerning the completeness or accuracy of any item of information contained in a consumer report on such consumer produced by the reseller, the reseller shall, within 5 business days of receiving the notice, and free of charge--
``(A) determine whether the item of information is incomplete or inaccurate as a result of an act or omission of the reseller; and
``(B) if--
``(i) <<NOTE: Deadline.>> the reseller determines that the item of information is
incomplete or inaccurate as a result of an act or omission of the reseller, not later than 20 days after receiving the notice, correct the information in the consumer report or delete it; or
``(ii) if the reseller determines that the item of information is not incomplete or inaccurate as a result of an act or omission of the reseller, convey the notice of the dispute, together with all relevant information provided by the consumer, to each consumer reporting agency that provided the reseller with the information that is the subject of the dispute, using an address or a notification mechanism specified by the consumer reporting agency for such notices.
``(3) Responsibility of consumer reporting agency to notify consumer through reseller.--Upon the completion of a reinvestigation under this section of a dispute concerning the completeness or accuracy of any information in the file of a consumer by a consumer reporting agency that received notice of the dispute from a reseller under paragraph (2)--
``(A) the notice by the consumer reporting agency under paragraph (6), (7), or (8) of subsection (a) shall be provided to the reseller in lieu of the consumer; and
``(B) the reseller shall immediately re-convey such notice to the consumer, including any notice of a deletion by telephone in the manner required under paragraph (8)(A).
``(4) Reseller reinvestigations.--No provision of this subsection shall be construed as prohibiting a reseller from conducting a reinvestigation of a consumer dispute directly.''.

(c) Technical and Conforming Amendment.--Section 611(a)(2)(B) of the Fair Credit Reporting Act (15 U.S.C. 1681i(a)(2)(B)) is amended in the subparagraph heading, by striking ``from consumer''.

SEC. 317. REASONABLE REINVESTIGATION REQUIRED.

Section 611(a)(1)(A) of the Fair Credit Reporting Act (15 U.S.C. 1681i(a)(1)(A)) is amended by striking ``shall reinvestigate free of charge'' and inserting ``shall, free of charge, conduct a reasonable reinvestigation to determine whether the disputed information is inaccurate''.

SEC. 318. <<NOTE: 15 USC 1681 note.>> FTC STUDY OF ISSUES RELATING TO THE FAIR CREDIT REPORTING ACT.

(a) Study Required.--
(1) In general.--The Commission shall conduct a study on ways to improve the operation of the Fair Credit Reporting Act.
(2) Areas for study.--In conducting the study under paragraph (1), the Commission shall review--

(A) the efficacy of increasing the number of points of identifying information that a credit reporting agency is required to match to ensure that a consumer is the correct individual to whom a consumer report relates before releasing a consumer report to a user, including--

(i) the extent to which requiring additional points of such identifying information to match would--

(I) enhance the accuracy of credit reports; and

(II) combat the provision of incorrect consumer reports to users;

(ii) the extent to which requiring an exact match of the first and last name, social security number, and address and ZIP Code of the consumer would enhance the likelihood of increasing credit report accuracy; and

(iii) the effects of allowing consumer reporting agencies to use partial matches of social security numbers and name recognition software on the accuracy of credit reports;

(B) requiring notification to consumers when negative information has been added to their credit reports, including--

(i) the potential impact of such notification on the ability of consumers to identify errors on their credit reports; and

(ii) the potential impact of such notification on the ability of consumers to remove fraudulent information from their credit reports;

(C) the effects of requiring that a consumer who has experienced an adverse action based on a credit report receives a copy of the same credit report that the creditor relied on in taking the adverse action, including--

(i) the extent to which providing such reports to consumers would increase the ability of consumers to identify errors in their credit reports; and

(ii) the extent to which providing such reports to consumers would increase the ability of consumers to remove fraudulent information from their credit reports;

(D) any common financial transactions that are not generally reported to the consumer reporting agencies, but would provide useful information in determining the credit worthiness of consumers; and

(E) any actions that might be taken within a voluntary reporting system to encourage the reporting of the types of transactions described in subparagraph (D).

(3) Costs and benefits.--With respect to each area of study described in paragraph (2), the Commission shall consider the extent to which such requirements would benefit consumers, balanced against the cost of implementing such provisions.

(b) Report Required.--Not <<NOTE: Deadline.>> later than 1 year after the date of enactment of this Act, the chairman of the Commission shall submit a report to the Committee on Banking, Housing, and Urban Affairs of the Senate and the Committee on Financial Services of the House of Representatives containing a detailed summary of the findings and conclusions of the study under this section, together with such recommendations for legislative or administrative actions as may be appropriate.

SEC. 319. <<NOTE: 15 USC 1681 note.>> FTC STUDY OF THE ACCURACY OF CONSUMER REPORTS.

(a) Study Required.--Until the final report is submitted under subsection (b)(2), the Commission shall conduct an ongoing study of the accuracy and completeness of information contained in consumer reports prepared or maintained by consumer reporting agencies and methods for improving the accuracy and completeness of such information.

(b) Biennial Reports Required.--

(1) Interim reports.--The Commission shall submit an interim report to the Congress on the study conducted under subsection

(a) at the end of the 1-year period beginning on the date of enactment of this Act and biennially thereafter for 8 years.

(2) Final report.--The Commission shall submit a final report to the Congress on the study conducted under subsection

(a) at the end of the 2-year period beginning on the date on which the final interim report is submitted to the Congress under paragraph (1).

(3) Contents.--Each report submitted under this subsection shall contain a detailed summary of the findings and conclusions of the Commission with respect to the study required under subsection (a) and such recommendations for legislative and administrative action as the Commission may determine to be appropriate.

TITLE IV--LIMITING THE USE AND SHARING OF MEDICAL INFORMATION IN THE FINANCIAL SYSTEM

SEC. 411. PROTECTION OF MEDICAL INFORMATION IN THE FINANCIAL SYSTEM.

(a) In General.--Section 604(g) of the Fair Credit Reporting Act (15 U.S.C. 1681b (g)) is amended to read as follows:

``(g) Protection of Medical Information.--
``(1) Limitation on consumer reporting agencies.--A consumer reporting agency shall not furnish for employment purposes, or in connection with a credit or insurance transaction, a consumer report that contains medical information about a consumer, unless--
``(A) if furnished in connection with an insurance transaction, the consumer affirmatively consents to the furnishing of the report;
``(B) if furnished for employment purposes or in connection with a credit transaction--
``(i) the information to be furnished is relevant to process or effect the employment or credit transaction; and
``(ii) the consumer provides specific written consent for the furnishing of the report that describes in clear and conspicuous language the use for which the information will be furnished; or
``(C) the information to be furnished pertains solely to transactions, accounts, or balances relating to debts arising from the receipt of medical services, products, or devises, where such information, other than account status or amounts, is restricted or reported using codes that do not identify, or do not provide information sufficient to infer, the specific provider or the nature of such services, products, or devices, as provided in section 605(a)(6).
``(2) Limitation on creditors.--Except as permitted pursuant to paragraph (3)(C) or regulations prescribed under paragraph (5)(A), a creditor shall not obtain or use medical information pertaining to a consumer in connection with any determination of the consumer's eligibility, or continued eligibility, for credit.
``(3) Actions authorized by federal law, insurance activities and regulatory determinations.--Section 603(d)(3) shall not be construed so as to treat information or any communication of information as a consumer report if the information or communication is disclosed--
``(A) in connection with the business of insurance or annuities, including the activities described in section 18B of the model Privacy of Consumer Financial and Health Information Regulation issued by the National Association of Insurance Commissioners (as in effect on January 1, 2003);
``(B) for any purpose permitted without authorization under the Standards for Individually Identifiable Health Information promulgated by the Department of Health and Human Services pursuant to the Health Insurance Portability and Accountability Act of 1996, or referred to under section 1179 of such Act, or described in section 502(e) of Public Law 106-102; or
``(C) as otherwise determined to be necessary and appropriate, by regulation or order and subject to paragraph (6), by the Commission, any Federal banking agency or the National Credit Union Administration (with respect to any financial institution subject to the jurisdiction of such agency or Administration under paragraph (1), (2), or (3) of section 621(b), or the applicable State insurance authority (with respect to any person engaged in providing insurance or annuities).
``(4) Limitation on re-disclosure of medical information.--Any person that receives medical information pursuant to paragraph (1) or (3) shall not disclose such information to any other person, except as necessary to carry out the purpose for which the information was initially disclosed, or as otherwise permitted by statute, regulation, or order.
``(5) Regulations and effective date for paragraph (2).--
``(A) Regulations required.--Each Federal banking agency and the National Credit Union Administration shall, subject to paragraph (6) and after notice and opportunity for comment, prescribe regulations that permit transactions under paragraph (2) that are determined to be necessary and appropriate to protect legitimate operational, transactional, risk, consumer, and other needs (and which shall include permitting actions necessary for administrative verification purposes), consistent with the intent of paragraph (2) to restrict the use of medical information for inappropriate purposes.
``(B) Final <<NOTE: Deadline.>> regulations required.--The Federal banking agencies and the National Credit Union Administration shall issue the regulations required under subparagraph (A) in final form before the end of the 6-month period beginning on the date of enactment of the Fair and Accurate Credit Transactions Act of 2003.
``(6) Coordination with other laws.--No provision of this subsection shall be construed as altering, affecting, or superseding the applicability of any other provision of Federal law relating to medical confidentiality.".

(b) Restriction on Sharing of Medical Information.--Section 603(d) of the Fair Credit Reporting Act (15 U.S.C. 1681a (d)) is amended--

(1) in paragraph (2), by striking "The term" and inserting Except as provided in paragraph (3), the term"; and

(2) by adding at the end the following new paragraph:

"(3) Restriction on sharing of medical information.--Except for information or any communication of information disclosed as provided in section 604(g)(3), the exclusions in paragraph (2) shall not apply with respect to information disclosed to any person related by common ownership or affiliated by corporate control, if the information is--

"(A) medical information;

"(B) an individualized list or description based on the payment transactions of the consumer for medical products or services; or

"(C) an aggregate list of identified consumers based on payment transactions for medical products or services.".

(c) Definition.--Section 603(i) of the Fair Credit Reporting Act (15 U.S.C. 1681a(i)) is amended to read as follows:

"(i) Medical Information.--The term 'medical information'--

"(1) means information or data, whether oral or recorded, in any form or medium, created by or derived from a health care provider or the consumer, that relates to--

"(A) the past, present, or future physical, mental, or behavioral health or condition of an individual;

"(B) the provision of health care to an individual; or

"(C) the payment for the provision of health care to an individual.

"(2) does not include the age or gender of a consumer, demographic information about the consumer, including a consumer's residence address or e-mail address, or any other information about a consumer that does not relate to the physical, mental, or behavioral health or condition of a consumer, including the existence or value of any insurance policy.".

(d) Effective Dates.--This <<NOTE: 15 USC 1681a note.>> section shall take effect at the end of the 180-day period beginning on the date of enactment of this Act, except that paragraph (2) of section 604(g) of the Fair Credit Reporting Act (as amended by subsection (a) of this section) shall take effect on the later of--

(1) the end of the 90-day period beginning on the date on which the regulations required under paragraph (5)(B) of such section 604(g) are issued in final form; or

(2) the date specified in the regulations referred to in paragraph (1).

SEC. 412. CONFIDENTIALITY OF MEDICAL CONTACT INFORMATION IN CONSUMER REPORTS.

(a) Duties of Medical Information Furnishers.--Section 623(a) of the Fair Credit Reporting Act (15 U.S.C. 1681s-2(a)), as amended by this Act, is amended by adding at the end the following:

"(9) Duty to provide notice of status as medical information furnisher.--A person whose primary business is providing medical services, products, or devices, or the person's agent or assignee, who furnishes information to a consumer reporting agency on a consumer shall be considered a medical information furnisher for purposes of this title, and shall notify the agency of such status.".

(b) Restriction of Dissemination of Medical Contact Information.--Section 605(a) of the Fair Credit Reporting Act (15 U.S.C. 1681c(a)) is amended by adding at the end the following:

"(6) The name, address, and telephone number of any medical information furnisher that has notified the agency of its status, unless--

"(A) such name, address, and telephone number are restricted or reported using codes that do not identify, or provide information sufficient to infer, the specific provider or the nature of such services, products, or devices to a person other than the consumer; or

"(B) the report is being provided to an insurance company for a purpose relating to engaging in the business of insurance other than property and casualty   insurance.".

(c) No Exceptions Allowed for Dollar Amounts.--Section 605(b) of the Fair Credit Reporting Act (15 U.S.C. 1681c(b)) is amended by striking "The provisions of subsection (a)" and inserting "The provisions of paragraphs (1) through (5) of subsection (a)".

(d) Coordination <<NOTE: 15 USC 1681b note.>> With Other Laws.--No provision of any amendment made by this section shall be construed as altering, affecting, or superseding the applicability of any other provision of Federal law relating to medical confidentiality.

(e) FTC Regulation of Coding of Trade Names.--Section 621 of the Fair Credit Reporting Act (15 U.S.C.1681s), as amended by this Act, is amended by adding at the end the following:

``(g) FTC Regulation of Coding of Trade Names.--If the Commission determines that a person described in paragraph (9) of section 623(a) has not met the requirements of such paragraph, the Commission shall take action to ensure the person's compliance with such paragraph, which may include issuing model guidance or prescribing reasonable policies and procedures, as necessary to ensure that such person complies with such paragraph.''.

(f) Technical and Conforming Amendments.--Section 604(g) of the Fair Credit Reporting Act (15 U.S.C. 1681b(g)), as amended by section 411 of this Act, is amended--

(1) in paragraph (1), by inserting ``(other than medical contact information treated in the manner required under section 605(a)(6))'' after ``a consumer report that contains medical information''; and

(2) in paragraph (2), by inserting ``(other than medical information treated in the manner required under section 605(a)(6))'' after ``a creditor shall not obtain or use medical information''.

(g) Effective Date.--The amendments made by this section shall take effect at the end of the 15-month period beginning on the date of enactment of this Act.

TITLE V--FINANCIAL <<NOTE: Financial Literacy and Education Improvement Act.>> LITERACY AND EDUCATION IMPROVEMENT

SEC. 511. <<NOTE: 20 USC 9701 note.>> SHORT TITLE.

This title may be cited as the ``Financial Literacy and Education Improvement Act''.

SEC. 512. <<NOTE: 20 USC 9701.>> DEFINITIONS.

As used in this title--

(1) the term ``Chairperson'' means the Chairperson of the Financial Literacy and Education Commission; and

(2) the term ``Commission'' means the Financial Literacy and Education Commission established under section 513.

SEC. 513. <<NOTE: 20 USC 9702.>> ESTABLISHMENT OF FINANCIAL LITERACY AND EDUCATION COMMISSION.

(a) In General.--There is established a commission to be known as the ``Financial Literacy and Education Commission''.

(b) Purpose.--The Commission shall serve to improve the financial literacy and education of persons in the United States through development of a national strategy to promote financial literacy and education.

(c) Membership.--

(1) Composition.--The Commission shall be composed of--

(A) the Secretary of the Treasury;

(B) the respective head of each of the Federal banking agencies (as defined in section 3 of the Federal Deposit Insurance Act), the National Credit Union Administration, the Securities and Exchange Commission, each of the Departments of Education, Agriculture, Defense, Health and Human Services, Housing and Urban Development, Labor, and Veterans Affairs, the Federal Trade Commission, the General Services Administration, the Small Business Administration, the Social Security Administration, the Commodity Futures Trading Commission, and the Office of Personnel Management; and

(C) <<NOTE: President.>> at the discretion of the President, not more than 5 individuals appointed by the President from among the administrative heads of any other Federal agencies, departments, or other Federal Government entities, whom the President determines to be engaged in a serious effort to improve financial literacy and education.

(2) Alternates.--Each member of the Commission may designate an alternate if the member is unable to attend a meeting of the Commission. Such alternate shall be an individual who exercises significant decision making authority.

(d) Chairperson.--The Secretary of the Treasury shall serve as the Chairperson.

(e) Meetings.--The Commission shall hold, at the call of the Chairperson, at least 1 meeting every 4 months. All such meetings shall be open to the public. The Commission may hold, at the call of the Chairperson, such other meetings as the Chairperson sees fit to carry out this title.

(f) Quorum.--A majority of the members of the Commission shall constitute a quorum, but a lesser number of members may hold hearings.

(g) Initial Meeting.--The <<NOTE: Deadline.>> Commission shall hold its first meeting not later than 60 days after the date of enactment of this Act.

SEC. 514. <<NOTE: 20 USC 9703.>> DUTIES OF THE COMMISSION.

(a) Duties.--

(1) In general.--The Commission, through the authority of the members referred to in section 513(c), shall take such actions as it deems necessary to streamline, improve, or augment the financial literacy and education programs, grants, and materials of the Federal Government, including curricula for all Americans.

(2) Areas of emphasis.--To improve financial literacy and education, the Commission shall emphasize, among other elements, basic personal income and household money management and planning skills, including how to--

(A) create household budgets, initiate savings plans, and make strategic investment decisions for education, retirement, home ownership, wealth building, or other savings goals;

(B) manage spending, credit, and debt, including credit card debt, effectively;

(C) increase awareness of the availability and significance of credit reports and credit scores in obtaining credit, the importance of their accuracy (and how to correct inaccuracies), their effect on credit terms, and the effect common financial decisions may have on credit scores;

(D) ascertain fair and favorable credit terms;

(E) avoid abusive, predatory, or deceptive credit offers and financial products;

(F) understand, evaluate, and compare financial products, services, and opportunities;

(G) understand resources that ought to be easily accessible and affordable, and that inform and educate investors as to their rights and avenues of recourse when an investor believes his or her rights have been violated by unprofessional conduct of market intermediaries;

(H) increase awareness of the particular financial needs and financial transactions (such as the sending of remittances) of consumers who are targeted in multilingual financial literacy and education programs and improve the development and distribution of multilingual financial literacy and education materials;

(I) promote bringing individuals who lack basic banking services into the financial mainstream by opening and maintaining an account with a financial institution; and

(J) improve financial literacy and education through all other related skills, including personal finance and related economic education, with the primary goal of programs not simply to improve knowledge, but rather to improve consumers' financial choices and outcomes.

(b) Website.--

(1) In general.--The Commission shall establish and maintain a website, such as the domain name``FinancialLiteracy.gov", or a similar domain name.

(2) Purposes.--The website established under paragraph (1) shall--

(A) serve as a clearinghouse of information about Federal financial literacy and education programs;

(B) provide a coordinated entry point for accessing information about all Federal publications, grants, and materials promoting enhanced financial literacy and education;

(C) offer information on all Federal grants to promote financial literacy and education, and on how to target, apply for, and receive a grant that is most appropriate under the circumstances;

(D) as the Commission considers appropriate, feature website links to efforts that have no commercial content and that feature information about financial literacy and education programs, materials, or campaigns; and

(E) offer such other information as the Commission finds appropriate to share with the public in the fulfillment of its purpose.

(c) Toll-Free Hotline.--The Commission shall establish a toll-free telephone number that shall be made available to members of the public seeking information about issues pertaining to financial literacy and education.

(d) Development and Dissemination of Materials.--The Commission shall--

(1) develop materials to promote financial literacy and education; and

(2) disseminate such materials to the general public.

(e) Coordination of Efforts.--The Commission shall take such steps as are necessary to coordinate and promote financial literacy and education efforts at the State and local level, including promoting partnerships among Federal, State, and local governments, nonprofit organizations, and private enterprises.

(f) National Strategy.--

(1) In general.--The Commission shall--

(A) <<NOTE: Deadline.>> not later than 18 months after the date of enactment of this Act, develop a national strategy to promote basic financial literacy and education among all American consumers; and

(B) coordinate Federal efforts to implement the strategy developed under subparagraph (A).

(2) Strategy.--The strategy to promote basic financial literacy and education required to be developed under paragraph

(1) shall provide for--

(A) participation by State and local governments and private, nonprofit, and public institutions in the creation and implementation of such strategy;

(B) the development of methods--

(i) to increase the general financial education level of current and future consumers of financial services and products; and

(ii) to enhance the general understanding of financial services and products;

(C) review of Federal activities designed to promote financial literacy and education, and development of a plan to improve coordination of such activities; and

(D) the identification of areas of overlap and duplication among Federal financial literacy and education activities and proposed means of eliminating any such overlap and duplication.

(3) National strategy review.--The Commission shall, not less than annually, review the national strategy developed under this subsection and make such changes and recommendations as it deems necessary.

(g) Consultation.--The Commission shall actively consult with a variety of representatives from private and nonprofit organizations and State and local agencies, as determined appropriate by the Commission.

(h) Reports.--

(1) In general.--Not <<NOTE: Deadline.>> later than 18 months after the date of the first meeting of the Commission, and annually thereafter, the Commission shall issue a report, the Strategy for Assuring Financial Empowerment ("SAFE Strategy"), to the Committee on Banking, Housing, and Urban Affairs of the Senate and the Committee on Financial Services of the House of Representatives on the progress of the Commission in carrying out this title.

(2) Contents.--The report required under paragraph (1) shall include--

(A) the national strategy for financial literacy and education, as described under subsection (f);

(B) information concerning the implementation of the duties of the Commission under subsections (a) through

(g);

(C) an assessment of the success of the Commission in implementing the national strategy developed under subsection (f);and impact of Federal financial literacy and education materials;

(E) information concerning the content and public use of--

(i) the website established under subsection

(b); and

(ii) the toll-free telephone number established under subsection (c);

(F) a brief survey of the financial literacy and education materials developed under subsection (d), and data regarding the dissemination and impact of such materials, as measured by improved financial decision making;

(G) a brief summary of any hearings conducted by the Commission, including a list of witnesses who testified at such hearings;

(H) information about the activities of the Commission planned for the next fiscal year;

(I) a summary of all Federal financial literacy and education activities targeted to communities that have historically lacked access to financial literacy materials and education, and have been underserved by the mainstream financial systems; and

(J) such other materials relating to the duties of the Commission as the Commission deems appropriate.

(3) Initial report.--The initial report under paragraph (1) shall include information regarding all Federal programs, materials, and grants which seek to improve financial literacy, and assess the effectiveness of such programs.

(i) Testimony.--The Commission shall annually provide testimony by the Chairperson to the Committee on Banking, Housing, and Urban Affairs of the Senate and the Committee on Financial Services of the House of Representatives.

SEC. 515. <<NOTE: 20 USC 9704.>> POWERS OF THE COMMISSION.

(a) Hearings.--

(1) In general.--The Commission shall hold such hearings, sit and act at such times and places, take such testimony, and receive such evidence as the Commission deems appropriate to carry out this title.

(2) Participation.--In hearings held under this subsection, the Commission shall consider inviting witnesses from, among other groups--

(A) other Federal Government officials;

(B) State and local government officials;

(C) consumer and community groups;

(D) nonprofit financial literacy and education groups (such as those involved in personal finance and economic education); and

(E) the financial services industry.

(b) Information From Federal Agencies.--The Commission may secure directly from any Federal department or agency such information as the Commission considers necessary to carry out this title. Upon request of the Chairperson, the head of such department or agency shall furnish such information to the Commission.

(c) Periodic Studies.--The Commission may conduct periodic studies regarding the state of financial literacy and education in the United States, as the Commission determines appropriate.

(d) Multilingual.--The Commission may take any action to develop and promote financial literacy and education materialism languages other than English, as the Commission deems appropriate, including for the website established under section 514(b), at the toll-free number established under section 514(c), and in the materials developed and disseminated under section 514(d).

SEC. 516. <<NOTE: 20 USC 9705.>> COMMISSION PERSONNEL MATTERS.

(a) Compensation of Members.--Each member of the Commission shall serve without compensation in addition to that received for their service as an officer or employee of the United States.

(b) Travel Expenses.--The members of the Commission shall be allowed travel expenses, including per diem in lieu of subsistence, at rates authorized for employees of agencies under subchapter I of chapter 57 of title 5, United States Code, while away from their homes or regular places of business in the performance of services for the Commission.

(c) Assistance.--

(1) In general.--The Director of the Office of Financial Education of the Department of the Treasury shall provide assistance to the Commission, upon request of the Commission, without reimbursement.

(2) Detail of government employees.--Any Federal Government employee may be detailed to the Commission without reimbursement, and such detail shall be without interruption or loss of civil service status or privilege.

SEC. 517. <<NOTE: 20 USC 9706.>> STUDIES BY THE COMPTROLLER GENERAL.

(a) Effectiveness Study.--Not <<NOTE: Deadline. Reports.>> later than 3 years after the date of enactment of this Act, the Comptroller General of the United States shall submit a report to Congress assessing the effectiveness of the Commission in promoting financial literacy and education.

(b) Study and Report on the Need and Means for Improving Financial Literacy Among Consumers.--

(1) Study required.--The Comptroller General of the United States shall conduct a study to assess the extent of consumers' knowledge and awareness of credit reports, credit scores, and the dispute resolution process, and on methods for improving financial literacy among consumers.

(2) Factors to be included.--The study required under paragraph (1) shall include the following issues:

(A) The number of consumers who view their credit reports.

(B) Under what conditions and for what purposes do consumers primarily obtain a copy of their consumer report (such as for the purpose of ensuring the completeness and accuracy of the contents, to protect against fraud, in response to an adverse action based on the report, or in response to suspected identity theft) and approximately what percentage of the total number of consumers who obtain a copy of their consumer report do so for each such primary purpose.

(C) The extent of consumers' knowledge of the data collection process.

(D) The extent to which consumers know how to get a copy of a consumer report.

(E) The extent to which consumers know and understand the factors that positively or negatively impact credit scores.

(3) Report required.--Before <<NOTE: Deadline.>> the end of the 12-month period beginning on the date of enactment of this Act, the Comptroller General shall submit a report to Congress on the findings and conclusions of the Comptroller General pursuant to the study conducted under this subsection, together with

such recommendations for legislative or administrative action as the Comptroller General may determine to be appropriate, including recommendations on methods for improving financial literacy among consumers.

SEC. 518. <<NOTE: 20 USC 9707.>> THE NATIONAL PUBLIC SERVICE MULTIMEDIA CAMPAIGN TO ENHANCE THE STATE OF FINANCIAL LITERACY.

(a) In General.--The Secretary of the Treasury (in this section referred to as the "Secretary"), after review of the recommendations of the Commission, as part of the national strategy, shall develop, implement, and conduct a pilot national public service multimedia campaign to enhance the state of financial literacy and education in the United States.

(b) Program Requirements.--

(1) Public service campaign.--The Secretary, after review of the recommendations of the Commission, shall select and work with a nonprofit organization or organizations that are especially well-qualified in the distribution of public service campaigns, and have secured private sector funds to produce the pilot national public service multimedia campaign.

(2) Development of multimedia campaign.--The Secretary, after review of the recommendations of the Commission, shall develop, in consultation with nonprofit, public, or private organizations, especially those that are well qualified by virtue of their experience in the field of financial literacy and education, to develop the financial literacy national public service multimedia campaign.

(3) Focus of campaign.--The pilot national public service multimedia campaign shall be consistent with the national strategy, and shall promote the toll-free telephone number and the website developed under this title.

(c) Multilingual.--The Secretary may develop the multimedia campaign in languages other than English, as the Secretary deems appropriate.

(d) Performance Measures.--The Secretary shall develop measures to evaluate the effectiveness of the pilot national public service multimedia campaign, as measured by improved financial decision making among individuals.

(e) Report.--For each fiscal year for which there are appropriations pursuant to the authorization in subsection (e), the Secretary shall submit a report to the Committee on Banking, Housing, and Urban Affairs and the Committee on Appropriations of the Senate and the Committee on Financial Services and the Committee on Appropriations of the House of Representatives, describing the status and implementation of the provisions of this section and the state of financial literacy and education in the United States.

(f) Authorization of Appropriations.--There are authorized to be appropriated to the Secretary, not to exceed $3,000,000 for fiscal years 2004, 2005, and 2006, for the development, production, and distribution of a pilot national public service multimedia campaign under this section.

SEC. 519. <<NOTE: 20 USC 9708.>> AUTHORIZATION OF APPROPRIATIONS.

There are authorized to be appropriated to the Commission such sums as may be necessary to carry out this title, including administrative expenses of the Commission.

TITLE VI--PROTECTING EMPLOYEE MISCONDUCT INVESTIGATIONS

SEC. 611. CERTAIN EMPLOYEE INVESTIGATION COMMUNICATIONS EXCLUDED FROM DEFINITION OF CONSUMER REPORT.

(a) In General.--Section 603 of the Fair Credit Reporting Act (15 U.S.C. 1681a), as amended by this Act is amended by adding at the end the following:

``(x) Exclusion of Certain Communications for Employee Investigations.--

``(1) Communications described in this subsection.--A communication is described in this subsection if-

``(A) but for subsection (d)(2)(D), the communication would be a consumer report;

``(B) the communication is made to an employer in connection with an investigation of--

``(i) suspected misconduct relating to employment; or

``(ii) compliance with Federal, State, or local laws and regulations, the rules of a self-regulatory organization, or any preexisting written policies of the employer;

``(C) the communication is not made for the purpose of investigating a consumer's credit worthiness, credit standing, or credit capacity; and

``(D) the communication is not provided to any person except--

``(i) to the employer or an agent of the employer;

"(ii) to any Federal or State officer, agency, or department, or any officer, agency, or department of a unit of general local government;

"(iii) to any self-regulatory organization with regulatory authority over the activities of the employer or employee;

"(iv) as otherwise required by law; or

"(v) pursuant to section 608.

"(2) Subsequent disclosure.--After taking any adverse action based in whole or in part on a communication described in paragraph (1), the employer shall disclose to the consumer a summary containing the nature and substance of the communication upon which the adverse action is based, except that the sources of information acquired solely for use in preparing what would be but for subsection (d)(2)(D) an investigative consumer report need not be disclosed.

"(3) Self-regulatory organization defined.--For purposes of this subsection, the term `self-regulatory organization' includes any self-regulatory organization (as defined in section

3(a)(26) of the Securities Exchange Act of 1934), any entity established under title I of the Sarbanes-Oxley Act of 2002, any board of trade designated by the Commodity Futures Trading Commission, and any futures association registered with such Commission.".

(b) Technical and Conforming Amendment.--Section 603(d)(2)(D) of the Fair Credit Reporting Act (15 U.S.C. 1681a(d)(2)(D)) is amended by inserting "or (x)" after "subsection (o)".

TITLE VII--RELATION TO STATE LAWS

SEC. 711. RELATION TO STATE LAWS.

Section 625 of the Fair Credit Reporting Act (15 U.S.C. 1681t), as so designated by section 214 of this Act, is amended--

(1) in subsection (a), by inserting "or for the prevention or mitigation of identity theft," after "information on consumers,";

(2) in subsection (b), by adding at the end the following:

"(5) with respect to the conduct required by the specific provisions of--

"(A) section 605(g);

"(B) section 605A;

"(C) section 605B;

"(D) section 609(a)(1)(A);

"(E) section 612(a);

"(F) subsections (e), (f), and (g) of section 615;

"(G) section 621(f);

"(H) section 623(a)(6); or

"(I) section 628."; and

(3) in subsection (d)--

(A) by striking paragraph (2);

(B) by striking "(c)--" and all that follows through "do not affect" and inserting "(c) do not affect"; and

(C) by striking "1996; and" and inserting "1996.".

TITLE VIII--MISCELLANEOUS

SEC. 811. CLERICAL AMENDMENTS.

(a) Short Title.--Section 601 of the Fair Credit Reporting Act (15 U.S.C. 1601 note) is amended by striking "the Fair Credit Reporting Act." and inserting "the `Fair Credit Reporting Act'.".

(b) Section 604.--Section 604(a) of the Fair Credit Reporting Act (15 U.S.C. 1681b(a)) is amended in paragraphs (1) through (5), other than subparagraphs (E) and (F) of paragraph (3), by moving each margin 2 ems to the right.

(c) Section 605.--

(1) Section 605(a)(1) of the Fair Credit Reporting Act (15 U.S.C. 1681c(a)(1)) is amended by striking "(1) cases" and inserting "(1) Cases".

(2)(A) <<NOTE: 15 USC 1681c.>> Section 5(1) of Public Law 105-347 (112 Stat. 3211) is amended by striking "Judgments which" and inserting "judgments which".

(B) <<NOTE: 15 USC 1681c note.>> The amendment made by subparagraph (A) shall be deemed to have the same effective date as section 5(1) of Public Law 105-347 (112 Stat. 3211).

(d) Section 609.--Section 609(a) of the Fair Credit Reporting Act (15 U.S.C. 1681g(a)) is amended--

(1) in paragraph (2), by moving the margin 2 ems to the right; and
(2) in paragraph (3)(C), by moving the margins 2 ems to the left.

(e) Section 617.--Section 617(a)(1) of the Fair Credit Reporting Act (15 U.S.C. 1681o(a)(1)) is amended by adding ``and" at the end.

(f) Section 621.--Section 621(b)(1)(B) of the Fair Credit Reporting Act (15 U.S.C. 1681s(b)(1)(B)) is amended by striking ``25(a)" and inserting ``25A".

(g) Title 31.--Section 5318 of title 31, United States Code, is amended by re-designating the second item designated as subsection (l) (relating to applicability of rules) as subsection (m).

(h) Conforming Amendment.--Section 2411(c) of Public Law 104-208 (110 Stat. 3009-445) <<NOTE: 15 USC 1681m.>> is repealed.

Approved December 4, 2003.

LEGISLATIVE HISTORY--H.R. 2622 (S. 1753):

HOUSE REPORTS: Nos. 108-263 and Pt.2 (Comm. on Financial Services) and 108-396 (Comm. of Conference).SENATE REPORTS: No. 108-166 accompanying S. 1753 (Comm. on Banking, Housing, and Urban Affairs).CONGRESSIONAL RECORD, Vol. 149 (2003):
    Sept. 10, considered and passed House.
    Nov. 5, considered and passed Senate, amended, in lieu of S. 1753.
    Nov. 21, House agreed to conference report.
    Nov. 22, Senate agreed to conference report.
WEEKLY COMPILATION OF PRESIDENTIAL DOCUMENTS, Vol. 39 (2003):
    Dec. 4, Presidential remarks.

Chapter 15

FAIR DEBT COLLECTION

As amended by Public Law 104-208, 110 Stat. 3009 (Sept. 30, 1996)

To amend the Consumer Credit Protection Act to prohibit abusive practices by debt collectors.

Be it enacted by the Senate and House of Representatives of the United States of America in Congress assembled, That the Consumer Credit Protection Act (15 U.S.C. 1601 et seq.) is amended by adding at the end thereof the following new title:

TITLE VIII - DEBT COLLECTION PRACTICES [Fair Debt Collection Practices Act]

Sec.
801. Short Title
802. Congressional findings and declaration of purpose
803. Definitions
804. Acquisition of location information
805. Communication in connection with debt collection
806. Harassment or abuse
807. False or misleading representations
808. Unfair practice
809. Validation of debts
810. Multiple debts
811. Legal actions by debt collectors
812. Furnishing certain deceptive forms
813. Civil liability
814. Administrative enforcement
815. Reports to Congress by the Commission
816. Relation to State laws
817. Exemption for State regulation
818. Effective date

§ 801. Short Title [15 USC 1601 note]

This title may be cited as the "Fair Debt Collection Practices Act."

§ 802. Congressional findings and declarations of purpose [15 USC 1692]

(a) There is abundant evidence of the use of abusive, deceptive, and unfair debt collection practices by many debt collectors. Abusive debt collection practices contribute to the number of personal bankruptcies, to marital instability, to the loss of jobs, and to invasions of individual privacy.

(b) Existing laws and procedures for redressing these injuries are inadequate to protect consumers.

(c) Means other than misrepresentation or other abusive debt collection practices are available for the effective collection of debts.

(d) Abusive debt collection practices are carried on to a substantial extent in interstate commerce and through means and instrumentalities of such commerce. Even where abusive debt collection practices are purely intrastate in character, they nevertheless directly affect interstate commerce.

(e) It is the purpose of this title to eliminate abusive debt collection practices by debt collectors, to insure that those debt collectors who refrain from using abusive debt collection practices are not competitively disadvantaged, and to promote consistent State action to protect consumers against debt collection abuses.

§ 803. Definitions [15 USC 1692a]

As used in this title --

(1) The term "Commission" means the Federal Trade Commission.

(2) The term "communication" means the conveying of information regarding a debt directly or indirectly to any person through any medium.

(3) The term "consumer" means any natural person obligated or allegedly obligated to pay any debt.

(4) The term "creditor" means any person who offers or extends credit creating a debt or to whom a debt is owed, but such term does not include any person to the extent that he receives an assignment or transfer of a debt in default solely for the purpose of facilitating collection of such debt for another.

(5) The term "debt" means any obligation or alleged obligation of a consumer to pay money arising out of a transaction in which the money, property, insurance or services which are the subject of the transaction are primarily for personal, family, or household purposes, whether or not such obligation has been reduced to judgment.

(6) The term "debt collector" means any person who uses any instrumentality of interstate commerce or the mails in any business the principal purpose of which is the collection of any debts, or who regularly collects or attempts to collect, directly or indirectly, debts owed or due or asserted to be owed or due another. Notwithstanding the exclusion provided by clause (F) of the last sentence of this paragraph, the term includes any creditor who, in the process of collecting his own debts, uses any name other than his own which would indicate that a third person is collecting or attempting to collect such debts. For the purpose of section 808(6), such term also includes any person who uses any instrumentality of interstate commerce or the mails in any business the principal purpose of which is the enforcement of security interests. The term does not include --

(A) any officer or employee of a creditor while, in the name of the creditor, collecting debts for such creditor;

(B) any person while acting as a debt collector for another person, both of whom are related by common ownership or affiliated by corporate control, if the person acting as a debt collector does so only for persons to whom it is so related or affiliated and if the principal business of such person is not the collection of debts;

(C) any officer or employee of the United States or any State to the extent that collecting or attempting to collect any debt is in the performance of his official duties;

(D) any person while serving or attempting to serve legal process on any other person in connection with the judicial enforcement of any debt;

(E) any nonprofit organization which, at the request of consumers, performs bona fide consumer credit counseling and assists consumers in the liquidation of their debts by receiving payments from such consumers and distributing such amounts to creditors; and

(F) any person collecting or attempting to collect any debt owed or due or asserted to be owed or due another to the extent such activity (i) is incidental to a bona fide fiduciary obligation or a bona fide escrow arrangement; (ii) concerns a debt which was originated by such person; (iii) concerns a debt which was not in default at the time it was obtained by such person; or (iv) concerns a debt obtained by such person as a secured party in a commercial credit transaction involving the creditor.

(7) The term "location information" means a consumer's place of abode and his telephone number at such place, or his place of employment.

(8) The term "State" means any State, territory, or possession of the United States, the District of Columbia, the Commonwealth of Puerto Rico, or any political subdivision of any of the foregoing.

§ 804. Acquisition of location information [15 USC 1692b]

Any debt collector communicating with any person other than the consumer for the purpose of acquiring location information about the consumer shall --

(1) identify himself, state that he is confirming or correcting location information concerning the consumer, and, only if expressly requested, identify his employer;

(2) not state that such consumer owes any debt;

(3) not communicate with any such person more than once unless requested to do so by such person or unless the debt collector reasonably believes that the earlier response of such person is erroneous or incomplete and that such person now has correct or complete location information;

(4) not communicate by post card;

(5) not use any language or symbol on any envelope or in the contents of any communication effected by the mails or telegram that indicates that the debt collector is in the debt collection business or that the communication relates to the collection of a debt; and

(6) after the debt collector knows the consumer is represented by an attorney with regard to the subject debt and has knowledge of, or can readily ascertain, such attorney's name and address, not communicate with any person other than that attorney, unless the attorney fails to respond within a reasonable period of time to the communication from the debt collector.

§ 805. Communication in connection with debt collection [15 USC 1692c]

(a) COMMUNICATION WITH THE CONSUMER GENERALLY. Without the prior consent of the consumer given directly to the debt collector or the express permission of a court of competent jurisdiction, a debt collector may not communicate with a consumer in connection with the collection of any debt --

(1) at any unusual time or place or a time or place known or which should be known to be inconvenient to the consumer. In the absence of knowledge of circumstances to the contrary, a debt collector shall assume that the convenient time for communicating with a consumer is after 8 o'clock anti-meridian and before 9 o'clock postmeridian, local time at the consumer's location;

(2) if the debt collector knows the consumer is represented by an attorney with respect to such debt and has knowledge of, or can readily ascertain, such attorney's name and address, unless the attorney fails to respond within a reasonable period of time to a communication from the debt collector or unless the attorney consents to direct communication with the consumer; or

(3) at the consumer's place of employment if the debt collector knows or has reason to know that the consumer's employer prohibits the consumer from receiving such communication.

(b) COMMUNICATION WITH THIRD PARTIES. Except as provided in section 804, without the prior consent of the consumer given directly to the debt collector, or the express permission of a court of competent jurisdiction, or as reasonably necessary to effectuate a post judgment judicial remedy, a debt collector may not communicate, in connection with the collection of any debt, with any person other than a consumer, his attorney, a consumer reporting agency if otherwise permitted by law, the creditor, the attorney of the creditor, or the attorney of the debt collector.

(c) CEASING COMMUNICATION. If a consumer notifies a debt collector in writing that the consumer refuses to pay a debt or that the consumer wishes the debt collector to cease further communication with the consumer, the debt collector shall not communicate further with the consumer with respect to such debt, except-

(1) to advise the consumer that the debt collector's further efforts are being terminated;

(2) to notify the consumer that the debt collector or creditor may invoke specified remedies which are ordinarily invoked by such debt collector or creditor; or

(3) where applicable, to notify the consumer that the debt collector or creditor intends to invoke a specified remedy.

If such notice from the consumer is made by mail, notification shall be complete upon receipt.

(d) For the purpose of this section, the term "consumer" includes the consumer's spouse, parent (if the consumer is a minor), guardian, executor, or administrator.

§ 806. Harassment or abuse [15 USC 1692d]

A debt collector may not engage in any conduct the natural consequence of which is to harass, oppress, or abuse any person in connection with the collection of a debt. Without limiting the general application of the foregoing, the following conduct is a violation of this section:

(1) The use or threat of use of violence or other criminal means to harm the physical person, reputation, or property of any person.

(2) The use of obscene or profane language or language the natural consequence of which is to abuse the hearer or reader.

(3) The publication of a list of consumers who allegedly refuse to pay debts, except to a consumer reporting agency or to persons meeting the requirements of section 603(f) or 604(3)[1] of this Act.

(4) The advertisement for sale of any debt to coerce payment of the debt.

(5) Causing a telephone to ring or engaging any person in telephone conversation repeatedly or continuously with intent to annoy, abuse, or harass any person at the called number.

(6) Except as provided in section 804, the placement of telephone calls without meaningful disclosure of the caller's identity.

§ 807. False or misleading representations [15 USC 1692e]

A debt collector may not use any false, deceptive, or misleading representation or means in connection with the collection of any debt. Without limiting the general application of the foregoing, the following conduct is a violation of this section:

(1) The false representation or implication that the debt collector is vouched for, bonded by, or affiliated with the United States or any State, including the use of any badge, uniform, or facsimile thereof.

(2) The false representation of --

(A) the character, amount, or legal status of any debt; or

(B) any services rendered or compensation which may be lawfully received by any debt collector for the collection of a debt.

(3) The false representation or implication that any individual is an attorney or that any communication is from an attorney.

(4) The representation or implication that nonpayment of any debt will result in the arrest or imprisonment of any person or the seizure, garnishment, attachment, or sale of any property or wages of any person unless such action is lawful and the debt collector or creditor intends to take such action.

(5) The threat to take any action that cannot legally be taken or that is not intended to be taken.

(6) The false representation or implication that a sale, referral, or other transfer of any interest in a debt shall cause the consumer to --

(A) lose any claim or defense to payment of the debt; or

(B) become subject to any practice prohibited by this title.

(7) The false representation or implication that the consumer committed any crime or other conduct in order to disgrace the consumer.

(8) Communicating or threatening to communicate to any person credit information which is known or which should be known to be false, including the failure to communicate that a disputed debt is disputed.

(9) The use or distribution of any written communication which simulates or is falsely represented to be a document authorized, issued, or approved by any court, official, or agency of the United States or any State, or which creates a false impression as to its source, authorization, or approval.

(10) The use of any false representation or deceptive means to collect or attempt to collect any debt or to obtain information concerning a consumer.

(11) The failure to disclose in the initial written communication with the consumer and, in addition, if the initial communication with the consumer is oral, in that initial oral communication, that the debt collector is attempting to collect a debt and that any information obtained will be used for that purpose, and the failure to disclose in subsequent communications that the communication is from a debt collector, except that this paragraph shall not apply to a formal pleading made in connection with a legal action.

(12) The false representation or implication that accounts have been turned over to innocent purchasers for value.

(13) The false representation or implication that documents are legal process.

(14) The use of any business, company, or organization name other than the true name of the debt collector's business, company, or organization.

(15) The false representation or implication that documents are not legal process forms or do not require action by the consumer.

(16) The false representation or implication that a debt collector operates or is employed by a consumer reporting agency as defined by section 603(f) of this Act.

§ 808. Unfair practices [15 USC 1692f]

A debt collector may not use unfair or unconscionable means to collect or attempt to collect any debt. Without limiting the general application of the foregoing, the following conduct is a violation of this section:

(1) The collection of any amount (including any interest, fee, charge, or expense incidental to the principal obligation) unless such amount is expressly authorized by the agreement creating the debt or permitted by law.

(2) The acceptance by a debt collector from any person of a check or other payment instrument postdated by more than five days unless such person is notified in writing of the debt collector's intent to deposit such check or instrument not more than ten nor less than three business days prior to such deposit.

(3) The solicitation by a debt collector of any postdated check or other postdated payment instrument for the purpose of threatening or instituting criminal prosecution.

(4) Depositing or threatening to deposit any postdated check or other postdated payment instrument prior to the date on such check or instrument.

(5) Causing charges to be made to any person for communications by concealment of the true propose of the communication. Such charges include, but are not limited to, collect telephone calls and telegram fees.

(6) Taking or threatening to take any non-judicial action to effect dispossession or disablement of property if --

(A) there is no present right to possession of the property claimed as collateral through an enforceable security interest;

(B) there is no present intention to take possession of the property; or

(C) the property is exempt by law from such dispossession or disablement.

(7) Communicating with a consumer regarding a debt by post card.

(8) Using any language or symbol, other than the debt collector's address, on any envelope when communicating with a consumer by use of the mails or by telegram, except that a debt collector may use his business name if such name does not indicate that he is in the debt collection business.

§ 809. Validation of debts [15 USC 1692g]

(a) Within five days after the initial communication with a consumer in connection with the collection of any debt, a debt collector shall, unless the following information is contained in the initial communication or the consumer has paid the debt, send the consumer a written notice containing --

(1) the amount of the debt;

(2) the name of the creditor to whom the debt is owed;

(3) a statement that unless the consumer, within thirty days after receipt of the notice, disputes the validity of the debt, or any portion thereof, the debt will be assumed to be valid by the debt collector;

(4) a statement that if the consumer notifies the debt collector in writing within the thirty-day period that the debt, or any portion thereof, is disputed, the debt collector will obtain verification of the debt or a copy of a judgment against the consumer and a copy of such verification or judgment will be mailed to the consumer by the debt collector; and

(5) a statement that, upon the consumer's written request within the thirty-day period, the debt collector will provide the consumer with the name and address of the original creditor, if different from the current creditor.

(b) If the consumer notifies the debt collector in writing within the thirty-day period described in subsection (a) that the debt, or any portion thereof, is disputed, or that the consumer requests the name and address of the original creditor, the debt collector shall cease collection of the debt, or any disputed portion thereof, until the debt collector obtains verification of the debt or any copy of a judgment, or the name and address of the original creditor, and a copy of such verification or judgment, or name and address of the original creditor, is mailed to the consumer by the debt collector.

(c) The failure of a consumer to dispute the validity of a debt under this section may not be construed by any court as an admission of liability by the consumer.

§ 810. Multiple debts [15 USC 1692h]

If any consumer owes multiple debts and makes any single payment to any debt collector with respect to such debts, such debt collector may not apply such payment to any debt which is disputed by the consumer and, where applicable, shall apply such payment in accordance with the consumer's directions.

§ 811. Legal actions by debt collectors [15 USC 1692i]

(a) Any debt collector who brings any legal action on a debt against any consumer shall --

(1) in the case of an action to enforce an interest in real property securing the consumer's obligation, bring such action only in a judicial district or similar legal entity in which such real property is located; or

(2) in the case of an action not described in paragraph (1), bring such action only in the judicial district or similar legal entity --

(A) in which such consumer signed the contract sued upon; or

(B) in which such consumer resides at the commencement of the action.

(b) Nothing in this title shall be construed to authorize the bringing of legal actions by debt collectors.

§ 812. Furnishing certain deceptive forms [15 USC 1692j]

(a) It is unlawful to design, compile, and furnish any form knowing that such form would be used to create the false belief in a consumer that a person other than the creditor of such consumer is participating in the collection of or in an attempt to collect a debt such consumer allegedly owes such creditor, when in fact such person is not so participating.

(b) Any person who violates this section shall be liable to the same extent and in the same manner as a debt collector is liable under section 813 for failure to comply with a provision of this title.

§ 813. Civil liability [15 USC 1692k]

(a) Except as otherwise provided by this section, any debt collector who fails to comply with any provision of this title with respect to any person is liable to such person in an amount equal to the sum of --

(1) any actual damage sustained by such person as a result of such failure;

(2) (A) in the case of any action by an individual, such additional damages as the court may allow, but not exceeding $1,000; or

(B) in the case of a class action, (i) such amount for each named plaintiff as could be recovered under subparagraph (A), and (ii) such amount as the court may allow for all other class members, without regard to a minimum individual recovery, not to exceed the lesser of $500,000 or 1 per centum of the net worth of the debt collector; and

(3) in the case of any successful action to enforce the foregoing liability, the costs of the action, together with a reasonable attorney's fee as determined by the court. On a finding by the court that an action under this section was brought in bad faith and for the purpose of harassment, the court may award to the defendant attorney's fees reasonable in relation to the work expended and costs.

(b) In determining the amount of liability in any action under subsection (a), the court shall consider, among other relevant factors --

(1) in any individual action under subsection (a)(2)(A), the frequency and persistence of noncompliance by the debt collector, the nature of such noncompliance, and the extent to which such noncompliance was intentional; or

(2) in any class action under subsection (a)(2)(B), the frequency and persistence of noncompliance by the debt collector, the nature of such noncompliance, the resources of the debt collector, the number of persons adversely affected, and the extent to which the debt collector's noncompliance was intentional.

(c) A debt collector may not be held liable in any action brought under this title if the debt collector shows by a preponderance of evidence that the violation was not intentional and resulted from a bona fide error notwithstanding the maintenance of procedures reasonably adapted to avoid any such error.

(d) An action to enforce any liability created by this title may be brought in any appropriate United States district court without regard to the amount in controversy, or in any other court of competent jurisdiction, within one year from the date on which the violation occurs.

(e) No provision of this section imposing any liability shall apply to any act done or omitted in good faith in conformity with any advisory opinion of the Commission, notwithstanding that after such act or omission has occurred, such opinion is amended, rescinded, or determined by judicial or other authority to be invalid for any reason.

§ 814. Administrative enforcement [15 USC 1692*l*]

(a) Compliance with this title shall be enforced by the Commission, except to the extend that enforcement of the requirements imposed under this title is specifically committed to another agency under subsection (b). For purpose of the exercise by the Commission of its functions and powers under the Federal Trade Commission Act, a violation of this title shall be deemed an unfair or deceptive act or practice in violation of that Act. All of the functions and powers of the Commission under the Federal Trade Commission Act are available to the Commission to enforce compliance by any person with this title, irrespective of whether that person is engaged in commerce or meets any other jurisdictional tests in the Federal Trade Commission Act, including the power to enforce the provisions of this title in the same manner as if the violation had been a violation of a Federal Trade Commission trade regulation rule.

(b) Compliance with any requirements imposed under this title shall be enforced under --

(1) section 8 of the Federal Deposit Insurance Act, in the case of --

(A) national banks, by the Comptroller of the Currency;

(B) member banks of the Federal Reserve System (other than national banks), by the Federal Reserve Board; and

(C) banks the deposits or accounts of which are insured by the Federal Deposit Insurance Corporation (other than members of the Federal Reserve System), by the Board of Directors of the Federal Deposit Insurance Corporation;

(2) section 5(d) of the Home Owners Loan Act of 1933, section 407 of the National Housing Act, and sections 6(i) and 17 of the Federal Home Loan Bank Act, by the Federal Home Loan Bank Board (acting directing or through the Federal Savings and Loan Insurance Corporation), in the case of any institution subject to any of those provisions;

(3) the Federal Credit Union Act, by the Administrator of the National Credit Union Administration with respect to any Federal credit union;

(4) subtitle IV of Title 49, by the Interstate Commerce Commission with respect to any common carrier subject to such subtitle;

(5) the Federal Aviation Act of 1958, by the Secretary of Transportation with respect to any air carrier or any foreign air carrier subject to that Act; and

(6) the Packers and Stockyards Act, 1921 (except as provided in section 406 of that Act), by the Secretary of Agriculture with respect to any activities subject to that Act.

(c) For the purpose of the exercise by any agency referred to in subsection (b) of its powers under any Act referred to in that subsection, a violation of any requirement imposed under this title shall be deemed to be a violation of a requirement imposed under that Act. In addition to its powers under any provision of law specifically referred to in subsection (b), each of the agencies referred to in that subsection may exercise, for the purpose of enforcing compliance with any requirement imposed under this title any other authority conferred on it by law, except as provided in subsection (d).

(d) Neither the Commission nor any other agency referred to in subsection (b) may promulgate trade regulation rules or other regulations with respect to the collection of debts by debt collectors as defined in this title.

§ 815. Reports to Congress by the Commission [15 USC 1692m]

(a) Not later than one year after the effective date of this title and at one-year intervals thereafter, the Commission shall make reports to the Congress concerning the administration of its functions under this title, including such recommendations as the Commission deems necessary or appropriate. In addition, each report of the Commission shall include its assessment of the extent to which compliance with this title is being achieved and a summary of the enforcement actions taken by the Commission under section 814 of this title.

(b) In the exercise of its functions under this title, the Commission may obtain upon request the views of any other Federal agency which exercises enforcement functions under section 814 of this title.

§ 816. Relation to State laws [15 USC 1692n]

This title does not annul, alter, or affect, or exempt any person subject to the provisions of this title from complying with the laws of any State with respect to debt collection practices, except to the extent that those laws are inconsistent with any provision of this title, and then only to the extent of the inconsistency. For purposes of this section, a State law is not inconsistent with this title if the protection such law affords any consumer is greater than the protection provided by this title.

§ 817. Exemption for State regulation [15 USC 1692o]

The Commission shall by regulation exempt from the requirements of this title any class of debt collection practices within any State if the Commission determines that under the law of that State that class of debt collection practices is subject to requirements substantially similar to those imposed by this title, and that there is adequate provision for enforcement.

§ 818. Effective date [15 USC 1692 note]

This title takes effect upon the expiration of six months after the date of its enactment, but section 809 shall apply only with respect to debts for which the initial attempt to collect occurs after such effective date.

Approved September 20, 1977

ENDNOTES

1. So in original; however, should read "604(a)(3)."

LEGISLATIVE HISTORY:

Public Law 95-109 [H.R. 5294]

HOUSE REPORT No. 95-131 (Comm. on Banking, Finance, and Urban Affairs).

SENATE REPORT No. 95-382 (Comm. on Banking, Housing, and Urban Affairs).

CONGRESSIONAL RECORD, Vol. 123 (1977):

Apr. 4, considered and passed House.

Aug. 5, considered and passed Senate, amended.

Sept. 8, House agreed to Senate amendment.

WEEKLY COMPILATION OF PRESIDENTIAL DOCUMENTS, Vol. 13, No. 39:

Sept. 20, Presidential statement.

AMENDMENTS:

SECTION 621, SUBSECTIONS (b)(3), (b)(4) and (b)(5) were amended to transfer certain administrative enforcement responsibilities, pursuant to Pub. L. 95-473, § 3(b), Oct. 17, 1978. 92 Stat. 166; Pub. L. 95-630, Title V. § 501, November 10, 1978, 92 Stat. 3680; Pub. L. 98-443, § 9(h), Oct. 4, 1984, 98 Stat. 708.

SECTION 803, SUBSECTION (6), defining "debt collector," was amended to repeal the attorney at law exemption at former Section (6)(F) and to re-designate Section 803(6)(G) pursuant to Pub. L. 99-361, July 9, 1986, 100 Stat. 768. For legislative history, *see* H.R. 237, HOUSE REPORT No. 99-405 (Comm. on Banking, Finance and Urban Affairs). CONGRESSIONAL RECORD: Vol. 131 (1985): Dec. 2, considered and passed House. Vol. 132 (1986): June 26, considered and passed Senate.

SECTION 807, SUBSECTION (11), was amended to affect when debt collectors must state (a) that they are attempting to collect a debt and (b) that information obtained will be used for that purpose, pursuant to Pub. L. 104-208 § 2305, 110 Stat. 3009 (Sept. 30, 1996).

Chapter 16

EQUAL CREDIT OPPORTUNITY ACT

6500 - FDIC Consumer Protection

TITLE VII—EQUAL CREDIT OPPORTUNITY
Sec.

§ 701. Prohibited discrimination; reasons for adverse action
(a) It shall be unlawful for any creditor to discriminate against any applicant, with respect to any aspect of a credit transaction--   (1) on the basis of race, color, religion, national origin, sex or marital status, or age (provided the applicant has the capacity to contract);   (2) because all or part of the applicant's income derives from any public assistance program; or   (3) because the applicant has in good faith exercised any right under the Consumer Credit Protection Act.   (b) It shall not constitute discrimination for purposes of this title for a creditor--   (1) to make an inquiry of marital status if such inquiry is for the purpose of ascertaining the creditor's rights and remedies applicable to the particular extension of credit and not to discriminate in a determination of credit-worthiness;   (2) to make an inquiry of the applicant's age or of whether the applicant's income derives from any public assistance program if such inquiry is for the purpose of determining the amount and probable continuance of income levels, credit history, or other pertinent element of credit-worthiness as provided   in   regulations   of   the   Board;   {{4-30-04   p.6610.49}}
(3) to use any empirically derived credit system which considers age if such system is demonstrably and statistically sound in accordance with regulations of the Board, except that in the operation of such system the age of an elderly applicant may not be assigned a negative factor or value; or   (4) to make an inquiry or to consider the age of an elderly applicant when the age of such applicant is to be used by the creditor in the extension of credit in favor of such applicant.   (c) It is not a violation of this section for a creditor to refuse to extend credit offered pursuant to--   (1) any credit assistance program expressly authorized by law for an economically disadvantaged class of persons;   (2) any credit assistance program administered by a nonprofit organization for its members or an economically disadvantaged class of persons; or   (3) any special purpose credit program offered by a profit-making organization to meet special social needs which meets standards prescribed in regulations by the Board;   if such refusal is required by or made pursuant to such program.
(d)(1) Within thirty days (or such longer reasonable time as specified in regulations of the Board for any class of credit transaction) after receipt of a completed application for credit, a creditor shall notify the applicant of its action on the application.   (2) Each applicant against whom adverse action is taken shall be entitled to a statement of reasons for such action from the creditor. A creditor satisfies this obligation by--   {{2-28-92 p.6611}}   (A) providing statements of reasons in writing as a matter of course to applicants against whom adverse action is taken; or   (B) giving written notification of adverse action which discloses (i) the applicant's right to a statement of reasons within thirty days after receipt by the creditor of a request made within sixty days after such notification, and (ii) the identity of the persons or office from which such statement may be obtained. Such statement may be given orally if the written notification advises the applicant of his right to have the statement of reasons confirmed in writing on written request.   (3) A statement of reasons meets the requirements of this section only if it contains the specific reasons for the adverse action taken.
(4) Where a creditor has been requested by a third party to make a specific extension of credit directly or indirectly to an applicant, the notification and statement of reasons required by this subsection may be made directly by such creditor, or indirectly through the third party, provided in either case that the identity of the creditor is disclosed.   (5) The requirements of paragraph (2), (3), or (4) may be satisfied by verbal statements

or notifications in the case of any creditor who did not act on more than one hundred and fifty applications during the calendar year preceding the calendar year in which the adverse action is taken, as determined under regulations of the Board.   (6) For purposes of this subsection, the term "adverse action" means a denial or revocation of credit, a change in the terms of an existing credit arrangement, or a refusal to grant credit in substantially the amount or on substantially the terms requested. Such term does not include a refusal to extend additional credit under an existing credit arrangement where the applicant is delinquent or otherwise in default, or where such additional credit would exceed a previously established credit limit.   (e) Each creditor shall promptly furnish an applicant, upon written request by the applicant made within a reasonable period of time of the application, a copy of the appraisal report used in connection with the applicant's application for a loan that is or would have been secured by a lien on residential real property. The creditor may require the applicant to reimburse the creditor for the cost of the appraisal.

[Codified to 15 U.S.C. 1691] [Source: Section 701 of title VII of the Act of May 29, 1968 (Pub. L. No. 90--321), as added by section 503 of title V of the Act of October 28, 1974 (Pub. L. No. 93--495; 88 Stat. 1521), effective October 28, 1975, as amended by section 2 of the Act of March 23, 1976 (Pub. L. No. 94--239; 90 Stat. 251), effective March 23, 1977; section 223(d) of title II of the Act of December 19, 1991 (Pub. L. No. 102--242; 105 Stat. 2306), effective December 19, 1991]
NOTES

Findings and purpose. Section 502 of title V of the Act of October 28, 1974 provides as follows: **§ 502. Findings and purpose**   The Congress finds that there is a need to insure that the various financial institutions and other firms engaged in the extensions of credit exercise their responsibility to make credit available with fairness, impartiality, and without discrimination on the basis of sex or marital status. Economic stabilization would be enhanced and competition among the various financial institutions and other firms engaged in the extension of credit would be strengthened by an absence of discrimination on the basis of sex or marital status, as well as by the informed use of credit which Congress has heretofore sought to promote. It is the purpose of this [Equal Credit Opportunity] Act to require that financial institutions and other firms engaged in the extension of credit make that credit equally available to all creditworthy customers without regard to sex or marital status. {{2-28-92 p.6612}}

§ 702. Definitions
(a) The definitions and rules of construction set forth in this section are applicable for the purposes of this title.   (b) The term "applicant" means any person who applies to a creditor directly for an extension, renewal, or continuation of credit, or applies to a creditor indirectly by use of an existing credit plan for an amount exceeding a previously established credit limit.   (c) The term "Board" refers to the Board of Governors of the Federal Reserve System.   (d) The term "credit" means the right granted by a creditor to a debtor to defer payment of debt or to incur debts and defer its payment or to purchase property or services and defer payment therefore. (e) The term "creditor" means any person who regularly extends, renews, or continues credit; any person who regularly arranges for the extension, renewal, or continuation of credit; or any assignee of an original creditor who participates in the decision to extend, renew, or continue credit.   (f) The term "person" means a natural person, a corporation, government or governmental subdivision or agency, trust, estate, partnership, cooperative, or association.   (g) Any reference to any requirement imposed under this title or any provision thereof includes reference to the regulations of the Board under this title or the provision thereof in question.

[Codified to 15 U.S.C. 1691a] [Source: Section 702 of title VII of the Act of May 29, 1968 (Pub. L. No. 90--321), as added by section 503 of title V of the Act of October 28, 1974 (Pub. L. No. 93--495; 88 Stat. 1522), effective October 28, 1975]

§ 703. Regulations

(a)(1) The Board shall prescribe regulations to carry out the purposes of this title. These regulations may contain but are not limited to such classifications, differentiation, or other provision, and may provide for such adjustments and exceptions for any class of transactions, as in the judgment of the Board are necessary or proper to effectuate the purposes of this title, to prevent circumvention or evasion thereof, or to facilitate or substantiate compliance therewith.   (2) Such regulations may exempt from the provisions of this title any class of transactions that are not primarily for personal, family, or household purposes, or business or commercial loans made available by a financial institution, except that a particular type within a class of such transactions may be exempted if the Board determines, after making an express finding that the application of this title or of any provision of this title of such transaction would not contribute substantially to effecting the purposes of this title.   (3) An exemption granted pursuant to paragraph (2) shall be for no longer than five years and shall be extended only if the Board makes a subsequent determination, in the manner described by such paragraph, that such exemption remains appropriate.   (4) Pursuant to Board regulations, entities making business or commercial loans shall maintain such records or other data relating to such loans as may be necessary to evidence compliance with this subsection or enforce any action pursuant to the authority of this Act. In no event shall such records or data be maintained for a period of less than one year. The Board shall promulgate regulations to implement this paragraph in the manner prescribed by chapter 5 of title 5, United States Code.   (5) The Board shall provide in regulations that an applicant for a business or commercial loan shall be provided a written notice of such applicant's right to receive a written statement of the reasons for the denial of such loan.

[Codified to 15 U.S.C. 1691b] [Source: Section 703 of title VII of the Act of May 29, 1968 (Pub. L. No. 90--321), as added by section 503 of title V of the Act of October 28, 1974 (Pub. L. No. 93--495; 88 Stat. 1522), effective October 28, 1975, as amended by section 3 of the Act of March 23, 1976 (Pub. L. {{4-30-97 p.6613}}No. 94--239; 90 Stat. 252), effective March 23, 1976; section 301 of title III of the Act of October 25, 1988 (Pub. L. No. 100--533; 102 Stat. 2692), effective October 25, 1988]

§ 704. Administrative enforcement   (a) Compliance with the requirements imposed under this title shall be enforced under: (1) section 8 of the Federal Deposit Insurance Act, in the case of--   (A) national banks, and Federal branches and Federal agencies of foreign banks, by the Office of the Comptroller of the Currency;
   (B) member banks of the Federal Reserve System (other than national banks), branches and agencies of foreign banks (other than Federal branches, Federal agencies, and insured State branches of foreign banks), commercial lending companies owned or controlled by foreign banks, and organizations operating under section 25 or 25(a) of the Federal Reserve Act, by the Board of Governors of the Federal Reserve System; and
   (C) banks insured by the Federal Deposit Insurance Corporation (other than members of the Federal Reserve System) and insured State branches of foreign banks, by the Board of Directors of the Federal Deposit Insurance Corporation;   (2) Section 8 of the Federal Deposit Insurance Act, by the Director of the Office of Thrift Supervision, in the case of a savings association the deposits of which are insured by the Federal Deposit Insurance Corporation.   (3) The Federal Credit Union Act, by the Administrator of the National Credit Union Administration with respect to any Federal Credit Union.   (4) The Acts to regulate commerce, by the Secretary of Transportation, with respect to all carriers subject to the jurisdiction of the Surface Transportation Board.   (5) The Federal Aviation Act of 1958, by the Civil Aeronautics Board with respect to any carrier or foreign air carrier subject to that Act.   (6) The Packers and Stockyards Act, 1921 (except as provided in section 406 of that Act), by the Secretary of Agriculture with respect to any activities subject to that Act.
   (7) The Farm Credit Act of 1971, by the Farm Credit Administration with respect to any Federal land bank, Federal land bank association, Federal intermediate credit bank, and production credit association;   (8) The Securities Exchange Act of 1934, by the Securities and Exchange Commission with respect to brokers and dealers; and   (9) The Small Business Investment Act of 1958, by the Small Business Administration, with respect to small business investment companies.   The terms used in paragraph (1) that are not defined in this title or otherwise defined in section 3(s) of the Federal Deposit Insurance Act (12 U.S.C. 1813(s)) shall have the meaning given to them in section 1(b) of the International Banking Act of 1978 (12 U.S.C. 3101).   (b) For the purpose of the exercise by any agency referred to in subsection (a) of its powers under any Act referred to in that subsection, a violation of any requirement imposed under this title shall be deemed to be a violation of a requirement imposed under that Act. In addition to its powers under any provision of law specifically referred to in subsection (a), each of the agencies referred to in that subsection may exercise for the purpose of enforcing compliance with any requirement imposed under this title, any other authority conferred on it by law. The exercise of the authorities of any of the agencies referred to in subsection (a) for the purpose of enforcing compliance with any requirement imposed under this title shall in no way preclude the exercise of such authorities for the purpose of enforcing compliance with any other provision of law not relating to the prohibition of discrimination on the basis of sex or marital status with respect to any aspect of a credit transaction.   (c) Except to the extent that enforcement of the requirements imposed under this title is specifically committed to some other Government agency under subsection (a), the Federal Trade Commission shall enforce such requirements. For the purpose of the exercise by the Federal Trade Commission of its functions and powers under the Federal Trade Commission Act, a violation of any requirement imposed under this title shall be {{4-30-97 p.6614}}deemed a violation of a requirement imposed under that Act. All of the functions and powers of the Federal Trade Commission under the Federal Trade Commission Act are available to the Commission to enforce compliance by any person with the requirements imposed under this title, irrespective of whether that person is engaged in commerce or meets any other jurisdictional tests in the Federal Trade Commission Act, including the power to enforce any Federal Reserve Board regulation promulgated under this title in the same manner as if the violation had been a violation of a Federal Trade Commission trade regulation rule.   (d) The authority of the Board to issue regulations under this title does not impair the

authority of any other agency designated in this section to make rules respecting its own procedures in enforcing compliance with requirements imposed under this title.

[Codified to 15 U.S.C. 1691c] [Source: Section 704 of title VII of the Act of May 29, 1968 (Pub. L. No. 90--321), as added by section 503 of title V of the Act of October 28, 1974 (Pub. L. No. 93--495; 88 Stat. 1522), effective October 28, 1975, and as amended by section 4 of the Act of March 23, 1976 (Pub. L. No. 94--239; 90 Stat. 253), effective March 23, 1976; section 744(m) of title VII of the Act of August 9, 1989 (Pub. L. No. 101--73; 103 Stat. 439), effective August 9, 1989; section 212(d) of title II of the Act of December 19, 1991 (Pub. L. No. 102--242; 105 Stat. 2301), effective December 19, 1991; section 1604(a)(8) of title XVI of the Act of October 28, 1992 (Pub. L. No. 102--550, 106 Stat. 4082), effective December 19, 1991; section 315 of title III of the Act of December 29, 1995 (Pub. L. No. 104--88; 109 Stat. 948), effective December 29, 1995]

§ 704A. Incentives for self-testing and self-correction. (a) PRIVILEGED INFORMATION.-- (1) CONDITIONS FOR PRIVILEGE.--A report or result of a self-test (as that term is defined by regulations of the Board) shall be considered to be privileged under paragraph (2) if a creditor-- (A) conducts, or authorizes an independent third party to conduct, a self-test of any aspect of a credit transaction by a creditor, in order to determine the level or effectiveness of compliance with this title by the creditor; and (B) has identified any possible violation of this title by the creditor and has taken, or is taking, appropriate corrective action to address any such possible violation. (2) PRIVILEGED SELF-TEST.--If a creditor meets the conditions specified in subparagraphs (A) and (B) of paragraph (1) with respect to a self-test described in that paragraph, any report or results of that self-test-- (A) shall be privileged; and (B) may not be obtained or used by any applicant, department, or agency in any-- (i) proceeding or civil action in which one or more violations of this title are alleged; or (ii) examination or investigation relating to compliance with this title. (b) RESULTS OF SELF-TESTING.-- (1) IN GENERAL.--No provision of this section may be construed to prevent an applicant, department, or agency from obtaining or using a report or results of any self-test in any proceeding or civil action in which a violation of this title is alleged, in any examination or investigation of compliance with this title if-- (A) the creditor or any person with lawful access to the report or results-- (i) voluntarily releases or discloses all, or any part of, the report or results to the applicant, department, or agency, or to the general public; or (ii) refers to or describes the report or results as a defense to charges of violations of this title against the creditor to whom the self-test relates; or (B) the report or results are sought in conjunction with an adjudication or admission of a violation of this title for the sole purpose of determining an appropriate penalty or remedy. {{4-30-97 p.6614.01}} (2) Disclosure for determination of penalty or remedy.--Any report or results of a self-test that are disclosed for the purpose specified in paragraph (1)(B)-- (A) shall be used only for the particular proceeding in which the adjudication or admission referred to in paragraph (1)(B) is made; and (B) may not be used in any other action or proceeding. (c) ADJUDICATION.--An applicant, department, or agency that challenges a privilege asserted under this section may seek a determination of the existence and application of that privilege in-- (1) a court of competent jurisdiction; or (2) an administrative law proceeding with appropriate jurisdiction.

[Codified to 15 U.S.C. 1691c-1] [Section 704 of title VII of the Act of May 29, 1968 (Pub. L. No. 90-321), as added by section 2302 of title II of the Act of September 30, 1996 (Pub. L. No. 104-208; 110 Stat. 3009-420), effective September 30, 1996]

§ 705. Relation to State laws
(a) A request for the signature of both parties to a marriage for the purpose of creating a valid ien, passing clear title, waiving inchoate rights to property, or assigning earnings, shall not constitute discrimination under this title: *Provided, however,* That this provision shall not be construed to permit a creditor to take sex or marital status into account in connection with the evaluation of creditworthiness of any applicant. (b) Consideration or application of State property laws directly or indirectly affecting creditworthiness shall not constitute discrimination for purposes of this title. (c) Any provision of State law which prohibits the separate extension of consumer credit to each party to a marriage shall not apply in any case where each party to a marriage voluntarily applies for separate credit from the same creditor: *Provided,* That in any case where such a State law is so preempted, each party to the marriage shall be solely responsible for the debt so contracted. (d) When each party to a marriage separately and voluntarily applies for and obtains separate credit accounts with the same creditor, those accounts shall not be aggregated or otherwise combined for purposes of determining permissible finance charges or permissible loan ceilings under the laws of any State or of the United States. (e) Where the same act or omission constitutes a violation of this title and of applicable State law, a person aggrieved by such conduct may bring a legal action to recover monetary damages either under this title or under such State law, but not both. This election of remedies shall not apply to court actions in which the relief sought does not include monetary damages or to administrative actions. (f) This title does not annul, alter, or

affect, or exempt any person subject to the provisions of this title from complying with, the laws of any State with respect to credit discrimination, except to the extent that those laws are inconsistent with any provision of this title, and then only to the extent of the inconsistency. The Board is authorized to determine whether such inconsistencies exist. The Board may not determine that any State law is inconsistent with any provision of this title if the Board determines that such law gives greater protection to the applicant. (g) The Board shall by regulation exempt from the requirements of sections 701 and 702 of this title any class of credit transactions within any State if it determines that under the law of that State that class of transactions is subject to requirements substantially similar to those imposed under this title or that such law gives greater protection to the applicant, and that there is adequate provision for enforcement. Failure to comply with any {{2-28-92 p.6615}} requirement of such State law in any transaction so exempted shall constitute a violation of this title for the purposes of section 706. *[Codified to 15 U.S.C. 1691d] [Source: Section 705 of title VII of the Act of May 29, 1968 (Pub. L. No. 90--321), as added by section 503 of title V of the Act of October 28, 1974 (Pub. L. No. 93--495; 88 Stat. 1523), effective October 28, 1975, and as amended by section 5 of the Act of March 23, 1976 (Pub. L. No. 94--239; 90 Stat. 253), effective March 23, 1976]*

§ **706. Civil liability** (a) Any creditor who fails to comply with any requirement imposed under this title shall be liable to the aggrieved applicant for any actual damages sustained by such applicant acting either in an individual capacity or as a member of a class. (b) Any creditor, other than a government or governmental subdivision or agency, who fails to comply with any requirement imposed under this title shall be liable to the aggrieved applicant for punitive damages in an amount not greater than $10,000, in addition to any actual damages provided in subsection (a), except that in the case of a class action the total recovery under this subsection shall not exceed the lesser of $500,000 or 1 per centum of the net worth of the creditor. In determining the amount of such damages in any action, the court shall consider, among other relevant factors, the amount of any actual damages awarded, the frequency and persistence of failures of compliance by the creditor, the resources of the creditor, the number of persons adversely affected, and the extent to which the creditor's failure of compliance was intentional. (c) Upon application by an aggrieved applicant, the appropriate United States district court or any other court of competent jurisdiction may grant such equitable and declaratory relief as is necessary to enforce the requirements imposed under this title. (d) In the case of any successful action under subsection (a), (b), or (c), the costs of the action, together with a reasonable attorney's fee as determined by the court, shall be added to any damages awarded by the court under such subsection. (e) No provision of this title imposing liability shall apply to any act done or omitted in good faith in conformity with any official rule, regulation, or interpretation thereof by the Board or in conformity with any interpretation or approval by an official or employee of the Federal Reserve System duly authorized by the Board to issue such interpretations or approvals under such procedures as the Board may prescribe therefore, notwithstanding that after such act or omission has occurred, such rule, regulation, interpretation, or approval is amended, rescinded, or determined by judicial or other authority to be invalid for any reason. (f) Any action under this section may be brought in the appropriate United States district court without regard to the amount in controversy, or in any other court of competent jurisdiction. No such action shall be brought later than two years from the date of the occurrence of the violation, except that-- (1) whenever any agency having responsibility for administrative enforcement under section 704 commences an enforcement proceeding within two years from the date of the occurrence of the violation, (2) whenever the Attorney General commences a civil action under this section within two years from the date of the occurrence of the violation, then any applicant who has been a victim of the discrimination which is the subject of such proceeding or civil action may bring an action under this section not later than one year after the commencement of that proceeding or action. (g) The agencies having responsibility for administrative enforcement under section 704, if unable to obtain compliance with section 701, are authorized to refer the matter to the Attorney General with a recommendation that an appropriate civil action be instituted. Each agency referred to in paragraphs (1), (2), and (3) of section 704(a) shall refer the matter to the Attorney General whenever the agency has reason to believe that 1 or more creditors has engaged in a pattern or practice of discouraging or denying applications for {{2-28-92 p.6616}}credit in violation of section 701(a). Each such agency may refer the matter to the Attorney General whenever the agency has reason to believe that 1 or more creditors has violated section 701(a). (h) When a matter is referred to the Attorney General pursuant to subsection (g), or whenever he has reason to believe that one or more creditors are engaged in a pattern or practice in violation of this title, the Attorney General may bring a civil action in any appropriate United States district court for such relief as may be appropriate, including actual and punitive damages and injunctive relief. (i) No person aggrieved by a violation of this title and by a violation of section 805 of the Civil Rights Act of 1968 shall recover under this title and section 812 of the Civil Rights Act of 1968, if such violation is based on the same transaction. (j) Nothing in this title shall be construed to prohibit the discovery of a creditor's credit granting standards under appropriate discovery procedures in the court or agency in which an action or proceeding is brought. (k) NOTICE TO HUD OF

VIOLATIONS.--Whenever an agency referred to in paragraph (1), (2), or (3) of section 704(a)-- (1) has reason to believe, as a result of receiving a consumer complaint, conducting a consumer compliance examination, or otherwise, that a violation of this title has occurred; (2) has reason to believe that the alleged violation would be a violation of the Fair Housing Act; and (3) does not refer the matter to the Attorney General pursuant to subsection (g), the agency shall notify the Secretary of Housing and Urban Development of the violation, and shall notify the applicant that the Secretary of Housing and Urban Development has been notified of the alleged violation and that remedies for the violation may be available under the Fair Housing Act.

[Codified to 15 U.S.C. 1691e] [Source: Section 706 of title VII of the Act of May 29, 1968 (Pub. L. No. 90--321), as added by section 503 of title V of the Act of October 28, 1974 (Pub. L. No. 93--495; 88 Stat. 1524), effective October 28, 1975, and as amended by section 6 of the Act of March 23, 1976 (Pub. L. No. 94--239; 90 Stat. 253), effective March 23, 1976; sections 223(a)--(c) of title II of the Act of December 19, 1991 (Pub. L. No. 102--242; 105 Stat. 2306), effective December 19, 1991]

§ 707. Annual reports to Congress Each year, the Board and the Attorney General shall, respectively, make reports to the Congress concerning the administration of their functions under this title, including such recommendations as the Board and the Attorney General, respectively, deem necessary or appropriate. In addition, each report of the Board shall include its assessment of the extent to which compliance with the requirements of this title is being achieved, and a summary of the enforcement actions taken by each of the agencies assigned administrative enforcement responsibilities under section 704.

[Codified to 15 U.S.C. 1691f] [Source: Section 707 of title VII of the Act of May 29, 1968 (Pub. L. No. 90--321), as added by section 7 of the Act of March 23, 1976 (Pub. L. No. 94--239; 90 Stat. 255), effective March 23, 1976; as amended by section 610 of title VI of the Act of March 31, 1980 (Pub. L. No. 96--221; 94 Stat. 174), effective April 1, 1982

§ 708. Effective date
This title takes effect upon the expiration of one year after the date of its enactment. The amendments made by the Equal Credit Opportunity Act Amendments of 1976 shall take effect on the date of enactment thereof and shall apply to any violation occurring on or after such date, except that the amendments made to section 701 of the Equal Credit Opportunity Act shall take effect 12 months after the date of enactment. {{2-28-92 p.6616.01}} *[Codified to 15 U.S.C. 1691 note]*

[Source: Section 708 (formerly 707) of title VII of the Act of May 29, 1968 (Pub. L. No. 90--321), as added by section 503 of title V of the Act of October 28, 1974 (Pub. L. No. 93--495; 88 Stat. 1525), effective October 28, 1975, as re-designated by section 7, and as amended by section 8, of the Act of March 23, 1976 (Pub. L. No. 94--239; 90 Stat. 255), effective March 23, 1976]

§ 709. Short title This title may be cited as the "Equal Credit Opportunity Act." [Codified to 15 U.S.C. 1691 note] [Source: Section 709 of title VII of the Act of May 29, 1968 (Pub. L. No. 90--321), as added by section 1(b) of the Act of March 23, 1976 (Pub. L. No. 94--239; 90 Stat. 251), effective March 23, 1976]

Chapter 17

GLOSSARY

Acknowledgement: A formal declaration before a public official that one has signed a specific document.

Adjustable rate loan: Adjustable rate mortgage, ARM; a loan that allows adjustments in the interest rate at specified times based on a named index.

Adjusted basis: The original cost plus capital improvements minus depreciation. Use adjusted basis to compute taxable gain or loss on the sale of a home.

Agent: A person authorized by another, the principle, to act for him or her in dealing with third parties.

Annual percentage rate: APR; an interest rate that includes interest, discount points, origination fees, and loan broker's commission.

Appraisal: An examination of a property by a qualified professional to estimate the property's market value as of a specific date.

APR: *See* Annual Percentage Rate.

Arbitration: Taking of a controversy to an unbiased third person. This person holds a hearing wt which both parties may speak and then issues an opinion.

Assessment: Tax or charge by governmental body for a specific public improvement covering the property owner's portion of costs. Assessments are in addition to normal property taxes.

Assign: Transfer.

Assignee: The person to whom interest is transferred.

Assignment: The transfer of any property from one party to another. It can also be the delegation of duties and rights from one party to another.

Assignor: The person from whom interest is transferred.

Assume: Buyers taking over primary responsibility for payment of existing loan. Sellers then become secondarily liable for the loan and for any deficiency judgment.

Assumption fee: Transfer fee; the fee a lender may charge for work involved in allowing buyers to assume primary liability for payment on an existing loan.

Attorney: A person licensed to practice law by giving legal advice or assistance, as well as prosecuting and defending cases in courts.

Authorization to sell: a listing contract allowing a real estate professional to act as an agent in the sale of property.

Bankruptcy: Relief by a court of an obligation to pay money owed after turning over all property to a court-appointed trustee.

Basis: The cost of a home when purchased, including down payment, loans, and closing costs.

Beneficiary: The lender of money on a property used in a trust deed type of loan.

Bid Down: This is where you "Bid Down" the interest rate to the amount of interest you are willing to accept. (Example: if the interest starts at 18% and you "bid it down" to 14% to secure the Tax Lien Certificate, you will receive 14% and the county will receive the balance of the 18%, which is 4%).

Binder: An informal contract listing an agreement's main points, later replaced by a formal, detailed written contract.

Broker: *See* Real estate broker.

Buyer's fees: Chargers that are paid for the buyers.

Buyer's market: A condition in which there are more sellers than buyers; prices generally decrease.

Call: Demand payment on debt.

Capital asset: Property, both real and personal, held by a taxpayer and not excluded by tax laws.

Capital gain: Profit from selling or exchanging a capital asset in excess of the cost.

Capital improvements: Additions to property that are permanent, increase property value, and have a useful life of more than one year.

Capitalization rate: The rate of return an investment receives.

Capital loss: Loss from selling or exchanging property other than a personal residence at less than its cost.

Cashier's check: A bank's own check guaranteed to be good by the bank at which it is drawn.

Casualty: Loss of or damage to structures or personal property.

Casualty insurance: *See* Hazard insurance.

Certificate of title: A report, produced by a party providing abstracts of titles, stating that based on an examination of public records, the title is properly vested in the present owner.

Classified advertisements: Advertisements that are separated by type and listed accordingly.

Closing: Closing escrow, settlement; the final phase of a real estate transaction that involves signing loan documents, paying closing costs, and delivering the deed. (*See* also Escrow).

Closing costs: Costs of sale; the additional expenses over and above the purchase price of buying and selling real estate.

Closing escrow: *See* Closing.

Closing fee: *See* Closing.

Due-on-sale clause: Alienation clause; an acceleration clause in a loan giving the lender the right to demand all sums owed due at once and payable if the property owner transfers title.

Equity: The part of a property's current value that is owned and on which no money is owed; the property's value minus the liens owed against the property.

Escrow: A process in the transfer of real property in which buyers and sellers deposit documents or money with a neutral third party (the escrow holder). Buyers and sellers give instructions to the escrow holder to hold and deliver documents and money if certain conditions are met.

Escrow instructions: A written agreement between the seller and buyer that extrapolates the purchase contract into a form that is to be used as directed on how to conduct and close the escrow.

Fire insurance: See Hazard insurance.

Foreclosure: The process by which a property on which a borrower has not paid is sold to satisfy a loan against the property.

Fraud: Willfully concealing or misrepresenting a material fact in order to influence another person to take action. The action results in the person's loss of property or legal rights.

Gift deed: A deed given for love or affection.

Guarantee of title: A warranty that title is vested in the party shown on the deed.

Hazard insurance: Casualty insurance, fire insurance; insurance protection against stated specific hazards such as fire, hail windstorms, earthquakes, floods, civil disturbances, explosions, riots, theft, and vandalism.

Homeowner's insurance: A policy protecting a homeowner from liability and casualty hazards listed in the policy. (See also Hazard insurance).

Market value: The amount buyers are willing to pay and sellers are willing to accept within a reasonable time.

Marshal's deed: *See* Sheriff's deed.

Mortgage: A contract to secure a loan by which you promise your property without giving up possession or title.

Mortgagee: Lender of money on property using a mortgage.

Mortgagor: Property owner who borrows money using a mortgage.

Notary fee: A charge paid to a notary public to witness signatures on some of the legal documents in a transaction.

Notice of default: Warning sent to a borrower on a loan cautioning the borrower that the payment is delinquent.

Personal property: Items that are not permanently attached to your home or other structures on your property.

Power of attorney: A document that gives one person the power to sign documents for another person.

Power of sale clause: A provision in a loan allowing the lender to foreclose and sell borrower's property publicly without a court procedure.

Premium Bid: This is where you Bid above the interest rate charged. In most but not all cases, you will only receive the interest on the Tax Lien. The balance is an interest free loan to the county. When the Tax Lien is redeemed you will receive the interest free loan amount plus the Tax Lien cost and interest.

Principle residence: An IRS term denoting the residence wherein you spend the most time during the tax year.

Promissory note: The written contract you sign promising to pay a definite amount of money by a definite future date.

Property Interest Bid: This is the same as a *Straight Bid*; where you receive the interest rate in full and are bidding on the amount of the Tax Lien Certificate only. The winner is the investor who will accept the lowest amount of personal interest in the property.

Property taxes: Taxes; taxes assessed on a property at a uniform rate so that eh amount of the tax depends on the value.

Property tax statements: Documents that the county assessor's office mails to homeowners itemizing the semiannual or annual tax bill on a home and indicating the payment due date.

Quitclaim deed: A deed using the word quitclaim in the clause granting ownership and thus releasing the grantor from any claim to the property. A quitclaim deed has no warranties.

Real estate: *See* Real property.

Real estate broker: A real estate agent who represents another person in dealing with third parties. This person must take required courses, pass a broker's exam, and be state licensed. A broker may employ other qualified individuals and is responsible for their actions.

Real estate professional: A real estate broker or sales associate.

Real estate sales agent: A person who is licensed by state and who represents a real estate broker in transactions.

Real property: Real estate; land and whatever is built on, growing on, or attached to the land.

Sheriff's deed: Marshal's deed; a deed used by courts in foreclosure or in carrying out a judgment. This deed transfers a debtor's title to a buyer.

Straight Bids: This is where you receive the interest rate in full. You are bidding on the amount of the Tax Lien Certificate only.

Sub escrow fee: A fee charged by some escrow holders for their costs when they handle money.

Survey fee: A fee charged for a survey showing the exact locations and boundaries of a property.

Tax deed: Controller's deed; a deed used by a state to transfer title to the buyers.

Taxes: *See* Property taxes.

Tax parcel number: The number assigned to a piece of property by the local taxing authority.

Title:_ Evidence of one's right to a property and the extent of that right.

Title insurance: The policy issued to you by the title company on completion of the final title search protecting against claims in the future based on circumstances in the past.

Title Insurance Companies: These are companies issuing title insurance policies.

Title search: An examination of information recorded on your property at the county recorder's office. This examination verifies that the property has no outstanding claims or liens against it to adversely affect the buyer or lender and that you can transfer clear legal title to the property.

Transfer fee: *See* Assumption fee.

Transfer tax: Documentary transfer tax; a tax that some states allow individual counties or cities to place on the transferring of the real property.

Trust deed: A document, used as a security device for the loan on your property, by which you transfer bare (naked) legal title with the power of sale to a trustee. This transfer is in effect until you have totally paid off the loan.

Trust funds: Funds held by a closing agent or escrow holder for the benefit of the buyers or seller.

Unconditional lien release: Waiver of liens; a release, usually signed by a contractor, after a job is complete and you made the final payments waiving and releasing all rights and claims against your home.

Void: To have no effect; unenforceable at law.

Waive: Unilateral voluntary relinquish of a right of which one is aware.

Warranties: Printed or written documents guaranteeing the condition of property or its components.

Warranty deed: A deed in which the grantor explicitly guarantees the title to be as indicated in the deed. The grantor agrees to protect buyers against all claimants to the property.

Yield: The return on investment including interest and principal expressed annually.

Zoning: Governmental laws establishing building codes and governing the specific uses of land and building.